GLOBE TERRESTRE ET AQUATIQUE EN DEUX PLAN[S HEMISPHE]RES ;
L'EAU , SUIVANT LES RELATIONS LES PLUS NOUVELLES . Par le Sr. SANSON, [...] oy . 1719.

Discovery

Discovery
Exploration Through the Centuries
ERIC FLAUM

GALLERY BOOKS

An Imprint of W.H. Smith Publishers, Inc.
112 Madison Avenue
New York, New York 10016

A FRIEDMAN GROUP BOOK

Published by GALLERY BOOKS
An imprint of WH Smith Publishers, Inc.
112 Madison Avenue
New York, New York 10016

ISBN 0-8317-2381-5

DISCOVERY: *Exploration Through the Centuries*
was prepared and produced by
Michael Friedman Publishing Group, Inc.
15 West 26th Street
New York, New York 10010

Editor: Sharon Kalman
Art Director: Jeff Batzli
Designer: Devorah Levinrad
Photography Editor: Ede Rothaus
Senior Photo Editor: Christopher Bain
Photo Researcher: Gerhard Gruitrooy
Editorial Research Assistants: Kal Raustiala, Dave Pandy
Production: Karen L. Greenberg

Typeset by B.P.E. Graphics, Inc.
Color separation by Universal Colour Scanning Ltd.
Printed and bound in Hong Kong by Leefung-Asco Printers Ltd.

Gallery Books are available for bulk purchase for sales promotions
and premium use. For details write or telephone the Manager of
Special Sales, W.H. Smith Publishers, Inc., 112 Madison Avenue,
New York, New York 10016. (212) 532-6600

Dedication

for Casey Lee,
the future

Acknowledgments

First, as always, to Seija, without whom this would be impossible. You make it all worthwhile.

Thanks, once again, to Karla, who made this all possible in the first place. You always know when to encourage and when to get tough. I'm forever in your debt.

Special thanks to Sharon, once again, on our second round together. Your patience and support throughout these projects has made all the difference in the world and I appreciate it greatly.

And many thanks to Devorah, whose personal committment to the project transformed my words into a beautiful book. I'm not sure you realize how much I've appreciated your input and your patience.

Big-time thanks to K.L. and Dave, who came through with fact, quotes, and musical accompaniment. Boy, that was fun.

Thanks to Geoff for steering me through turbulent waters with his maritime expertise.

Gratiae pro libris to "Biff" Giersbach for his classics, Mom and Dad for the use of their library, New York for the use of its Public Library, and H.G. Wells for his *Outline of History*. And also to Roland Huntford, whose books reminded me how wonderful nonfiction can be.

Official apologies to all the friends who got tired of hearing about every phase of history, in turn, and about how I'd be able to hang out with them as soon as this was done. Sorry Shecky, C-man, Kenny Benny (and company), AV, Robert, et al.

Unrelated thanks to Therese and Bob, my favorite 'toons, for making sure things were always kept in perspective, skewed as that perspective might have been; and especially to Mr. Butch, who has always shared his own discoveries with me. I miss you Chairman.

No more filmstrips.

Contents

AUTHOR'S NOTE

The history of exploration is by no means a closed book. Interpretations and revisions are based on the period of time during which the history is rewritten, reflecting as much about the audience as the subjects it recounts. One generation's heroes become the butchers of another. Those who died in ignominious poverty are celebrated long afterward. I have tried to present as objective a picture as possible, but regret that such is not always the case. The overwhelming European bias of this work is primarily on account of the fact that their explorations lead to worldwide expansion and power. The people and countries that benefited from their discoveries were subsequently in the position to celebrate them. The accomplishments of long-lost cultures are usually long lost themselves.

In addition, there is a heavy emphasis on maritime exploration and on instantaneous discovery. Surely, the peoples of North Africa and Southeast Asia were familiar with one another long before the Portuguese sailed among them. The act of discovery seems to indicate the need for someone to be in a place none of his or her people had ever been before. When those discoveries are simply tiny additions to a large picture they are quickly forgotten. Only when great changes in technology or political power allow for great leaps in travel does discovery on a grand scale come about. This results in an emphasis on instantaneous, often unexpected discoveries, as opposed to more natural progressions that lead to expansion over the course of years or decades. The individuals who extend boundaries a mile or kilometer at a time are mostly forgotten, whereas those who leapt across continents and oceans are more easily remembered.

As Eurocentric as this study tends to be, it's even more limited in the gender of its participants. Unfortunately, the history of exploration is almost completely monosexual. Some might suggest that the unnatural circumstances of a group of men traveling together, without the balancing effect of female companions, accounts for some of the nastier episodes in the history of exploration, which might have been avoided had a more natural way of traveling for long periods of time been devised. The use of male-dominated language grows wearisome, but remains necessary nonetheless. Similarly, we have the used the term B.C. throughout this book, as its common usage in the literature of early history permeates our literature and our perceptions. While the term is obviously religious in origin, it has come to serve as an inescapable unit of time measurement. To avoid using it, as I quickly discovered, becomes more postured than practical.

We've tried to provide you with maps and illustrations that bring these words to life. It's not always possible, however, to represent all of the islands, capes, ports, and rivers mentioned in the course of a text. So, please, for your own enjoyment, be sure to have a good globe or atlas handy. Nothing puts these accomplishments into perspective as well, and without a handy reference the flow of names and places can quickly become overwhelming.

Finally, it's important to make it clear that this is by no means a thorough or complete examination of all the names in the history of exploration. Each period offers up scores of fascinating personalities and predicaments, of which only the grandest, most famous can be incorporated. The nature of this book prevents us from examining the lives of so many brave, adventurous people. The process of selection has been a difficult one and is by no means perfect—the gaps are there, to be discovered and explored.

I hope you enjoy this book.

Eric Flaum
June 1989

> "... *man is usually a wandering and enterprising animal, for whom there exist few insurmountable barriers.*"
> —H.G. Wells

1

FROM MYTH TO MAYBE

hirty-five hundred years ago, the Egyptian queen Hatshepsut organized a mission to the distant land of Punt. There, she believed, her crews would find limitless stores of gold and incense. As much as their ships could carry. As much as they could barter for.

The queen relied on reports dating from nearly fifteen hundred years earlier, around 3000 B.C., the time of the dynasty of Sahu-Re. The stories told of early, treacherous voyages were thought to have been something of a secret, guarded closely by the powerful religious establishment. Perhaps they were simply waiting for a monarch capable of—and inclined toward—putting their valuable information to use. Queen Hatshepsut was an ambitious ruler who realized that a successful reopening of a trade route with Punt could finance her reign while establishing for her a place in history.

The queen's men first traveled across the eastern deserts to the shores of the Red Sea. There they collaborated with members of the ascendant Phoenician maritime community on the construction of their vessels. Phoenician ships had visited nearly all the bodies of water surrounding Asia Minor and had encountered the technologies of many pelagic peoples. They were great adapters and refiners upon the accomplishments of others; incorporating Arab, Indian, and Mediterranean features in their own designs, the Phoenician hybrids were versatile vessels.

Using Lebanese cedar and a good helping of Phoenician efficiency, Queen Hatshepsut's crew constructed five ships and launched them south along the familiar waters of the Red Sea. The argosy passed into the vaguely known Gulf of Aden before plunging south into uncertainty. That Punt existed was accepted as fact. Where it was, however, was anyone's guess. The experience gained from previous journeys measured by time instead of distance, under unknown conditions with more

Below: *Artifacts from the age of Queen Hatshepsut suggest a civilization juggling ancient traditions with innovative new ideas. The delicate balance crumbled when external forces created an environment that could no longer support adventurous exploration.*

primitive vessels, was difficult to apply to the comparatively advanced capabilities of the Queen's expedition.

It is unlikely the five ships often left sight of the African coast. The crew's navigational skills were fairly rudimentary, and the expedition's best chance lay in hugging close to freshwater and food-laden shores. At what point that shore became the place they were looking for, the site of historic Punt, remains unknown. At the least, the queen's men reached the southeast coast of Somalia. It is one of the uncertainties in the early history of exploration just how much farther they might have traveled. The frescoes and bas-reliefs from which historians learned of the queen's mission were essentially an inventory of the goods

her men brought back with them. Based on those commodities, others have placed Punt farther south, anywhere along the African coast from Kenya to Mozambique. Some historians have suggested Punt was actually an Indian, or even South American, port, but those theories seem to take great liberties with the few facts at our disposal. That such contact might have occurred is not as unlikely as it may seem, but there remains little historic evidence to support those theories.)

The queen's expedition along the western coast of the African continent is considered to be the subject of the earliest known travelogue. It celebrates the accomplishments of its captain, Nehsi, and his men, but is frustratingly vague in geographic detail. Shortly before Moses is reported to have crossed the very same desert off to the north, these men set out for a land shrouded in the mysterious quasi-history of earlier generations. They reached that distant land and returned from it with great riches. Though Queen Hatshepsut celebrated the benefits she reaped from the mission, she thought little of acknowledging the land from which they'd been harvested.

This early mention of exploration is itself the rediscovery of a route used centuries earlier. Go to Cape Guardarfui, the ancient horn of Africa, and head south, they were told; there you'll find Punt. More specific directions, it turns out, weren't necessary. The mission was profitable, but the route eventually fell back into disuse. The sea-wary Egyptians, often distracted by internal strife or external aggression, had little interest in maritime expansion. Punt was forgotten.

The earliest known depiction of a sailboat was created some time around the turn of the third millenium B.C. (probably *after* the earliest Egyptian voyages to Punt). Thereafter it is safe to assume that numerous individuals and communities took to the seas. River travel had certainly

been taking place for some time before that, available to anyone who could bind reeds or logs to one another. But sailing the great waters was quite a different matter. The first sailors stayed close to the shore. They fished just off the coast and probably didn't stray too far from their home ports at first. Only as they grew more confident in their crafts, and their own abilities to control them, did they venture further out. Travel between ports became an increasingly feasible alternative.

The Egyptians ruled the upper Nile and made their presence felt at times along the Mediterranean and Red seas. But as the Egyptian dynasties weakened, their domination of the surrounding waters gave way to a succession of smaller powers. The Egyptians had never placed a great priority on exploration, and as matters at home became critical, it came to seem even less enticing. The Phoenicians, constricted to a small terrestrial toehold on the shores of Asia Minor, began to venture out across the Mediterranean. Their interaction with the Egyptians had been incorporated into their maritime technology, and the Phoenicians soon exceeded anything their predecessors had been able to accomplish upon the waters. In the process, the Phoenicians were embarking upon the second generation of vaguely documented exploration. Again, the dearth of tangible informa-

The sarcophagus of Ramses III (below), dating back to the twelfth century B.C., offers a host of information about contemporary maritime travel. Depictions of the crew are supplemented by a series of hieroglyphs recounting the facts and figures of this mission.

These two reliefs (above) *depict the construction of the Argo and Jason's departure for the land of Colchis. While the scene of Jason's departure appears to be more mythological in origin* (top), *the other relief* (bottom) *offers insights into the technology of the day.*

Opposite page: *Lorenzo Costa, an Italian Renaissance artist, transposed Jason's Argo, and his Argonauts, into a strange amalgam of technologies and costuming. Whatever the reality of Jason's voyage might have been, it is unlikely to have had much in common with this oarless craft.*

tion available to us leaves us guessing at the accomplishments of these long-forgotten voyagers.

By now it becomes apparent how impossible it is to say for sure who the first true explorer was. The names we encounter are nothing more than fleeting references—hired hands—who were not explorers in the same sense of the word as those found in later times. They are based as much in fiction as in fact, handed down by generations of storytellers. Odysseus was just a soldier trying to get home from war, and Jason ventured to the end of the Earth as an alternative to execution. One fell into disfavor with Poseidon, the mythological god of the sea; the other was a victim of an insecure king. In cases such as that of the ambitious Queen Hatshepsut (married to successive pharaohs), the sponsor received more acclaim than the brave souls who actually made the journey.

The Cretans and Mycenaeans had been playing connect-the-dots among countless Aegean islands for a few centuries before Queen Hatshepsut's mission, but they left no specific rec-

ords of their journeys. They'd learned to use the islands as convenient stepping-stones for adventurous (or unlucky) crews far from home. The concept of recorded history being relatively new, we are left to rely on mythology to sketch out our earliest history—not considered as reliable as more traditional historical disciplines, such as archaeology and anthropology. There is an indeterminant amount of reality in the stories that have been handed down over the centuries, and it is from these tales that theories surrounding our earliest explorers take shape.

The voyage of Jason's *Argo* is likely to have occurred. It may have been a singularly spectacular accomplishment by one intrepid crew or the culmination of increasingly extensive exploration by a succession of expeditions. Compressed into a single mission, or simply elaborated upon for entertainment's sake (even then it was important that history serve as good drama worth passing along), the result was a natural progression in the development of the civilized world. Jason and his crew, which came to be known as the Argonauts, weren't looking to discover new lands so much as find a more direct route to one they already knew existed.

Whether Jason was fulfilling a prophecy of the gods or simply seeking cultural expansion and commercial interaction is nearly irrelevant, because the result was the same: the opening of a highly profitable pathway to lucrative trade with distant lands. The mythological voyage of the *Argo* from Ioclus (now known as Vólos, a small trading port on Greece's eastern coast) contains tales beyond credulity. Fantastic descriptions of vicious Harpies and wandering rocks make it difficult to accept that such a story could have any claim to historic importance. But at some time, or series of times, Mediterranean people sat poised at the edge of the known sea, wondering what lay beyond. Whether Jason and Heracles were among those who did is hard to say. It

Le prologue du premier livre qui parle ra du fait des gregois et de plusieurs hystoires de poetrie.

Pour mon principe ensuiv a linception et commencement de ceste matiere soit en mon cœur et de nant mes yeulx lo stencion de la benoite croix ou le precieux sang fut jadis espandu afin de enluminer mon povre esperit et desfermer la porte de mon entendement et moy donner vertu de sapience Come saint Iherome escrit en ses paroles. Au commencement de chune œuvre me tez devant oroison a messeigneur. et en vre front le signe de la croix. D cest principe vueil premier demonstrer

comme pour les sieges de paradis rem plir et enluminer les obscures tenebres qui estoient sur la fontaine dabisme voulut dieu nre createur creer le ciel quil nomma troisne. Et fist adonc le soleil et la lune et composa les autres planetes en ordonnant chune en son espere et ou hault ciel mist les estoilles du zodiaque donna cours naturel. et ou cours du soleil ordonna douze signes. et composa aux zones leurs co entre les polles naturelment. Et tout en la maniere que la trinite sainte et glorieuse enlumine de sa parfaitte gloire la sainte compaignie qui habite ou ce lestiel troisne et de son regard les fait re splendir car sans lui ne peuent recevoir lumiere fait le soleil qui est la principal planete par la clarte de lui les autres is difficult to imagine the feelings of those involved in such missions so very long ago—men venturing toward oceans believed infinite. Unfortunately, mythology's attention to the heroic and grandiose does little to convey the personal experiences and concerns of those venturing off into the unknown. We know more about the men who purposely set out to conquer the unexplored (such as diary-happy polar explorers, who spent so much time holed up that they pursued writing with a passion) than those who may have been unwitting—and sometimes unwilling—adventurers. It would be some time before captains, no less crewmen, were sufficiently inspired—and literate—to recount their adventures.

By the fourteenth century B.C., seafaring traffic along the Aegean Sea had already made its way to the Dardanelles (the straits at the entrance to the Black Sea). Confused reports of a treacherous passage and boundless waters on the opposite side had filtered back to the Grecian peninsula, resulting in a jumble of fact and fiction. The land of Colchis was said to sit on a distant shore, with great wonders beyond ominous obstacles. As the riches offered grew more fantastic, so did the dangers. The confusion made a difficult journey sound nearly impossible, conjuring up expectations of strange, sinister creatures and treacherous travel.

The slow trickle of goods that made their way through countless middlemen overland made access to a sea route quite rewarding. Essential commodities and exotic trinkets for the wealthy were just out of reach. They dangled enticingly in front of the Mediterranean merchants. The Golden Fleece, different things to different people, was within reach, waiting for some ambitious hand to snatch it up. (Perhaps the Golden Fleece referred to the golden fields of Asian grain more plentiful than any Mediterranean dweller could imagine; grain to feed family and livestock, unlike anything that could be grown along the rocky Aegean shores. Possibly, the phrase was derived from the use of shorn fleece to trap flecks of gold carried upon local rivers. Instead of panning for gold like later prospectors, the residents of Colchis found that fleece did a fine job of collecting the valuable ore as the river water filtered through. If this was indeed the fleece in question, the term is more literal than had once been imagined.)

———————————————

Pindar, a Greek lyrical poet of the fifth century B.C., offers one of the earliest references to Jason of Ioclus in his *Pythean Ode*. Around the same time, Herodotus, "the Father of History," makes casual mention in *The Histories* of "the grandsons of the crew of the ship *Argo*", taking it for granted that such a crew existed. More than a millennium after the voyage of the *Argo* is believed to have taken place, Apollonius of Rhodes passed along an already well-traveled tale that has itself been lost to us. The fragments that have survived from his version are more at home in the canon of ancient mythology than alongside the classics of exploratory reportage, given greater coverage in Robert Graves' twentieth-century mythological compendiums than in H.G. Wells' contemporary histories. They have been patched together and "reinterpreted" to suit the explanations of many scholars, but continue to be frustratingly incomplete. The facts remain elusive, even today leaving much to the imagination.

The *Argo* sailed during a period when Greece was under Phoenician rule; it traveled among a series of island empires known to one another. The Phoenicians had traveled extensively upon the waters of the Mediterranean and would remain important until their absorption into the prominent Hellenic culture of the first millenium B.C. It is safe to credit the Phoenicians with precedence as discoverers and explorers in the modern sense, yet their own tactics have obscured their place in history. We would know much more of their ac-

The city of Argos, its history presented in a fifteenth-century French chronicle by Jean de Courcy (opposite page), possessed the knowledge to produce the type of vessel pictured above. Jason and his men would have employed the sail whenever possible, but knew that a great deal of their travel would be dependant upon long turns at the oars.

This Athenian fresco (below), *currently residing in that city's Museo Nazionale, suggests the prevalence and importance of maritime travel to this seaside community. Depictions of Odysseus* (opposite page), *here being recognized by his long-time servant upon his homecoming, began to crop up on pottery shortly after his return and the triumphant reclamation of his position and property.*

complishments were it not for their habit of hiding them behind fabulous tales and purported dangers. (We should note here that the term *Phoenician* was coined long after their peak—probably by the Greeks—and was not one the people used to describe themselves. They thought of themselves as Tyrians or Byblians, Sidonians or Motyans, depending upon their home port. Similarly, most Greeks were quite parochial in their allegiances, uniting only when it was strategically necessary.)

In the ancient world, knowledge was one of the most valuable commodities of all. There are stories of increasing credibility that recount the lengths to which Phoenicians went to protect their geographic knowledge. Instead of publicizing or boasting about their accomplishments, they veiled them behind tales of diabolical sea monsters and voracious waters. Such fears were planted in the hope of deterring those adventurous enough to consider horning in on a piece of the Phoenicians' action.

Sometimes a physical deterrence was needed to turn back more aggressive competitors. One apocryphal tale has a Phoenician captain running his ship aground rather than allowing spies to follow him through safe waters to profitable ports. The story concludes with the captain's sponsors reimbursing him for his brave defense of their exclusive information. The value of the ship was that much less than the knowledge of safe passageways to friendly traders.

Opting for wealth instead of fame, the earliest Phoenician adventurers were suspicious traders desirous of anonymity. By the time Jason set off on his journey, the Phoenicians had already extended their domain throughout the coastal Mediterranean and even out past the Strait of Gibraltar into the Atlantic Ocean. They had already settled a colony at Utica (near where Carthage would rise to prominence a few centuries later) and had established contact with a number of ancient Iberian cities. Their control of the western portion of the known

of the Argonauts portaging their ship across regions incorporated within modern Romania or Bulgaria. The Argonauts would then have followed one of several rivers south and emerged into either the Adriatic or the Aegean. From there it would be a short skip to Ioclus.

A few interpretations still suggest that the *Argo* was stranded inland somewhere along the North African coast, but this seems particularly unlikely. Many scenarios rely on some fairly great leaps of faith on the part of the listener and often seem to contradict one another. But such exaggerated possibilities have often been found to conceal small nuggets of reality. Perhaps the story's residence in the world of mythology accounts for its ability to mean different things to different people, while still succeeding as a tale of great adventure. Jason lived, we are told, to a rather advanced age, and in a plot twist worthy of great fiction, he is said to have met his end by the seashore when the rotting prow of the decaying *Argo* fell and struck him.

On account of such uncertainty, the journey of the *Argo* represents the point of time in the history of exploration where there was still a lot more myth than maybe. Left with the scraps of a well-worn tale, interpretations of *The Argonautica* often reflect as much about the beliefs and wishes of the interpreter than the story itself. The myth tantalizes us with possibilities and sets the stage for the next chapter in the chronicle of man's explorations.

It is possible, in fact, that the next chapter was also literally the next generation. The victorious return of Odysseus from Troy is believed to have occurred within a century of Jason's travels. A number of the same individuals appear in both stories, but this is probably due to the fact that certain stock characters were often inserted into such tales like heavily typecast actors. And, as with *The Argonautica*, *The Odyssey* focuses a ge-

body of water at that time may well be one reason Jason and his men headed north toward the Dardanelles rather than south and west into the Phoenicians' domain.

Whether the actual circumstances of Jason's journey and ascension to power were special enough to have worked their way into a history of the times or were inflated by a well-paid bard to make them appear so is impossible to say. If such a voyage took place, we are left to create our own plausible scenarios for the path Jason's *Argo* may have taken and what it was that happened along the way. The Argonauts reached the Dardanelles with ease, passing through well-known waters along the northern Aegean. Their goal was Aea ("the land"), in the ancient kingdom of Colchis. It sat upon the western side of a swath of land that separates the Black and Caspian seas. Today the region encompasses that part of the Soviet Union that incorporates the Caucasus mountain range. Three thousand years ago it was a mysterious kingdom with access to a number of alluring products. It is where Jason's people believed they would find the Golden Fleece. The

benefits of such a mission, however, could never have been limited to any one single commodity. Along with whichever Golden Fleece he might have been looking for, Jason brought back a wife, some immigrants, and enough wonders from foreign lands to make him a wealthy man.

The *Argo* was aided either by good fortune and communication with knowledgable locals or by the divine guidance of a number of helpful deities. Jason and the Argonauts reached the land of Colchis and obtained not only the Golden Fleece but the king's daughter as well. The king and his people were not particularly pleased with the loss of either, and set out after them. At this point the uncertainties of the *Argo*'s route leave us grasping at vague clues and veiled references. Interpretation of the myth has led some people to determine that Jason and his men took the long route counterclockwise along the coast of the Black Sea and emerged back out through the Dardanelles. This would certainly have been the easiest route. Others rely on tales of enormous waves stranding the Argo far inland as indicating the possibility

A Tunisian mosaic (above, top) *and an* Etruscan urn (above, bottom) *both offer a portrayal of Odysseus' encounter with the Sirens, probably somewhere off of Italy's west coast along the Tyrrhenian Sea. There were those who suggested that Odysseus' misfortunes were a result of the ruthlessness with which he and his men laid waste to Troy* (opposite page) *following their victory there.*

ographic spotlight on the Dardanelles. While Jason offered proof that the Black Sea was not an infinite ocean, so Odysseus leaves the Dardanelles behind and establishes that the western Mediterranean was also essentially landlocked. Many had already known this, but remember that the Phoenicians had gone a long way toward misrepresenting such truths.

Though we have been told that Troy was invaded on account of Helen, "the Fairest of her Sex," it's more likely that the city's position overlooking the Dardanelles had a lot more to do with it. Even today the area remains a place of global strategic importance. In Odysseus' time it was worth going to war over, back when going to war was a hands-on affair. Odysseus survived the decade-long Trojan War, but experienced further suffering on his return voyage, traveling the length of the Mediterranean in the process.

Homer, the man responsible for immortalizing brave Odysseus, did so five hundred years after the fact, from somewhere in Asia Minor. His place

in time during the reign of Greek civilization allowed his works to become sufficiently widespread, and copies survived long after the original Greek versions were lost. Following the fall of the Roman Empire, copies of *The Iliad* and *The Odyssey* did not reappear in Europe until the late fifteenth century. These classics survived through the foresight of Mideastern scholars who preserved that which Homer's own descendants could not.

It's worth noting that the first two elaborated tales of travel we come upon (those of Jason and Odysseus) feature individuals who turn a handsome profit from their endeavors. While this tells us a lot about the rewards for such adventures, it also raises the question of whether the "heroes" of these tales might have bought their way into history. A mission of great geographic significance that failed to "turn a profit" would be quickly forgotten. (As we will see in a few centuries.) Those who had accomplished more commercially successful voyages would also have the financial wherewithal to immortalize themselves. A bard such as Homer, for the right price, could probably have been coerced into glorifying the accomplishments of a wealthy man, intent on having others sing his praise and know of his accomplishments. Perhaps Jason himself subsidized the early tales that eventually grew into *The Argonautica.*

In his time, Homer was a very successful poet, known to the finest Mediterranean palaces. He is believed to have done a good deal of traveling in his early years, particularly those following the composition of *The Iliad.* (Homer may have been blinded in his later years, making it difficult for him to leave the employment of a ruler who took pleasure from his tales. This is believed to have been a custom of the times, to prevent entertaining storytellers from leaving one's kingdom, giving an ironic twist to the concept of a captive audience.) *The Odyssey,* written after his extensive travels, picks up with the conquest of Troy by the men from Ithaca, their mission accomplished in a far away land at great cost; mighty warriors such as Achilles had met their end, leaving the victorious few to head home.

Odysseus and his men left for Ithaca, with a few delays along the way for some last-minute sacking and pillaging. From there they were waylaid to the land of the lotus-eaters, where many of Odysseus' men took up the local custom. As a chronicle of foreign engagements, one of *The Odyssey*'s most portentous passages hints at the difficulty in keeping the enlisted men away from enticing regional inebriants. Odysseus' difficulty in the land of the lotus-eaters sounds quite similar to that of the Americans in Vietnam or Soviets in Afghanistan, where the troops proved vulnerable to the exotic narcotics of foreign lands.

Odysseus dragged his men from the lotus, somewhere along the coast of modern Libya, only to lead them into greater difficulties on the island of the Cyclopes. A series of further encounters resulted in the gradual decimation of his entire crew, until Odysseus was alone. (Odysseus deserves a lot of credit as a survivor, but the demise of his crew may indicate a certain lacking as a leader.) His voyage took him from the Black Sea to the Atlantic Ocean, with stops along the northern and southern Mediterranean coasts. And when he finally returned to Ithaca, he did so as a beggar.

In the end, as great tales are wont to do, our hero wins out and lives to a happy, prosperous old age. Like Jason, Odysseus was directed by the gods to enter infinite oceans, this time westwardly (the Atlantic), and also like Jason, the events Odysseus encountered are quite fantastic. Much of Homer's tale remains firmly ensconced in the storytelling form of his time, which still had more to do with heroes and the celebration of certain lineages than with factual his-

tory. As a result, his travels included episodes with spirits from the dead, enormous one-eyed barbarians, and highly possessive goddesses.

To show how easily fanciful descriptions of actual occurrences can be turned into fantastic "fact," consider the following passage:

> We sailed past a strange berg that resembled a pig-faced prehistoric monster. It rolled slowly to the swell. For five minutes at a time the grotesque face rolled down 100 feet into the sea. A long pause and it slowly rolled up again, the water pouring in torrents down the monster's face. It seemed to us to be weeping tears of rage at our escape from the pack.

The quote is not from Homer or any other ancient voyager. It is, in fact, from a narrative by F. A. Worsley, a twentieth-century ship captain who was a member of Sir Ernest Henry Shackleton's *Endurance* party during

the peak of Antarctic exploration. The description, edited of a few conditional phrases, could quickly come to sound as farfetched as the most fantastic Homeric tales, when it is instead found in a work considered particularly credible. So before Homer's tale is discredited for the liberties it takes with the reality of our knowledge, it is important to remember how easily, and how quickly, such tales could be distorted in their own time. Like a centuries-old game of telephone, the tale was altered with each telling, embellishing some details while discarding others. Regional "translations" could quickly turn the impressive into the impossible.

Until the nineteenth century, *The Iliad* and *The Odyssey* were believed to have been purely fictitious, as likely to have happened as the mythological torments of Prometheus or the symbolic rapture of Narcissus. During that century, however, an increasing number of wealthy adventurers and

"We were thankful enough when we got into open water out of reach of the rocks [the Laestrygonians] hurled at us." This scene from The Odyssey *(below) resides in the Vatican Library. Sea monsters, such as the one the god Nereid is shown riding* (opposite page) *could be found adorning many works from this era.*

fledgling archaeologists began to wonder if the city of Troy, site of *The Iliad* and point of departure for *The Odyssey*, might in fact have existed. Heinrich Schliemann, a German archaeologist, discovered ancient Troy, Homer in hand. Though Schliemann's discovery was most notable for its help in establishing the science of archaeology, it also served as a milestone in the history of exploration. Now the most famous tale of travel and adventure was beginning to look like the first great history of discovery as well.

Homer's words have served as a reliable guide for those who have attempted to retrace Odysseus' route, much of which has generally been agreed upon by contemporary scholars and adventurers. *The Odyssey* was the first epic to give sufficient navigational details to inspire numerous "experts" of varying authority to suggest particular locations for Odysseus' exploits. Several books are currently available documenting the tra-

vels of those who claim to have followed the Ithacan's twisted path, each with their own arguments regarding specific locales or radical alternatives. As with *The Argonautica*, the hard facts aren't necessarily as important as the impressions of Odysseus and his men and the peripheral historical details that shed light on the Greek way of life. The ease with which Telamachus, Odysseus' son, traveled between Ithaca and the Peloponnesus in search of his father indicates a level of regular contact among such ports and generally safe passage. (The Peloponnesus, the southernmost portion of the continental Greek peninsula, was named for Pelops, grandfather of Menelaus—whose wife, Helen, is credited with having instigated the Trojan War—and Agamemnon—commander in chief of the Greek forces sent to bring her back.)

As a historical document, *The Odyssey* has grown increasingly useful. It helps establish the geographic param-

"Here lived many enterprising people that occupy themselves with commerce and who navigate the monster-filled ocean far and wide in small ships."
—Avienus

Bards such as Homer, sculpted centuries after his death by a Roman artisan (below), were responsible for immortalizing heroes such as Agamemnon (opposite page), whose strengths allowed him to emerge from Troy victorious, only to meet a bloody end at his wife's hand upon his return.

> "If a man did not have a mighty poet to make a song of his deeds he would be forgotten after the last grandfather of the last grandson died.
> —Harold Lamb

eters of a people in history, in addition to serving as one of the most famous pieces of ancient literature. To read Homer's work is to enter into another world. It is to accept the fantastic as a given and hold out the hope that all will resolve itself well in the end. And though *The Odyssey* takes the reader across the known world, it is based on the personal yearnings of a man who wanted only to return to his home. Others sought the limitless horizon. Odysseus pined for a familiar stretch of coast.

The great expansion of the known world before 1000 B.C. left much to keep the seafaring powers busy for a number of centuries. Development of the western Mediterranean coasts kept the Phoenicians occupied, while the Greeks had enough room to the east to begin their rise to prominence. The Hamites and Semites of the Middle East had already been in contact with numerous Asian communities and maintained trading relations with them. We know that the journey to India or Ceylon had been made for centuries, as Arabic seamen had a thing or two to teach even the accomplished Phoenicians. Lone ships were certainly encountering unknown coasts or bodies of water, but little was being added to the body of common knowledge. The state of maritime technology had reached its exploratory potential. If any missions crossed oceans or rounded continents, their deeds are almost completely lost to us today.

Around the fifth century B.C. the earliest histories were being compiled. Herodotus is credited with having written one of the first, or at least the earliest to survive, earning him a place as the Father of History. He was born some time around 485 B.C., in Halicarnassus, a city in the southwest corner of modern-day Turkey, just north of Rhodes. Herodotus didn't remain there long, however, traveling the length and breadth of Western

civilization during his lifetime. In *The Histories*, ostensibly about the Persian Wars, which raged during the early portion of Herodotus' life, the well-traveled author manages to offer all he had learned about history and geography along the way. As a result, the earliest tales of exploration provided by the first historian are reports of journeys that had occurred relatively recent to that era. Anything that had taken place much more than a century or two earlier had either worked its way into some form of mythological history or had been forgotten altogether.

In fact, Herodotus himself has often been accused of entering the world of mythology under the guise of "history." Many of the Greek's contemporaries, as well as subsequent generations of scholars, considered him a fraud. The Father of History to some, he was the Father of Lies to others. Though Herodotus managed to cover a good deal of ground on his own, he was forced to rely on the stories of others for much of his narrative. He always credited his sources, took editorial exception to some of their taller tales, and provided a great deal of information that was well ahead of its time. Unfortunately, Herodotus' credulousness occasionally reveals him to possess a good deal of gullibility. Some of the more fabulous-sounding tales were responsible for the derision he received in his own lifetime, but one of these tales has emerged as another famous debate in the study of early exploration that has taken centuries to decide.

At a time when the majority of the world still "knew" the earth to be flat, Herodotus believed otherwise. His controversial map presumed the presence of a body of water that completely surrounded the African continent, based upon reports of its circumnavigation. Though the author expresses skepticism regarding some specifics of the tale (which we now know make geographic sense), he recounts the first circumnavigation of Africa as essentially factual.

Other historians and mapmakers of the final centuries B.C. also assumed the presence of water all around the African continent, though later generations obscured these beliefs for more than a thousand years. The details that Herodotus provides, considered by his contemporary critics as proof of the story's absurdity, have since served to establish the plausibility of such a mission. In fact, a few ideas seemed so preposterous that it is unlikely that anyone of Herodotus' time would make them up. Only an incredulous firsthand observer could have stood by such seemingly outlandish contentions. The African continent was known as Libya, and *The Histories* states with great certainty that the landmass:

> is washed on all sides by the sea except where it joins Asia, as was first demonstrated, so far as our knowledge goes, by the Egyptian king Nec[h]o, who... set out a fleet manned by a Phoenician crew with orders to sail round and return to Egypt and the Mediterranean by way of the Pillars of Heracles [the Strait of Gibraltar]. The Phoenicians sailed from the Red Sea into the southern ocean, and every autumn put in where they were on the Libyan coast, sowed a patch of ground, and waited for next year's harvest. Then, having got in their grain, they put to sea again, and after two full years rounded the Pillars of Heracles in the course of the third, and returned to Egypt.

Necho was an ambitious Egyptian king of the twenty-sixth dynasty, who went to great lengths to expand his empire. He began construction of a canal between the Nile and the Red Sea and challenged the forces of the powerful Babylonian king Nebuchadnezzar (of biblical fame). Necho failed at both. His hired Phoenicians, however, met with great success. Their names were soon lost to history, and the idea that they could have circled the continent has met with skepticism from the very start. If indeed their

journey took place, they would be the only men to complete such a mission for two thousand years. In 1497, Vasco da Gama crowned a succession of Portuguese missions to round the southern tip of Africa, in much the same way the *Apollo* astronauts brought about the culmination of a project that began with *Mercury*, *Gemini*, and the like. The Phoenicians, plunging into unknown waters, were on their own.

Herodotus himself doubted the story's assertion that the sun had been to the right, or north, of the sailors as they rounded the southern edge of the Libyan continent. Today we realize that such would be the case since the ship had traveled far south of the equator and can appreciate Herodotus' dutifully passing along a piece of information he himself did not believe. In fact, the observation is the first mention of Western man's entrance into the southern hemisphere. Though the land of Punt is likely to have existed south of zero-degree latitude, its crew passed along no known information of the change in the sun's position in the sky and would not have traveled from east to west to be made as aware of the change. The observation was seen as proof of the story's unfeasibility by early historians but serves instead as evidence that

HΡΟΔΟΤΟΣ

such a mission was, in fact, introducing information its scholars could not interpret.

The Histories offers an interesting postscript to this tale. Some time after King Necho's mission, a Carthaginian was sent on a similar circumnavigation. The fact that it was possible is offered as a given. The man's name was Sataspes, and he'd been apprehended for raping the daughter of a powerful military family. As an alternative to impalement, Sataspes was

offered the penance of circling the continent. Encountering difficulties, Sataspes returned home. He believed that having made it far south, though not even around the southern cape, would be deemed sufficient. The king thought otherwise and impaled Sataspes anyway upon his return.

Herodotus provides us with a diverse assortment of fact and fiction. As a result, we find a number of exploratory tales from the preceding centuries transformed into vague possibilities. One story involves "a group of wild young fellows, sons of chieftains in their country" who set off southward to see what lay beyond the great Libyan desert. They passed through it in a westerly direction and eventually encountered strange men of small stature with black skin, who held them hostage for some time. The youths eventually returned home with wild tales of sorcery and fantastic creatures. Other curious souls are reported to have investigated the source of the Nile, which Herodotus came to believe took a sharp right west into the heart of the continent.

Given the state of Phoenician maritime technology, the journey of King Necho's men is conceivable. The Phoenicians had already traveled down the Red Sea and out into the Atlantic Ocean at least as far as the Canary Islands. The fact that it wouldn't be duplicated for two thousand years simply makes it that much more remarkable. That the Phoenicians never repeated—or exploited—such a journey has a good deal to do with the fact that their power soon gave way to the Greeks and Persians. In addition, the journey—possibly intended to discover an alternative way to reach the Canary Islands and their prized dyes—proved too difficult to establish it as a profitable trade route, rendering it useless to the Phoenicians. We are given little indication that their goal was ever curiosity rather than profit.

The survivors of the journey are thought to have met with little acclaim on their return. This is because they were fruitless in their search for wealth and returned to a country on the verge of war. Though King Necho's men had accomplished a great feat, its relevance and usefulness in terms of commercial success was negligible. The Phoenicians were under increasing land-based pressure from the Assyrians to the east, north, and south. Perhaps a successful, profitable circumnavigation would have at least delayed the Phoenician decline. Instead, the mission signaled the swan song of the Phoenicians' seafaring supremacy.

Herodotus (opposite page) bridged the gap from storyteller to historian, attempting to create a coherent, factual version of natural history and geography. Though he fell prey to the fantastic stories related by others, Herodotus offered more truths than any of his contemporaries.

Much of our information about this era also comes from frescoes such as this one (below), in which the depiction of maritime craft and their attendant technology can be deciphered to reveal useful clues to the capabilities and inclinations of early Mediterranean sailors.

2

EXPLORERS &
EXPANSIONISTS

he principal subject of Herodotus' *Histories* is the Persian Wars, in which the united Greek colonies revolted against Darius, King of Persia. He had begun with a considerable homeland in Asia Minor and expanded it as far east as the Indus River. Darius wisely halted his advance in that direction and turned his attention to the west. (A couple of centuries later, Alexander the Great was also halted by the footsteps of the Himalayas and the western rivers of the Indian subcontinent.)

Legend has it that Darius had initially intended to head northwest into central Europe, but was swayed by a homesick Greek adviser who wished to return to his native peninsula. The Greeks, emboldened by Darius' failure to subdue the Scyths north of the Black Sea on his way back from the east, challenged his advance. Though Darius defeated them soundly at first, the Greek resistance outlived him, and the Greeks eventually gained independence from his successor, Xérxes, who was content to retreat to the Persian stronghold in Asia Minor. Darius' empire was short-lived, but it was impressive nonetheless. "The greater part of Asia," wrote Herodotus, ignoring those who actually lived there, "was discovered by Darius."

Darius' empire stretched from the tip of Cyrenaica in northern Libya (off the Gulf of Sidra) to the foothills of the Himalayas. In some ways his empire laid the foundation for that of Alexander the Great, who employed many of the economic and military strategies Darius had experimented with to cope with his own rapid expansion. Alexander, however, would insist on going everywhere himself, whereas Darius was content with allowing others to do the exploring. One of his trusted men appears to have been Scylax the Caryandian. Scylax, about whom little seems to be known but his name and his Greek heritage, had already spent time charting the Mediterranean. Upon reaching the Indus with Darius,

The ruins of Carthage (above) *stand as a testament to a once-great city. The architecture, though reduced to rubble and a few standing remains, was state-of-the-art in its day, the site of a bustling city at the heart of Mediterranean trade and travel.*

he was dispatched to follow the unfamiliar river south. Scylax sailed along until the waterway spilled out into the Arabian Sea, across which he traveled home.

With the rise of the Greeks, the once-powerful Phoenicians were beginning to find themselves subject to the will of others. The Greek repulsion of Xérxes had marked a turning point in Persian expansion, with which the old Phoenician states had aligned themselves. The era of Eastern Phoenicia's domination over its western colonies was coming to an end. As the home ports of Tyre and Sidon struggled to maintain their sovereignty, the rise of western Phoenicia found itself centered around the city of Carthage.

Carthage had been settled by early Phoenicians in the ninth century B.C., out on the northern tip of modern Tunisia. Eventually the Carthaginians, freed from the constraints of their founders, emerged as a major force in the western Mediterranean.

With access to the center of Africa and all the major harbors of Mediterranean maritime commerce, Carthage was in the right place at the right time. Goods emerging from the depths of Libya were prized throughout the Western world, and the city occupied the very center of regional commerce. It continued to grow throughout the era of Greek civilization and remained an important influence until it was conquered and subsequently destroyed by the Romans at the turn of the second century B.C. (Scipio Africanus Major was responsible for the defeat; his adopted grandson, Scipio Africanus Minor, handled the destruction.)

As Carthage grew, it established a sense of community that relied heavily upon its reputation as a center of trade. In their effort to expand business, the Carthaginians sent men across land and sea in hope of establishing safe ports along the way and discovering new trading partners. Settlements were planted in and around northern Africa, while other intrepid merchants ventured north across the Mediterranean into the European continent. Gold, ivory, and incense came from Africa, but tin—equally precious—came from Europe. The further the Carthaginians could travel, both in Africa and Europe, the greater their potential profit.

Though economic factors were certainly the primary impetus, there was apparently an ethnocentric ideal at work behind Carthaginian exploration that presages the collective enthusiasm of pole-crazy Britain or moon-mad America. The Carthaginians are known to have underwritten a number of exploratory expeditions, and the earliest on record was led by a man named Hanno. We know of Hanno's mission from a Greek translation of an account found in the ruins of the Temple of Cronos in Carthage. The work has come to be known as *The Periplus of Hanno* and provides, in unprecedented detail, a chronicle of his mission.

The record indicates Hanno led a colonizing contingency of sixty-seven ships, containing thirty thousand potential settlers from the harbor of Carthage. The trip was originally thought to have taken place around 520 B.C., but recent estimates suggest it occurred at least fifty years later, during the decline of Persia under Xérxes. The shrewd Carthaginians would certainly have put Hanno's information to use for business opportunities, but there didn't seem to be any great urgency to the mission. *The Periplus* offers the impression of a relaxed, inquisitive excursion, with extended stopovers when friendly natives were encountered. As long as the conditions seemed favorable, a settlement was undertaken. Inhospitable coasts were quickly passed by. (Hanno's mission is leisurely to any that preceeded it, but pales in comparison with Pytheas' a few centuries later.)

Of course, the big question regarding Hanno's voyage concerns how far he traveled. The Carthaginians had

Xerxes may have been a wily general, as evidenced by such tactics as his "bridge" across the Hellespont (below), *but eventually his Persian Empire was chipped away, setting the stage for Alexander's ascent.*

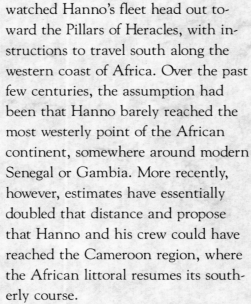

" . . . in the night we saw many fires burning and heard the sound of pipes, cymbals, drums and confused shouts. We were then afraid, and our diviners induced us to abandon the island."
—Hanno

watched Hanno's fleet head out toward the Pillars of Heracles, with instructions to travel south along the western coast of Africa. Over the past few centuries, the assumption had been that Hanno barely reached the most westerly point of the African continent, somewhere around modern Senegal or Gambia. More recently, however, estimates have essentially doubled that distance and propose that Hanno and his crew could have reached the Cameroon region, where the African littoral resumes its southerly course.

We know from *The Periplus* that Hanno passed what local interpreters referred to as the Horn of the West (Dakar? Cape Palmas?). There, he and his crew were frightened by the glow of distant fires and the sound of strange music. ("Fear seized us and the soothsayers told us to leave the island.") In fleeing southwards they eventually came upon something even more startling, around which much of the debate over Hanno's accomplishments is centered:

> We saw by night the land full of fire, and in the middle there was a fire bigger than the others, reaching to heaven. By day this revealed itself as a great mountain, called Theon Ochema.

Recently, Mount Cameroon has been championed as the site of Theon Ochema. Its thirteen-thousand-foot (four-thousand-meter) volcanic peak on the Gulf of Guinea is the highest in western Africa, just a few degrees north of the equator. Original estimates left Hanno considerably farther north than the Cameroon—some confining his mission to the coastline of modern-day Morocco—but recent historians are more generous with their estimations. If they are correct, his accomplishments are quite outstanding.

Hanno and his soothsayers agreed to put the flaming mountain quickly behind them. Even three days past Theon Ochema they were still "sailing past streams of fire." (Some scholars have suggested that the fires were ac-

tually seasonal slash-and-burn rituals, but Hanno's assertion that a particular mountainous peak had been observed by day seems to indicate something more specific.) The ship sailed on for an indeterminate period of time, eventually encountering an "island full of wild men." The Carthaginians' interpreters called them gorillas, and the reference is one of the first in Western literature.

The Periplus ends with the statement that Hanno turned back for Carthage on account of a dwindling food supply. That seems rather unlikely. King Necho's men had suggested that it was possible to support a mission along bountiful shores, and *The Periplus* indicates Hanno's crew was adept at maintaining trade relations with natives along the way. It is more likely that, if he had indeed reached Mount Cameroon, Hanno was daunted by the prospect of plunging any farther south, possibly even circumnavigating the continent. Perhaps the general purpose of his mission had been accomplished—or deemed unattainable. Maybe he had run out of colonists to plant like seedlings along the way.

The Carthaginians established a chain of settlements (making the difficult return voyage a bit easier) but seem to have come up empty-handed in the discovery of anything economically tangible. If Hanno was looking for something specific—gold, tin, copper—he doesn't seem to have found it. Whereas the record of Queen Hatshepsut's crew was focused on the spoils of a mission, offering little geographic information, *The Periplus*, rich in other details, has little to say about financial gains.

Hanno was not the first to pass from the Mediterranean into the Atlantic, nor was he the first to travel south along the African coast. He is, however, the first name we have, the first individual to have recorded and preserved his accomplishments. There are no pictures of the man nor any solid biographical information; in fact, we are left with little more than a translation of a dedication found in an ancient temple. But the long list of names begins here, where the facts of history begin to assert themselves over the dramatic enhancements of mythology.

The fact that Hanno's voyage was not particularly profitable for his country should not undermine our appreciation of the skills required for its safe completion. Traveling along unknown coasts, always close to land, Hanno's crew would have encountered navigational hazards, in unfamiliar waters, an assortment of creatures both strange and imagined, and the general trepidations of any early traveler. The Carthaginians were in the process of redirecting their focus to the north, and the limited success of Hanno's mission may have contributed to that change.

The Pillars of Hercules were a dreaded obstacle to centuries of maritime travelers. This tenth-century map shows their continued prominence, and the lingering notion of their position at the "edge of the world."

We know that Hanno wasn't the first man to undertake an exploratory voyage. He's just the first we know about. During his time the seas and oceans were thick with ships. Some Carthaginians had preceded Hanno to the near Moroccan coast, while others had ventured north after passing through the Pillars of Heracles. Tin had reached Carthage across the Mediterranean from European land routes, and if the source could be discovered, it could be exploited for great profit. If the Carthaginian senate was willing to underwrite Hanno's voyage south, there's no reason to doubt that a similar interest would be expressed in exploring to the north. An island rich with tin was said to lie off the northern European coast, and the discovery of a sea route would bypass the numerous middlemen. The journey would be a difficult one, but apparently seemed feasible to the Carthaginians. One attempt at discovering such a route is believed to have been commanded by a man named Himilco.

If we know little about Hanno, we know even less about Himilco. It is possible that they were brothers, though Phoenician names were somewhat generic, and establishing lineage is difficult. It's possible that Himilco led one of many voyages north or that his was in fact the farthest reaching of its kind. References to the voyage are vague and indicate that Himilco's ships reached the British Isles, but establish little else. The southern coast of Britain would certainly have been in active contact with the European continent by this time, and a ship coming around France's Brittany peninsula is almost certain to have encountered it.

There is evidence of Mediterranean interaction with the early British tin trade, though it is impossible to determine whether it arrived across land or over water. Extensive seaborne trade may not have been established this early, but it seems clear that initial forays had been launched. Those tentative introductions were developed steadily for the next few centuries, while interest in the southern European continent waned along the Mediterranean. While Hanno's mission was no more than a glorious probe into a veritable dead end (it would be nearly two thousand years before European merchants would venture much beyond Theon Ochema), Himilco's mission was an early step toward establishing some form of commercial interaction involving a large part of the European continent.

The vagaries that surrounded the Carthaginians' tentative exploration of the North Atlantic, coupled with their penchant for secrecy, allowed generations following Himilco to remain uninformed about the northern source of tin. That did not, however, prevent them from becoming curious. The Greek colony of Massilia (modern-day Marseilles in southern France) had served as a northern Mediterranean outlet for some of that tin and was certainly familiar with descriptions of its fountainhead. The Massilians were in direct competition with Carthage, aligning themselves over the centuries with Alexander, Ptolemy, other Greeks, and the Romans, who would eventually obliterate the once-great African city. Often the victim of Carthaginian secrecy and subterfuge, the Massilians decided to ignore the tall tales and investigate the northern waters for themselves.

Toward the end of the fourth century B.C., the city organized a mission chronicled by the first great explorer, Pytheas. It was not, like the Carthaginians, a mercenary affair; it seems to have had scientific curiosity and geographic exploration as its primary objectives. That Pytheas, a scholar and scientist, was chosen to lead the mission is itself a confirmation of that impression. The five- or six-year duration of his journey is another indication that the Massilians weren't simply looking for windfall profits. And the fact that Pytheas published two books about his journey (these sadly lost to time) indicates a willingness to share information that is contrary to the actions of a competitive trader.

Since Pytheas' own words have been lost and the generations that still had access to his volumes were quite skeptical (if not downright disdainful) of his claims, our information is once again sketchy. We are forced to rely on secondhand references and quotations found in the works of historians writing during the apex of Roman dominion within a century or two of the time of Christ. Were Pytheas' own *The Ocean and A Description of the Earth* available to us, we could easily chart his course north. The fact that

Pytheas was an astronomer well ahead of his time and a history-conscious scholar leads us to believe that his information could have proved infinitely more exacting than the traveled exaggerations of Odysseus or the second-hand recitations of Herodotus.

To begin his voyage, Pytheas measured the position of the solstitial sun from the docks of Massilia. His readings were astoundingly accurate, surpassing any that would be compiled for another five hundred years, lending further credence to subsequent latitudinal claims. Pytheas had learned a great deal about the heavens during his landed days and was able to apply them to a navigational understanding that eluded more experienced captains. His geographic discoveries may have been the greatest of their time, and his scientific accomplishments are nearly their equal. He introduced the concept of employing astronomical measurements to determine precise geographic location in strange waters (now known as celestial navigation) and introduced Mediterranean scientists to the relationship between the moon and tides. In addition, Pytheas served as something of an anthropologist during the mission.

Carthaginian merchants grew familiar with a wide variety of marketable goods, and the traders that looked to peddle them. Sometimes the merchandise represented the natural resources of an area, though a good deal of business involved the slave trade.

He was certainly more than just a roving cartographer.

It was once believed that Pytheas had begun his journey overland, traveling north through the European continent before embarking out to the tin island by boat. It's more likely, however, that Pytheas cast off into the Gulf of Lions and traveled southwest along the Iberian coast. This was still the domain of the Carthaginians, and it could be that this was the most dangerous portion of the journey. Warships prowled the strait itself but also kept watch from their Mediterranean and Atlantic ports. Strabo, a Greek geographer of the first century B.C., reports Pytheas' taking five days to travel from modern-day Cádiz to Portugal's Cape St. Vincent. Pytheas' ship, larger and sturdier than Columbus' *Santa Maria*, would certainly have been able to make better time than that but was probably traveling as inconspicuously as possible. Moving at night, veering away from ports or approaching sails, Pytheas' crew eventually eluded the blockade and headed off into the unknown.

What Pytheas observed and reported along his journey seemed incredible to some. Upon his return, Pytheas was hailed as a hero, but succeeding generations increasingly brought his work into question and eventually came to consider him a fool and a liar. He had reported tides in excess of 50 feet (about 19 meters) and waves nearly twice that high. Further north than any Mediterranean had ever traveled, Pytheas reported a place where the sun never set, where land, sea, and air came together in a misty state that was like none of the three—a state through which no ship could travel and upon which no man could walk. Pytheas' story, with the passage of time, came to sound like the ultimate seaman's yarn, and its dismissal is surely one reason his works have been lost to us.

Before reaching Britain, Pytheas cruised the Atlantic coast of modern France along the Bay of Biscay. He rounded the Brittany peninsula and sailed into the English Channel to Land's End, the farthest outpost of

Mediterranean contact. No one in history had claimed to have traveled farther from the warm southern waters, and none had any idea what might lie beyond.

Pytheas probably anchored for a while in the Cornwall region, repairing and restocking his ship while familiarizing himself with the island's inhabitants. Throughout his examination of the British islands, Pytheas appears to have made a number of treks inland, and it's impossible to determine where they led him or how long they lasted. Descriptions of the British people attributed to Pytheas range from the southern traders and maritime communities to the resourceful residents of the lonely Scottish Highlands. In the course of his travels, Pytheas also became the first Mediterranean to report the existence of a fermented intoxicant known as "*curmi*", a version of today's beer.

Heading north from Land's End, Pytheas began his circumnavigation of the British islands. He skirted the island's western coast, may have visited Ireland, passed the Hebrides, and payed a visit to the Orkneys: a chain of seventy small, barren islands he personally christened the Orcas. That Pytheas made it this far north is generally agreed upon. Where he proceeded to from here, however, remains another great debate in the early history of exploration.

Among the Orkney natives Pytheas heard talk about the land of Ultima Thule, a mythic island reported to lie six days north by boat of the northernmost British islands. We are told that Pytheas considered the Orkneys a part of Britain. It is possible that from there he merely managed to reach the Shetland or Faeroe Archipelagoes and believed them to have been Thule. Possibly Pytheas' ship actually took an easterly course and landed along the southern coast of Norway near the Lindesnes Cape. But maybe, taking a great leap into the unknown, Pytheas' journey north led him to Iceland.

Some doubt that Thule existed at all, but it seems very likely that Pytheas and his crew did travel beyond the Orkneys. In doing so they placed considerable confidence in information they'd gathered along the way. On treacherous, unfamiliar waters, in the midst of an ocean as vast as their imaginations, Pytheas led his men to a place they'd never been. Perhaps only a man of Pytheas' navigational capabilities could have found Thule, and—of equal importance—returned from it.

Students of Pytheas' voyage are usually forced to rely on quotations provided by Roman historians, many of whom selected the passages they imagined would make the Massilian appear as outlandish as possible. Strabo, in the first century B.C., relayed Pytheas' claim that he reached Thule and even attempted to explore beyond it. The Massilian found that:

> Thule is one day's sail from the congealed sea. In these regions ...there is no longer any distinction between land and sea and air, but a mixture of the three like a sea-lung which binds all together and can be transversed neither on foot nor by boat.

In summation, Strabo dryly informs his readers that "this Pytheas saw with his own eyes—or so he would have us believe!"

The concept of an ocean frozen over, shrouded in mist, was incomprehensible to most Mediterranean dwellers. The idea that it lay beyond a land where the sun never set in summer, never rose in winter, made it that much more difficult to believe. Today, however, there is increasing agreement that Pytheas may well have been the first explorer from the literate world to enter the Arctic Circle. Fridtjof Nansen, a pioneer of polar exploration in the nineteenth and twentieth centuries, credits Pytheas with having "pushed back the limit of the learned world's knowledge from the south coast of Britain to the Arctic Circle," a distance of some 1,100 miles (1,770 kilometers).

"*There will come a time in the long years of the world when the Ocean Sea will loosen its shackles and a great part of the earth will be opened up and a new sailor... shall discover a new world—and then shall Thule no longer be the last of lands.*"
—Seneca

Travel in the early stages of man's history was still a treacherous undertaking, dependant upon the kindness of strangers. Some cultures were quick to be hospitable (as in the scene, opposite page, of a woman giving water to a strange passerby), while others made it nearly impossible for a foreigner to pass through their lands.

Philip of Macedonia, his likeness seen on the above coin, did everything within his power to provide his son with the instruction that would make him a great general and a respected commander. Father and son are captured in fourth century B.C. ivory sculptures below. Maps show us how extensive Alexander's travels were, such as that on the opposite page showing his ill-fated foray into the subcontinent, while such depictions of Alexander's wedding (opposite page, bottom) or his entourage (preceding pages) blur the boundary between fact and fantasy.

That Pytheas, trained on the comparably calm waters of the Mediterranean, could navigate the rough waters of the North Atlantic is astounding. That he proceeded to explore much of the coastline along the European lowlands before returning home is usually mentioned as a peripheral aside. Upon his return, Pytheas appears to have spent much of his time compiling the accounts of his journey and defending them to the skeptical. Within a few short generations, Pytheas had increasingly more detractors than supporters. Ironically, today there are those who place the man among the elite in the history of exploration, expanding the known world as drastically as did Christopher Columbus or Ferdinand Magellan or Captain James Cook.

Around the time that Pytheas' small group was exploring the northern reaches of the known world, Alexander the Great was somewhere in the midst of the most extravagant militarily supported exploration of all time. Unfortunately, Alexander's accomplishments were inextricably woven in with his actions as a king, general,

politician, and demigod and have been ignored by many students of exploration. Instilled with a great curiosity about the world around him, and with a considerable empire at his disposal, Alexander mobilized his power and traveled the full extent of the known world. If he had to bring his army along and conquer a region to visit it, so be it.

Philip of Macedon is often overlooked in the tales of his son's accomplishments, but he laid much of the groundwork for Alexander's interests. Philip began as the king of a small landlocked peasant state and grew to reign over most of Greece by the time of his death. He infused his son with a strong will and great ambitions and prepared him throughout his youth for the crown that would one day pass to him. Philip had Alexander trained as a soldier, to merit the position he would take as general of the greatest fighting force of its time, and he had him tutored by the best teachers the Greek academies could offer. Toward that end, he brought Aristotle, eminent student of Plato, from Greece to teach his son and surrounded him with the brightest students in the realm.

The fact that Alexander was the ruler of the most extensive empire in history, one that has no rival for continuity and domination of so much of the known world, means that his life is well documented. His pronouncements and orders were recorded by scribes and passed along by politicians, bards, and courtiers. In the millenia that have followed his reign, Alexander has been portrayed in every light imaginable; as deity, egomaniac, explorer, and usurper. Dramatized biographies have portrayed him as a passionate, driven young man. On the other hand, some historians have described him as a capricious child, dead at an early age on account of his own folly and excess.

Alexander's reign lasted thirteen years, beginning in 336 B.C. with the assassination of Philip. Early on, the youth struggled to maintain all that

his father had assembled. But once he left his homeland, for battle-cum-exploration, Alexander never returned. The Macedonian king quickly abandoned his origins and adopted the customs of those he conquered. He took an Asiatic wife, to the chagrin of many Macedonians, and replaced many of his original advisers with foreign acquaintances. In many ways, Alexander may have been as driven by his wish to put Macedonia behind him as he was drawn forward to the unknown.

Alexander's greatest military victories came early in his travels, in lands relatively familiar to the Mediterranean forces he'd assembled. The subjugation of the Persians across Asia Minor ranks among the great military campaigns of ancient history, but has little to do with exploration. Alexander proceeded from there to Egypt, where he was greeted by the residents as their savior from their enemies, the Persians, and accorded great tribute.

By land and sea, Alexander's troops approached, encountered, and conquered (preceding pages). Some were more willing to accept the yoke of Macedonian rule; others even invited it in place of more oppressive regimes. Nonetheless, it is doubtful that Alexander's entrance into Babylon (below) was quite so orderly. Most towns, such as the one depicted in this fifteenth-century French manuscript (opposite page), offered as much resistance as possible, though the result was invariably the same.

The young king responded by respecting the Egyptians' religious architecture and adopting certain Egyptian practices. It was the first of many times that Alexander's encounter with a conquered land would seem as much like a cultural exchange as a military occupation.

Alexander established collaborative provisional governments in each of his acquisitions, and then moved on. (The idea corresponded with his Aristotilian education but broke down as the empire grew larger and larger and Alexander himself became increasingly less interested in its administration.) Once the land had been conquered and its delicacies sampled, Alexander had little inclination to linger, and his wanderlust quickly led him on. By the time the Macedonian army left recently conquered Babylon in 331 B.C. and crossed east of the Tigris River, it was leaving behind the last landmarks found on the Greek maps it had brought along. Alexander's geographers could no longer calculate distances in relation to where they had come from and had much less of an idea where they were headed.

As Alexander's increasing forces worked their way through Iran's Zagros Mountains, his men still believed they were involved in a war with the Persians. Once Darius II, the Persian king, was left on the verge of death by his fleeing generals, Alexander's

troops began to wonder what drove them on. They reached the southern coast of the Caspian Sea and dispatched an exploratory mission from its shores. They continued to march in and out of unknown mountain ranges, encountering new races of people, hitherto unfamiliar to Westerners. They skirted the Salt Desert of ancient Parthia (known today as the Dasht-e Kabir) only to run smack into the Caucuses Indicus mountains, known today as the Hindu Kush range. Though Alexander could not have known he was on the edge of the greatest concentration of mountainous peaks in the world, he did realize that his efforts were growing futile. And the more dead ends he led his troops

up, the more they grumbled. As a result, Alexander redirected his army and his focus to the south and led his men through the Khyber Pass toward the subcontinent.

In India, Alexander was welcomed by one of two warring factions, with whom he drove off the other. Alexander wished to go on, believing that he was very close to the eastern end of the world, just short of the "Infinite Ocean." Another great river was said to lie beyond—probably the Ganges—and beyond that: "the end of the world." But the Macedonian and Greek soldiers had had enough. The five rivers of western India were the final straws. Some men had been away from home for seven or eight years

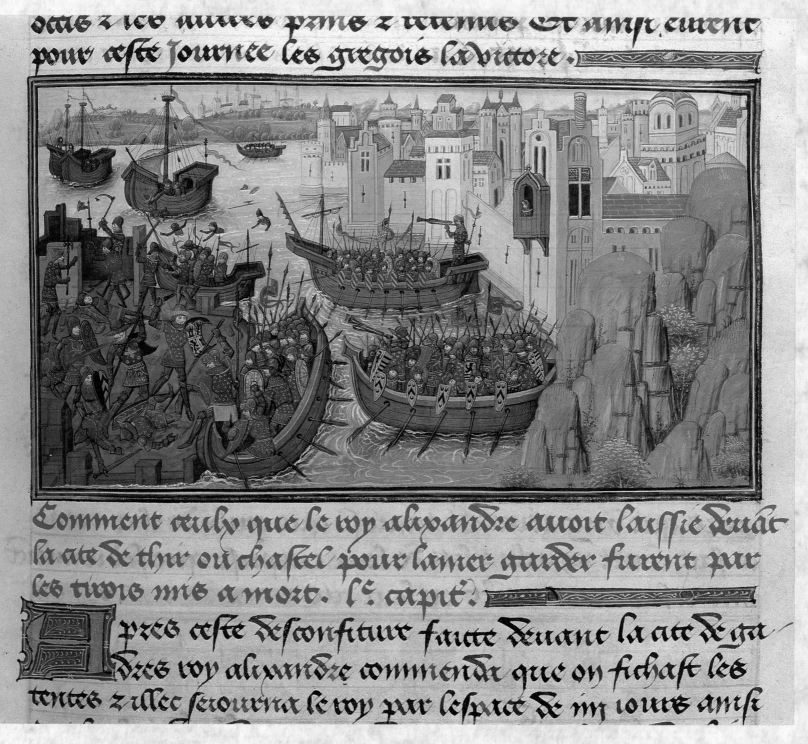

Above: *The funeral of Alexander, as envisioned in 1940 by Frenchman Andre Bauchant, took place far from his birthplace.* Opposite page: *There is no shortage of paintings and statuary that has attempted to capture some phase of Alexander's life, each imparting the artist's beliefs, prejudices, and surroundings. Alexander's personality has been lost to history, leaving room for a healthy dose of mythologization.*

"*It seemed to veteran Macedonians as if this was to be more an exploring venture than an invasion. Who had ever heard of a general keeping a daily journal?*"
—Harold Lamb

and wished to return in time to enjoy their considerable spoils. Who had ever heard of an army traveling so far for such nebulous reasons? Of a general who kept a daily diary? Of a self-proclaimed deity who spent more time mapping the earth than consulting the heavens?

It is impossible to guess how Alexander would have ruled the enormous empire he had amassed and whether he could have held it together. During the return voyage, he is portrayed as alternately despondent and agitated. On a side trip along the Euphrates, weakened by an assortment of war wounds and drinking binges, Alexander contracted a fever. His physical condition left him incapable of fighting the disease, and perhaps his will had been broken. Scarred and exhausted, obsessed by his failure to reach the very end of the world, Alexander died at the relatively young age of thirty-three. His body was never returned to his Macedonian birthplace,

but was taken instead to Egypt and entombed there.

Alexander's kingdom was eventually divided amongst his most trusted advisers and never again attained the cohesiveness it had under his rule. The ascending Roman Empire eventually took over much of Macedonia's lands, and Alexander himself passed quickly from the realm of the living to that of the historic. Though a personality cult shrouded his reputation, we can now view the traveling monarch in a relatively objective light.

Whether Alexander's exploratory motives were scientific or egotistic, they could certainly be no worse than the slave traders and abusive sots of later generations. That his travels were so inextricably tied to war and oppression makes his discoveries no less important. (The Spanish conquistadors of the sixteenth century introduced Europe to a whole new continent while committing crimes against humanity.) What Alexander did was link the continental caravan routes with the coastal terminals, establishing an unprecedented number of new cities along the way. Not until the Europeans had the entire North American continent to divide among themselves would man expand so rapidly.

Alexander discovered new regions and people and introduced a great many previously encountered lands to Mediterranean people who had never imagined their existence. He created expeditions to explore the southern coast of the Caspian Sea and the Arabian coast of the Persian Gulf, and carefully mapped regions that had only been rough sketches before. Whether Alexander was the most traveled man to this point in time is impossible to tell, though he certainly holds that honor among those who kept records of their movements. As such, it should be noted that Pytheas, Hanno, et al., traveled over the seas and made stops along the way, whereas Alexander did nearly all of

his traveling by land. He immersed himself in the cultures of the regions he visited, but never managed to compile in one place, as did Herodotus, his thoughts about all he had seen along the way.

Perhaps an older, settled Alexander could have made sense of all that he had seen and done. Perhaps Alexander, the wily general, could have resisted, if not actually subdued, the Romans, and changed the course of history. Neither, of course, ever happened. With the keen senses of a general and the heart of a wanderer, Alexander traveled pell-mell through Asia Minor, southwest Asia, and the Indian subcontinent. Where aggression gave way to exploration, greed to curiosity, is unclear. But in the same way that Alexander has of popping up in all aspects of history, so does he leave his mark in the world of exploration. It would be more than a millenium before any European would reach beyond his boundaries.

3

COLD,
FORGOTTEN SEAS

he rise of the Roman Empire marks the beginning of a remarkably unadventurous period in the history of exploration. The Romans reasoned that the only lands worth exploring were those that had something worth taking. They didn't visit; they invaded. In fact, one of the few travelogues that remains from that time recounts Julius Caesar's "journey of conquest" through Gaul into Britain. The best piece of Roman travel reportage extant was initially preserved to chronicle Caesar's military prowess. Used today by British scholars for insight into the history of the islands, *Gallic Wars* originally established Caesar as a preeminent general.

There were a handful of Roman exploratory expeditions dispatched over the centuries of the empire's existence, but there's little indication of any consistent cultural enthusiasm. Two years after Caesar met his bloody end, Paulinus led an expedition across the Atlas Mountains of northern Africa onto the edge of the vast Sahara Desert. Paulinus received great acclaim for his venture, but the lack of military or pecuniary reward in a harsh, barren land did little to inspire any imitators.

To the east, China's Han Dynasty rose around the same time as the Roman Empire. While the Romans expanded into lands that were already known to them through recent history (i.e., Darius, Alexander), the Chinese seem to have ventured toward lands they'd rarely felt safe enough to visit before. The fear of hostile nomadic tribes had been handed down from generation to generation, and only the unprecedented breadth of the Han expansion allowed the notion of distant travel to be seriously considered.

The story of Chang Chíen is probably the most noted example of how hazardous such travel could still be. Sent by his emperor to enlist allies against the Huns, Chíen was captured by them and held for a decade. Eventually he regained his freedom and continued his

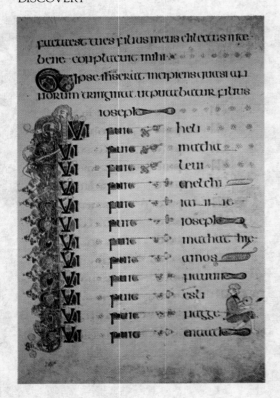

mission south through Kazakhstan (one of the southernmost Soviet republics) and into Afghanistan. Chíen had little success convincing anyone to return with him to fight the Huns, but he did play a role in establishing the path that eventually grew into the well-traveled Silk Route. Coming out of the heart of China, the Silk Route passed south of the Caspian Sea, skirting the Elburz Mountains in northern Iran in the vicinity of what is today Tehran. From there the route broke up and took several paths into Europe.

Along his travels, Chíen also helped introduce the hazy notion of a great eastern empire to the farthest outposts of Alexander's decayed legacy. They may have taken some time to work their way back to the Mediterranean, but the stories of Chang Chíen and countless other intrepid Oriental travelers lured Western explorers for more than a millenium. The promise of strange wonders and valuable commerce accompanied the imprecise information that filtered back to the heart of Europe and created an increasingly alluring notion of the Far East. Back home, Chang Chíen's stories fascinated his own people and eventually earned him another long, hazardous voyage west. To what extent Chíen's voyages specifically inspired others is unclear.

These entries from the Book of Kells *(above, right, and opposite page), an illuminated manuscript dating to approximately 800 A.D., are evidence of the artistic and religious spirit of the Irish monastics.*

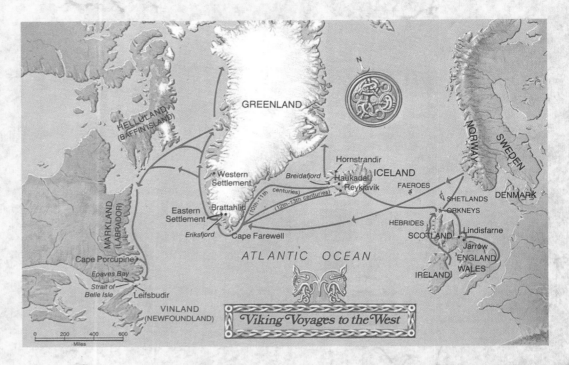

"I . . . have chosen to take upon myself this little task and recount the progress and outcome of our journey and navigation, not only in order to tell about it and make known the truth in the whole matter, but also in order to remove the temptation from many persons who may wish to relate this peregrination of ours or publish just the opposite of what we have experienced and seen. . . ."
—Brother Gaspar de Carvajal

Man's position at the center of the universe, as portrayed in this codex latinum *of St. Hildegard (opposite page), was essential to the development of Irish geographic theory. Peregrines headed out into the unknown, seeking the physical limits of their god's world.*

There were many others—from east and west—who set out for parts unknown during the centuries that followed, but just a handful of their names are known to us. Their stories are usually quite sketchy and the consequences of their discoveries more personally than culturally profound. (The early history of exploration is not all that picky; great detail *or* far-reaching ramifications are all that are needed for immortality, but hardly anyone seemed to possess either quality.) Middle Eastern and African traders expanded business along the Indian coasts and out towards the Orient, while their eastern counterparts ventured west. The Mediterranean, however, remained too politically chaotic to concern itself with exploration. Ships made regular voyages into the near North Atlantic, but the visions of early explorers were slowly fading from the collective consciousness of Europe. As Christianity rose to unify portions of the Continent, religious doctrine slowly veiled the rapidly diminishing geographic understanding of a waning civilization.

The adventurous cultures that eventually took up the spirit of exploration did so along the northern fringes of Western civilization. As a way of escaping local persecution, hardy souls struck out on their own into the uninhabited and unexplored regions. The Irish and Viking pioneers that plied the North Atlantic for much of the first millenium A.D. preferred to take their chances with the forces of nature than suffer the tyranny of others. Freed from the interference of a dominant power that extended into this territory, both groups skirted the fringe of the arctic world, undaunted by the treacherous waters of the cold northern seas.

Christianity had established a tenuous foothold in Ireland during the Roman occupation and grew slowly following its departure. It overcame a great deal of resistance within the island and looked to spread its message abroad. One reason for its eventual pervasiveness was the Irish Church's penchant for expansion. Some clerics set off as missionaries, looking to convert the pagans all around them; others, however, had more solitary aims. Many monks actively sought out the most forbidding, inclement, inhospitable surroundings in order to free themselves of intrusive neighbors and better live out their pious existences. (Surely the idea of self-denial is one that has appealed to the zealously devout throughout history. The Irish, however, excelled at a version of such abnegation novelly suited to their culture and technology. To the north were scores of remote, uninhabited islands, accessible only by boat. To the south, on the European continent, were the forbidding Alps. Both suited the Irish monastics' reclusive needs.)

52

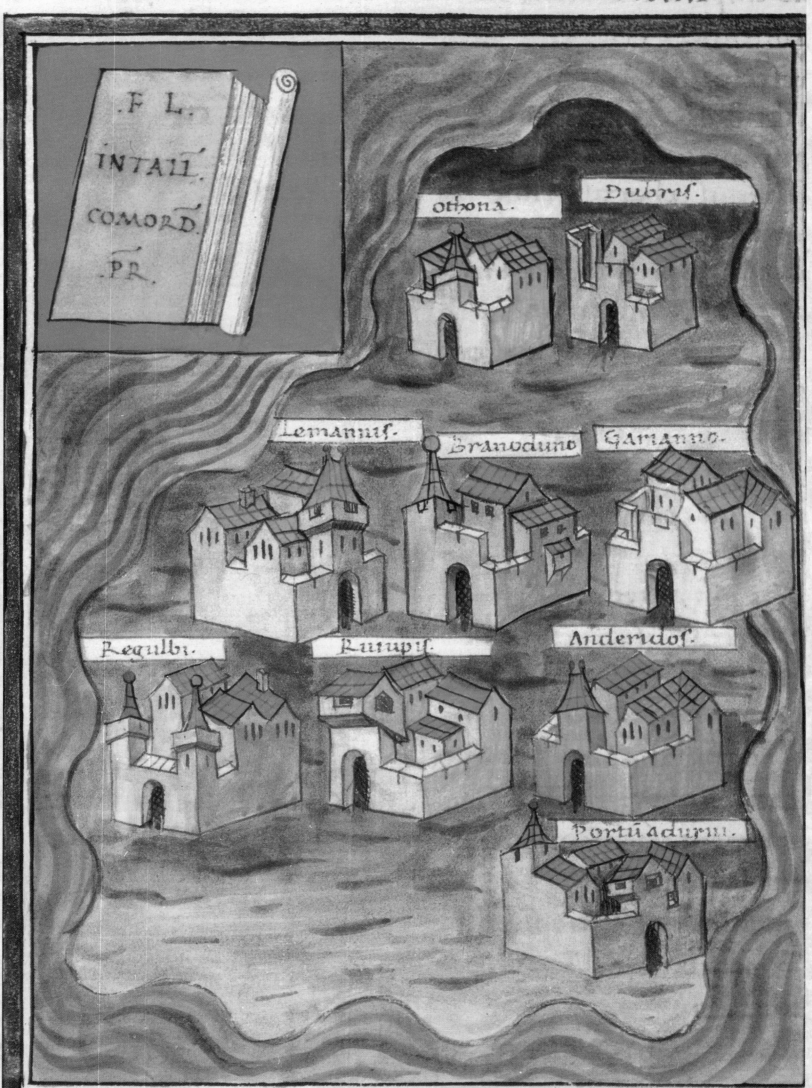

Totally independent of Mediterranean maritime evolution, the Irish developed their own seaworthy vessel well adapted to the cold, choppy waters of the northernmost Atlantic. The Irish *curragh* was made of tanned skins stretched across thin wooden frames and bobbed like a cork upon turbulent waters. It could be steered with surprising accuracy or simply left to drift. It was completely different from anything most Mediterranean skippers had ever encountered.

Some of the Irish saints that piloted curraghs out into the unknown may have been fleeing regional persecution. Others may have been simple wanderers metamorphosed into clerics by the religious historians who recorded their voyages. These tales, or *Imramha,* are filled with brave, hardy saints venturing out into the unknown. The most famous of them all is Saint Brendan, who sailed the seas in the fifth and sixth centuries A.D. and was immortalized by the *Navigatio Sancti Brendani (The Voyage of Brendan),* whose earliest remaining versions date back to the eighth century.

The *Imramha* are not exactly the greatest historic documents one could ask for; at times they make *The Agronautica* seem like fairly straightforward reportage. Voyages are usually a biblical forty days and forty nights in duration; distances are grossly imprecise; and any unfamiliar local phenomena are transformed into miraculous manifestations of the Promised Land. As a result, the *Imramha* have become fodder for a great deal of speculation.

It's accepted that the Irish were at least frequenting the near Atlantic. The geography of the *Imramha* may have been limited to islands that had been known to Greeks, Carthaginians, and Egyptians at various times during the preceding millenium: the Madeiras, Azores, Canaries, and Cape Verdes. Other Irish recluses were well established along the islands west of the Norwegian Sea (the Shetlands, Faeroes, and Iceland) during the eighth and ninth centuries, wherever the ever-expanding Norsemen seemed to go. Considering their abilities and peculiar inclinations, it seems reasonable to expect that Irish sailors extended that orbit even farther.

The solitary nature and religious fervor of the Irish anchorites makes it difficult to reconstruct this phase of discovery. By the time an anonymous Celtic cleric recorded the *Navigatio Sancti Brendani* toward the end of the ninth century, the tale had taken on fantastic proportions. Similar voyages were still taking place, but their personal, monastic nature made it impossible to create a unified picture from a mosaic of sources. The related *Imramha* present a jumbled, inexact story that many historians have chosen to disregard. The discrepancies

Saxon and Scandinavian art and crafts from the eighth and ninth centuries, such as those shown above and on the opposite page, are testament to the craftsmanship and creativity of the North Atlantic communities of this era. Inclement weather allowed artisans to spend a great deal of time honing their crafts, while others spent their time compiling the epic tales we rely upon when deciphering the history of this era.

and contradictions, they maintain, render the entire body of works historically inconclusive and unreliable. But there is a layer of truth beneath these tales that cannot be ignored. Since we are unable to document most of the specifics of Irish exploration during this period, we should not, as a result, belittle the anonymous accomplishments of generations of Irish anchorites.

There are those who have maintained that Saint Brendan—or one of a century's worth of his contemporaries, followers, and/or disciples—may even have beaten the Vikings to the New World. Perhaps the White Men's Land of *Erik's Saga*, recounting the Vikings' expansion several centuries later, was spawned by an Eskimo encounter with Irish anchorites. Maybe the inspiration for the Aztec god Quetzalcoatl, who paved the way for Hernán Cortés' devastation of that Mexican empire following Columbus' "discovery" of it, was in fact an Irish peregrine whose visitation became divine over the course of centuries. The extent of Irish exploration is impossible to determine for certain.

The effect of the *Imramha* on subsequent generations cannot be underestimated. As we will soon see, the Viking expansion west was certainly fueled by their encounters with Irishmen nearly everywhere they went. Though contact between the two was often reduced to invasion and pillage, it seems inevitable that some information would have been transferred between the two cultures.

The detailed work exhibited on this ninth-century Viking prow (left), as well as the wood head (opposite page) from the same time, are reflective of the Viking's nascent civilization. Drawing from their ancestors' roots, the Vikings blended their influences into a style suited to their nomadic lifestyle.

As such, they were sure to pass along some notion of still more islands unfamiliar to the Scandinavians. Perhaps the Vikings' failure to successfully colonize the North American continent could have been foreseen by the fact that they didn't find any Irishmen there upon their arrival.

More important than their influence on the Vikings, however, was the incentive the tales of Irish exploration provided the Europeans of a later century. It should be noted that the period of Irish exploration went hand in hand with their Golden Age of monastic scholarship. This is the period during which Ireland served as an alternate center of Christian learning for northern Europe. The arts of sculpture, metalwork, and illuminated manuscripts experienced periods of great vitality and were disseminated throughout the continent.

In the process of discovering the Irish arts, European scholars and cartographers were gleaning bits of information for their own studies. Mapmakers were soon filling the western Atlantic with a multitude of small islands as described in the *Imramha*. Each anchorite's discovery became a speck on a map, even though many were probably recounting previously chronicled specks. The concept of a "Land Promised to the Saints" lying west beyond the ocean planted a seed in the back of the European mind that would take nearly five centuries to come to fruition.

Though the Vikings were a great deal more specific in charting their travels to the New World, they actually provided very little inspiration for the brave Mediterraneans who later claimed it as their own. The tales of Brendan and his followers were a great deal more repercussive. Though the extent of their veracity is impossible to determine, their acceptance as fact by subsequent generations is undeniable. For a few centuries, small groups of men were climbing into small, buoyant crafts and sailing off to any place fortune had in store. Sometimes they remained close to

home, other times they traveled a bit farther away. How far is unclear.

One of the reasons the Irish kept moving was the encroachment of Scandinavian sailors. These Norsemen, or Vikings, plundered their way west like a nomadic horde on water. They were outcasts and outlaws from the Scandinavian peninsulas, and their aggressive way of life propelled them from one place to the next. Much has been made of, and exaggerated about, the Viking Expansion. While there is little doubt that they were a rough lot with little regard for those whose lands they took over, it's untrue that their aggression was based simply on greed or mean-spiritedness. "Land, not plunder," writes one contemporary scholar, "became their primary aim." They began as Danes, Swedes, and Norwegians. In many

cases, the Scandinavians who became Icelanders had departed on account of political persecution at home. (Norway's powerful King Harold Fair-hair was not as gentle as his name might suggest.) But, as they became more numerous and formulated a way of life suited to their peculiar existence, they developed a collective identity. (The term *Viking* is thought to derive from the Old Norse root *Vik*, meaning "creek" or "inlet", from whence the Norse ships were known to spring upon their unsuspecting victims. It should be remembered that the term was coined by those cultures that had served as the Vikings' prey, whose hand in recording Western history has had its revenge upon their ancestors' attackers. The term is vaguely equivalent to the contemporary notion of larcenous ambush.)

Most of the time the Vikings were simply looking for a hospitable piece of land on which to settle. All sources agree that by the time the Norse outcasts had made their way to Iceland there were Irish monastics scattered along the island's southern coasts. The Viking arrival convinced the anchorites to leave—whether it was on account of Norse force or Irish misanthropy varied from case to case.

The Vikings were the first to use rigged sails on the high seas and the first to venture out across the open northern waters instead of safely island-hopping the entire way. Their maritime technology was nearly five centuries ahead of the rest of Europe's, and once they settled into Iceland their nascent culture was equally impressive. The development of Icelandic literature during this period is one of the bright spots from a time

whose general "personality" was such that it has come to be known as the Dark Ages.

Within sixty years of the first permanent Norse resident of Iceland (in A.D. 870), the island's population grew to thirty thousand. All habitable land had been claimed, but the exiled and adventurous kept coming. Our information about the Viking Expansion is centered around the literature of that period, preserved in the form of epic sagas. As narrative history, they recount royal lineages and civil unrest. They provide heroes and villains and a handful of tales about murderers forced continuously west. Usually collected as the *Norse* or *Vinland Sagas*, those tales make for some of the most enjoyable reading of all exploratory literature.

Among those who made the western passage to Iceland was Erik the Red. He and his father left Norway around 960 in the wake of a bloody feud. The *Graenlendinga Saga* tells us of Erik's banishment "because of some killings" and creates an auspicious air for his departure. Before leaving, Erik is said to have confided to friends that he would seek a new land beyond Iceland, a land first brought to Viking attention some eighty years earlier.

Back then, Gunnbjorn Ulfsson had been blown off course on his way to Iceland and found an unknown coast far west of his destination. He landed upon a few rocky islands and quickly headed back for his original destination. Word of the Gunnbjorn Skerries was handed down within the community, and it was just a matter of time until someone investigated Ulfsson's discovery. (The word *skerry* is of Scandinavian origin, used to refer to rocky, essentially inhospitable, islands.) That time came when Iceland began to seem sufficiently occupied; we are told that Erik the Red was the man to do so, leaving more evidence of his homicidal nature behind.

The sagas indicate that Erik was involved in two more murderous encounters during his time in Iceland, the second of which led to his departure. With an angry posse close on his trail, Erik gathered up a crew and set out for Gunnbjorn's land around 981 or 982. (The route Erik took quickly established itself as the path of choice for an increasingly bustling trade between the new colonies and the established eastern nations.) Erik safely found Gunnbjorn's land, and spent the next three years exploring the large island off of which his ships lay. He skirted the southern coasts and eventually established a settlement just west of Cape Farewell (christened Hvarf's Peak by Erik), Greenland's southernmost point.

After three winters, Erik sailed back to Iceland. Whether he had originally intended to return is uncertain, though the sagas manage to suggest a predestination for all events. It is certainly possible—if the sagas are even correct in attributing all these exploratory accomplishments to one heroic family—that Erik's return was in fact a submission to the difficulties in establishing a new settlement on a foreign shore. Before the next spring had passed Erik was in trouble again, a result of another skirmish, more murders, and another banishment. Banishments were often limited to a set number of years.

The problem may not have been with the frequency of Erik's bloody battles (the sagas are full of such encounters) but with his apparent inability to win the political battles that accompanied them. His own survival must serve as some testament to his personal prowess, but his inability to remain in Iceland could well have been the primary motive for Erik's return to his distant settlement.

If Erik couldn't exist peacefully in the society of others, he would establish his own. And in order to do that successfully he needed settlers to follow him back. Toward that end, Erik established himself as one of the slickest public-relations men in the history of exploration. As the sagas relate it,

"He named it *Greenland*, for he said that people would be much more tempted to go there if it had an attractive name." Erik the Red's persuasiveness convinced some to follow, and the hard times Iceland had fallen upon were surely contributory. A decade earlier famine had ravaged much of Europe, and the entire chain of trade and communication essential to the outer settlement's survival became "temporarily" unreliable. The sagas report that twenty-five ships left with Erik some time around 985 or 986. Only fourteen completed the journey. Some had turned back; others had been lost.

Among those who accompanied Erik was Herjolf Bardarson, a land-

A lifeless Viking helmet (opposite page) *does little to suggest the fear its wearer must have struck in the hearts of those who encountered it a millennium ago. As nomadic invaders, however, the Vikings were sure to suffer casualties of their own, one of whose funeral is depicted in this stone carving* (below), *found in Stockholm's Museum of History.*

"The background was all glaciers, and right up to the glaciers from the sea as it were a single slab of rock. The land impressed them as baren and useless.
—The Greenland Saga

owner who seems to have maintained some wealth during the hard times. Despite an apparently comfortable situation at home, he left quickly for Greenland. Though this probably had little effect on his former compatriots, Herjolf's move came as quite a surprise to his son, Bjarni Herjolfsson. He had gone to Norway on business and had returned to Iceland expecting to winter with his father. Upon discovering that Herjolf had packed up and moved, Bjarni convinced his crew to follow his father's path west despite the fact that none of them had ever traveled the route before.

It's a testament to Bjarni's perseverance—if not his recklessness—that he undertook such a journey. He and his crew set out for a land few had ever visited and about which only those who had failed to reach could offer any information. Had Bjarni and his crew arrived safely at Herjolf's new home they might have just merited a quick mention in the sagas. Instead, their ship was blown off course and missed its target. After days of directionless drifting beneath cloudy skies and fog, the sun shone through and soon led them to land. "They closed the land quickly," according to the *Graenlendinga Saga*, "and saw that it was flat and wooded." Bjarni's men wished to examine this unknown beach, but their leader demurred, preferring to travel on.

Bjarni appears to have led his ship north along this new coast and eventually to have turned east across open waters. According to the sagas, Bjarni had the good fortune to circle back on Greenland at the very place his fa-

ther had settled. Bjarni spent some time with Herjolf and later traveled back to Norway to tell others of his discovery. There was considerable interest in it, but Bjarni was also subject to a good deal of derision for having shown so little curiosity in an unknown land. But the first Norseman to have laid eyes upon a great unknown continent cared little for exploration and subsequently settled down to an agrarian existence in Greenland at the Viking's Eastern Settlement. The glory of colonizing waited for someone else.

Word of Bjarni's voyage, despite his own lack of enthusiasm, sparked interest in many fellow Greenlanders, including one of Erik the Red's own sons. Leif Eriksson was an accomplished seaman who had already distinguished himself by establishing direct, nonstop routes between Greenland and Norway and between Greenland and Scotland. Leif travelled to Herjolfsness to speak with Bjarni and returned with the ship the farmer had sailed in when he stumbled upon that new land. The sagas tell of Leif acquiring a crew as well, and it seems likely that some of Bjarni's original men were among them.

Leif Eriksson appears to have intended for his father to have led the mission, but this may have been more of a literary device than a historical fact. An ill omen on the way to the ship is provided as Erik's incentive for remaining behind, allowing young Leif to take his place in history. So, with Leif in command, he and his crew headed west, and came upon the place that Bjarni had sighted last before reaching Greenland. In view of his predecessor's failure to so much as lay claim to his discoveries, Leif made sure to plant his foot upon the soil. "Now we have done better than Bjarni," he reasoned. "We at least have set foot on it." Leif named it *Helluland* (Slab- or Flat-Rock-Land) and quickly moved on. The saga's description of this first site suggests it may have been part of Baffin Island, which comes within two hundred miles (320 kilometers) of Greenland near the Arctic Circle.

From here, Leif and his men traveled southwest and stopped at a number of islands and continental harbors. They wintered overlooking the ocean they had just bridged, feeding off of a bountiful land they named *Vinland*. There was no snow in winter; the salmon were bigger than any they had ever seen; and the days and nights were nearly equal in length. Assuming that Vinland is indeed North America, the question arises as to where the Norse settlements might actually have been located.

The arguments regarding the location of these settlements themselves fill volumes and involve everything from astronomy and scientific prehistory to North American anthropology

Artifacts, such as those from the era just preceding the period of Viking expansion (opposite page), *offer much more insight than do such fanciful depictions* (below) *of the Viking landing in the New World. (We can state with relative certainty that the Vikings did not sport these kinds of hats!)*

and taxonomy. Currently, there is a good deal of agreement that a major site discovered on the northern tip of Newfoundland, near a small hamlet known as L'Anse-aux-Meadow, was the site of a Viking settlement. Whether it's Leif's first settlement or belonged to his doomed brother Thorvald is impossible to determine. Perhaps Thorvald's successor, Thorfinn Karlsnefi, established the camp as the southernmost point of Viking expansion. Until any discoveries farther south are found, definitive evidence of Norse occupation remains exclusively

Canadian in terms of contemporary geography.

Thorvald Eriksson was considerably more adventurous than his brother and paid for it with his life at the hands of the *Skraelings* (the Viking term for the native residents of Vinland). Subsequently, Thorfinn made the strongest bid at establishing a permanent colony in Vinland but was also unable to peacefully coexist with the Skraelings. It is possible that later colonizers made the journey from Greenland and most likely that regular visits were made across the Davis

Strait to easily reap the fruits of Baffin Island. Perhaps some of those later visitors, no longer deemed worthy of more than a passing mention in the sagas or annals, did actually establish successful colonies on Vinland. None of this, however, could have stemmed the forces of nature and the politics that soon put an end to the Viking Expansion.

The plausibility of exploring Vinland any further passed as life in Greenland became increasingly difficult. Iceland fell prey to Norwegian trading politics, and Norway subse-

quently fell prey to, and passed along, the Black Death. The more distant the Norse outpost, the more isolated it became. Christianity had only established a tentative foothold in Greenland—even early Vatican manuscripts provide evidence of a familiarity with the Norse discovery of a distant continent. Matters were further complicated by a period of global cooling that resulted in harsher conditions and increasingly frozen seas. Graves were dug shallower and shallower as the cold descended farther south. In the fourteenth century, Iceland fell

under Danish rule, and a once-thriving center of exploration had been sadly reduced to a small, near-forgotten community surrounded by perceptibly colder seas. Despite a distinct national voice and a former link to Rome and the centers of Mediterranean learning, the lessons of the Norsemen were quickly lost or forgotten. Eventually, some time after Columbus staked his claim on the New World, the Vikings had left Greenland. Supremacy of the oceans returned to Mediterranean sailors, whose gazes were focused elsewhere.

This eleventh-century French tapestry features Harold, King of Norway, crossing the seas. Despite the relatively unthreatening appearance of him and his crew, Harold was greatly feared, and helped spur the movement of Viking outcasts to remote settlements.

4

A BRIEF GLIMPSE OF THE EAST

From the time after Hanno through that of the Viking discovery of Iceland little exploration originated from continental Europe. Its inhabitants were too busy fighting barbarians, infidels, and one another to realize that the growing Islamic culture to the east would have menaced any further expansion in that direction anyway. Exotic goods still trickled on to the continent through the Middle East, but talk of exploring mysterious, distant lands seemed superfluous at a time when there were more pressing concerns.

Pirates upon the waters and bandits along the highways inhibited Europeans of the first millenium A.D. from venturing far from home. Certainly, some individuals led the sort of nomadic existences that took them from continent to continent, but they left no records of their journeys and seem to have had no lasting historical effect. A blanket of ignorance lay across Western civilization, while a policy of isolationism became entrenched in the East. And between the two arose a hostile force, disinclined toward accommodating their intercourse. It was not a time for people to be traveling about.

As we have seen, the Vikings weren't exploring so much as escaping. Europeans, however, had no place to run. They huddled together in defense of nomadic enemies, only to fight among themselves once their defense seemed assured. Technology and art stagnated, and religion grew to a new prominence in their stead. The Christian hierarchy, particularly that portion which would center itself around the Italian peninsula, seemed to thrive in the darkness of the times, able to keep its corruptions and indulgences obscured by shadows.

During the twelfth and thirteenth centuries, the mythological kingdom of Prester John was thought to exist far to the east. Prester (Priest) John was said to rule a varyingly large Christian empire farther away than any European had ever traveled. He was, it could be argued, a logical manifestation of a religious culture looking to confirm its ideologies by their existence—and success—elsewhere. Centuries later, when access to the East was cut off, the kingdom of Prester John mythologically worked its way down to the southern portion of the African continent. Once the reality of Marco Polo's East became known, it was easier to accept the repositioning of the fabled empire than to confront the evidence of its basis in fiction and the possibility that one's religion was simply one of many, and by no means the most pervasive or powerful.

The bright lights of intellectual curiosity were shaped, and contained, by the Catholic church. Explorers investigated distant lands under the auspices of the Catholic Church, but there is scant evidence of the Church having any inclination toward sharing its knowledge with the lay people, particularly when it was contradictory to Christian doctrine. Eventually, however, the general populace resumed its own interest in the mysterious East. Adventurers and foreign visitors rekindled old folklore and provided contemporary apocrypha to create an ever-changing caricature of the farthest reaches of Asia. When Europe redirected its eye towards the horizon, it found a great new empire to the east—an empire with which the Catholic church hoped to link itself and from which adventurous merchants hoped to profit.

Though it's likely that some might have gone searching for Prester John, we have no record of such journeys. Until the rise of the Mongols, travel was so treacherous most explorers either turned back quickly or never returned at all. By the time a few intrepid missionaries successfully ventured out toward the far reaches of Asia, they did so on account of the relative peace that arose throughout a continent that had never witnessed such unification. The first explorers to record their visits to the East were certainly not the first to make such journeys. Instead they were members of an organization committed to chronicling and preserving its own history—a church that has distinguished itself for its archival inclinations—a church that hoped to find an ally in the powerful force to the east.

The period of Mongol rule is a fascinating, misunderstood chapter in history that has often been reduced to unflattering, comedic stereotypes or fictionalized, utopian fantasies. Yet the empire that grew under Genghis Khan is greater than any that came before it or that have arisen since. The Mongolian Empire was more than twice the size of the Roman Empire at its peak. The Great Khan, as each of the rulers of the empire was known, exerted his will from the Black Sea to the Yellow Sea, the

Danube to the Yangtze. He received tribute from the arctic north and the ports of Southeast Asia. At a time when Europe was subject to constant infighting and conflict, the Mongol empire was a marvel of military power, social organization (complete with a welfare system), and cultural curiosity. The court of Kublai Khan was the apex of this impressive dynasty, as magnificent as it was different from anything any European had ever seen.

It is no accident that the century of Mongolian supremacy coincides with the first great era of modern exploration. Though inclined to aggression and ruthlessness abroad, the courts of the Great Khans were open to the beliefs of others and encouraged contact with distant travelers. Cities could be casually sacked, yet visitors were rarely received as enemies. It eventually became known that Mongols who escorted foreigners to their ruler would be rewarded well for their efforts, which was probably more compensation to them than anything the foreigners could be fleeced of.

The first European to travel deep into the heart of the Mongolian empire and provide a narrative of that journey upon his return was an Italian friar by the name of Giovanni di Piano Carpini. At the advanced age of sixty he was dispatched eastward by Pope Innocent IV in 1245. The pope had learned of the recent death of Ogödei Khan, Genghis' son and hoped that his successor might be inclined toward Christianity. To obtain more information he sent the elderly Franciscan to investigate.

Carpini traveled to Kiev, and then passed north of the Black, Caspian, and Aral seas. He eventually encountered one of Genghis' grandsons, Batu, who brought Carpini and his companions to the royal court at Syra Orda, on the northern border of the Gobi Desert. The friar arrived in time to see the coronation of the third Great Khan, Kuyuk. This Khan was presently occupied in a struggle to control the throne and had little time

to worry about foreign missionaries. There was a tolerance for the Italian's beliefs and pronouncements, but Carpini soon returned home with little tangible success.

The next Franciscan to venture east departed shortly after Carpini's return, though it's uncertain whether he was familiar with the developments of his predecessor's journey. Guillaume de Rubrouck made the long, uncertain journey into the heart of modern-day Mongolia in the name of the French king Louis IX. He outdid Carpini by reaching Karakorum, the capital of the Mongol Empire, where Mongu had just become the next Great Khan. Rubrouck might possibly have been the first European to visit the Mongolian capital and is certainly the first to report having done so. Despite this accomplishment, he too met with little success in converting the Great Khan. He eventually returned home with more wondrous tales to fire the reawakening European imagination.

Some time around 1260, two brothers who were Venetian merchants embarked on an eastward journey. They

These maps, from the fifteenth (above) *and sixteenth* (opposite page) *centuries, still relied on information hundreds of years old. The information Marco Polo brought back to Europe served as the basis for most maps of Asia's interior for another three or four hundred years.*

"*It is impossible to understand medieval conceptions of the inhabited world and to realize how very limited the geographical knowledge of even the most cultured men in the earlier Middle Ages was. . . .*"
—Arthur P. Newton

Marco, his father, and his uncle left the known world behind at Constantinople, which was an important commercial and religious outpost as far back as the sixth century, when the drawing above was made. The city they visited had more in common with that rendered on the opposite page, in which ships from Asia, Europe, and Africa converged.

" . . . he endeavoured, wherever he went, to obtain correct information on these subjects and made notes of all he saw and heard, in order to gratify the curiosity of his master."
—Eileen Power

set out for Constantinople, along an oft-traveled, comparatively safe road. Sometime after departing from Venice, unbeknownst to those who had seen them off, the brothers decided to extend their travels and continued east, trading about the enormous inland seas—the Polos were simply letting geography and economy direct them. Little did they realize they would eventually cross the Asian continent, making them perhaps the first "Latins" to do so. They sought adventure and economic gain and in doing so propelled themselves into the domain of the last truly great Great Khan, grandson of Genghis: Kublai.

Niccolo and Maffeo Polo, traders in fine gems and jewels, searching "in the hope of a profitable venture," first encountered Kublai's cousin, Barka, himself a Khan of the West. (The subdivisions within the Mongol empire, some of which spent as much time fighting among themselves as with others, are more complicated than a book of this nature can address. There were a number of lesser Khans, many with rather colorful titles, who usually deferred to the Great Khan's desires.) They traded with Barka, the Khan of the Golden Horde, at great profit, and spent a year within his lands. When a local war broke out,

the Polo's decided it was time to leave, but found their route back home had been blocked. With little alternative, they headed north, where they entered the domain of the Khan of Turkestan, another of Genghis' descendants. The Polos remained with him for three years.

An envoy of the Great Khan's paying a visit to this local capitol marveled at the Polos' penetration into the heart of the Mongol empire and assured them they would be well advised to visit the Great Khan himself at his distant palace. The brothers agreed and set out for Khan-balik, where modern Beijing sits today. The journey was probably not as hazardous as the ones they had already made, now that they were safely within Khan's border, and they appear to have reached him with relative ease.

The Westerners are said to have intrigued Kublai Khan, though it's important to remember that the source of that information was Niccolo's son, Marco. The Polo brothers spoke with Kublai at great length about their homeland, their fellow Europeans, and their beliefs. The Great Khan eventually asked the Polos to pay his respects to the Pope and request from him that as many as one hundred

MARE CONGELATU
TARTARICUM
i a Guilælmo
6 cœpit, nomine
Süne verõ N.
riente, necne,
inconsultè
Tabin Plinio

Tabin promontoriu

AMERICÆ
PARS

M Tranquillum

Bargu Campestria

Cacatora

ANIAN FRETUM

Ung quæ Gog.
nonnullis dicitur

Corus
lacus

Tartar fluvius

Tartar

TENDUC Regnum
in quo Christiani regnabant
anno 1290.

Razata ins.
hic à Plinio
ponitur

Taingin

CARLI.

Sumongul que
MAGOG Mercatori

Zacabir

Tenduc

Mongul

Carocaran

Mons Alchai in quo Regum
Tartariæ sepulchra sunt.

Unchiam castru
contra irruptiones
Tartarorum

Sindacui

Xandu

Cavona

BARSOL

CATAIO

Ahisis

C de Fortuna

Naiman

Belgian desertum

Calacia

Cianganor

COLMAK

ANNIBI Naina
vorum terra Ioã:
ni de Planocarpini

STINGUI

Erina

Sandri

Cingui

Cambalu R

Caidu

Exandu

MARI

Annibus
lacus

Pasamfu

Cambalu

Tingu

Brema

Erginul

Gousa

Tango

SCYTHIA
EXTRA IMA-
UM MONTEM

In deserto Lop et Belgi
ari mira phantasmata esse,
mirabilesq, stresetus
diabolicos audiri,
hominesq, ab ijs se:
duci aiunt.

Camul

Canglu

Achbaluch

PACIFI

Ciangli

Serra

Geueiganfu

Suidio

Camul

Campion cujus
incolæ partim sunt
Christiani
Gauta

In hac regione mons est ex quo
terra effoditur (terra Abessus
Plinio) tenuissimis fibris, instar
graminis, quæ aptatæ in filum tex:
yntur, pannusque ex eo in
ignem injectus non coburitur

PARS

Desertum
Davisaval

Turfon

Sachion

Mulon

Hoyam

Quicui

Imaus mons

Chialis

Ochardus flu.

Suecuir

Chinchitalas

Kitai
lacus

thay

ra Cataio

Emil

Cuthia

Cogicamri

LOP DESERT.

Cangi

CIARIAM

Murus quadringentarum Leucarum inter montium crepidines
à Rege China contra irruptiones Tartarorum extructus.

Taskent

Pinegle

Lop

SKENT

PEIM

Peim

Aceu

Cotam

Chulifu

BELOR

COTAM

Xuntien aliv
Quinsay id est
cæli civitas quod
rex Chinæ hic
sedem habeat

Tauxem

Siganfu

CHI-

Chinsam I

digen

ESERTUM

UX

Taitofu

Sancij

NÆ REG:

COREA INS

Caradris st

Loheuhudu

Tiachio

amasi

Tayhancon

NI PARS

Turris la:
pulea mons

Sazechiam

Chana quicu

Ceuchio

Raosa

Hoychioy

Pehiou

Carazan

Tubchu

Tanhau
cezim

Douchio

Mechenderi

Iratusi

Borata

Vociam

Paliamliu

SANCII

Micheu

Lacus
Cincunhay

AN

BRAMAS

Zaridohu

TARTARIA

Candatai

Venhiu

Medius Meridianus est 120.
reliqui ad hunc inclinantur (ad
circulu maxi.) pro ratione 40.

Quito

Canchu

Niachu

Quidchenu

Marco Polo returned to Venice, viewed from an intriguing perspective (below), after twenty-five years in Asia, only to be denied entrance to his own home (right).

learned Christians be sent to his court. Then Kublai and his people could hear these learned men present the tenets of this Western faith and determine whether or not it had merit.

The Great Khan bestowed a golden tablet upon the brothers, with which they were accorded all privileges throughout the empire. For three years the Polos traveled west, occasionally delayed by impenetrable passes, swollen waterways, and a variety of seasonal hazards. Upon their return, the adventurous merchants learned that Pope Clement IV had died a year earlier, with no successor yet named. Instead of waiting in Acre, where they heard the news, Niccolo and Maffeo decided to return home to Venice; it's interesting to note that this alternative was not considered until it became clear that it would be some time before the next Pope would be chosen.

Niccolo's wife had passed on during his absence. Upon his return, only his son Marco, now fifteen years old, was there to greet him. Father and son became reacquainted during the two years the Polo brothers awaited the selection of the new pope, and Marco's own wanderlust—probably fueled by his father's tales and wealth —became apparent. When Niccolo and Maffeo finally departed from Venice, distressed by the continued delay in selecting the next pontiff, Marco accompanied them. So began one of the greatest journeys in history.

In addition to Christian scholars, the Great Khan had also requested "oil from the lamp that burns above the sepulchre of God in Jerusalem." Without a pope to dispatch the Christian scholars, the Polos, anxious to return to the East, attempted to at least obtain the oil. In the process of doing so they encountered the man who would shortly be chosen the next pontiff and assume the name Pope Gregory of Piacenza. Their previous deal-

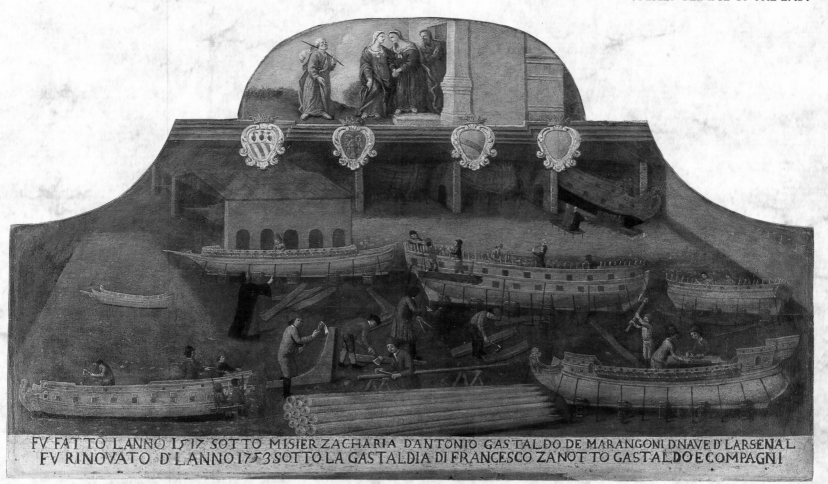

FV FATTO LANNO 1517 SOTTO MISIER ZACHARIA D'ANTONIO GASTALDO DE MARANGONI D'NAVE D'L'ARSENAL
FV RINOVATO D'LANNO 1753 SOTTO LA GASTALDIA DI FRANCESCO ZANOTTO GASTALDO E COMPAGNI

ings with the new pope had been fortuitous, and soon after Gregory was chosen, the three Polos headed east with two emissaries dispatched by him. Much has been made of the weak show the Church was able to muster in view of the potential benefits an alliance with the Mongol Empire could have realized. A stronger, unified effort on the part of Christianity may have had a great effect on the history of that era, though it's possible Pope Gregory was skeptical of anything more than simple curiosity on the part of the the Great Khan. Nearly all of the Khans were religiously permissive, though none exhibited any strong inclination toward conversion to the many religions being proffered. Had any of them developed real enthusiasm for the West's Christianity they could well have become later-day Constantines, injecting the words of the Church with new strength and vitality. Instead, they faded into obscurity and legend.

Before the Polo's entourage had made its way through Asia Minor, the pope's two emissaries decided such travel was far too hazardous and turned back. After finally obtaining the oil in Jerusalem, the Polos wasted no more time and began the long journey back to Khan-balik. In 1275, three and a half years after having left him, the brothers again paid their respects to the Great Khan in his palace and introduced him to Marco. Kublai Khan was quite taken with the bright young man (or so that young man would tell us many years later) and appears to have gained great respect for the young Venetian's intelligence and diligence.

So began a relationship that would span nearly two decades, during which an observant, interested young European traveled throughout the farthest reaches of the Asian continent. Marco "enjoyed facilities for extensive travel in the Mongol empire" and seems to have taken full advantage of them. He passed through much of China, skirted along the border of Tibet, and journeyed by sea along the eastern and southern coasts of Asia. He traveled north toward the Siberian Uplands and south among the islands comprising Indonesia. It is small exaggeration to suggest that it might be easier to list the places Marco Polo didn't visit than those he did.

A later history of Venetian shipbuilding (above), *pays homage to a maritime community that both launched Polo on his travels and subsequently led to his capture, providing the opportunity to record his incredible tale. Marco Polo's introduction to the Great Kublai Khan* (following page) *is chronicled in this thirteenth-century painting. Marco, in green, kneels behind his father and uncle.*

As a representative of the last great Mongol monarch, Marco Polo journeyed to places no Westerner would revisit until the twentieth century. He encountered unimaginable cultures throughout a wide variety of climates. Like countless other enterprising souls, Marco Polo traveled far and wide. But Marco, on a scale greater than anyone before him, returned to tell the tale.

The history of discovery can be a surprisingly subjective endeavor, and there are few individuals who have been the object of continuing appreciation. Ferdinand Magellan and Captain James Cook showed themselves to be such men in turn. Marco Polo seems to have been the first. Though mocked in his later years for his assumed tendency to exaggerate, Polo was undeniably the first great explorer. There were certainly financial motives underlying his curiosities, but here was a man who had seen things beyond imagination and who would eventually find himself with the time to record his experiences.

After seventeen years in the service of the Great Khan, the Polos began to consider a return to the West. Kublai was growing old, and Marco suggests that the Polos feared for their safety once their gracious friend was no longer alive to protect them. The Khan is said to have been reluctant to see his friends leave, but he eventually permitted their departure to escort a local woman betrothed to a regional khan in the West. The caravan set out on a voyage around Southeast Asia and the Indian subcontinent toward the Arabian Sea. Six hundred emissaries and attendants began the journey, of whom less than twenty arrived at their final destination.

The wily, well-traveled Polos all managed to survive the journey and eventually returned to Venice in 1295. They were initially met with skepticism by relatives who had long since given up hope of their return, but Maffeo, Niccolo, and Marco guaranteed themselves an enthusiastic reception by revealing the great wealth they had accumulated. And here the story could have come to its end, passed down as local folklore for a generation or two before fading into obscurity, were it not for a war that arose between Venice and Genoa in 1298. One of its participants was a gentleman commander of a Venetian galley named Marco Polo.

The Genoans dealt the Venetians a mighty blow at the Battle of Curzola, taking Polo and his crew prisoner in the process. The "gentleman commander" appears to have been accorded some privileges and shared a cell with a minor author of popular romances. Rustichello of Pisa listened as Polo regaled fellow prisoners, jailers—and even influential Genoans—with his anecdotes. The writer in Rustichello realized that these reminiscences were far better than any of the fictitious "travel books" enjoying a good deal of popularity during that time. "It would be a great pity," he wrote of Marco, "if he did not have a written record made of all the things that he had seen and heard by true report, so that those who have not seen them and do not know them may learn them from this

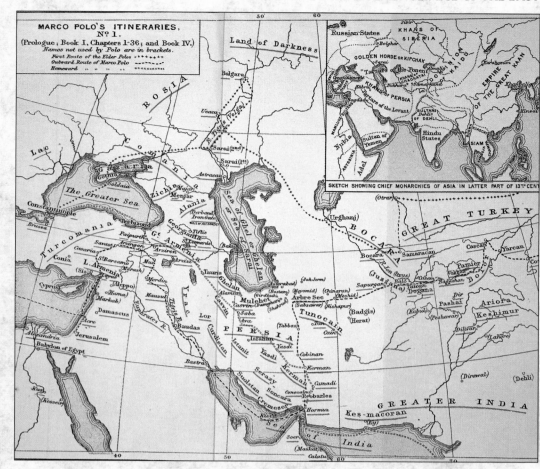

Polo's extensive travels, only a portion of which are incorporated into this map of central Asia (above), *exposed him to cultures few westerners had ever encountered. Along the way, Polo attempted to learn what he could of each region's customs and beliefs, such as the Tartars, whose garb he is shown wearing* (opposite page).

book." And so the composition of *The Travels of Marco Polo* was begun.

Marco was afforded the courtesy of obtaining the notes he had compiled during his time in the East, from which he recreated his travels for the writer and a fascinated audience. The task was barely completed when peace was established in 1299. The prisoners were released, sending Polo home to Venice and Rustichello to an uncertain fate. It appears that Polo led a comfortable existence thereafter, despite occasionally finding himself the subject of derision on account of his suspect stories. Branded *Il Milione* (*The Millions*) for the apparently unbelievable sizes and quantities he attributed to the Great Khan's possessions, copies of his book were spreading throughout the literate Mediterranean and European communities a century and a half before the revolution in printing technology made such things easier. It's important to keep in mind that *The Travels* enjoyed their initial popularity at a time when few lay works were deemed worthy of being copied by hand. The classics of Greek literature had yet to be reintroduced to European bookshelves, and just a handful of fictitious endeavors made their way throughout the scattered outposts of literacy. Some of those, such as *The Travels of Sir John Manville*, were highly imaginative precursors to the factual travelogues inspired by the collaboration of Polo and Rustichello.

Marco Polo told of cultures and regions no European had ever imagined existed. He was the first European to describe the Malay Archipelago and the first to report the presence of an island empire east of the Asian continent. Polo never visited *Cipangu* (Japan), but his time along the Yellow Sea made him familiar with those who claimed to have been there. Further south he visited a place "teeming with elephants, unicorns, and other wild beasts". Historians think this lies within modern-day Burma. Another time he traveled by boat to India. Possessing a keen eye and the appraising instinct of a good Venetian trader, Polo was able to retain a wealth of facts and figures.

Unfortunately, however, Polo was by no means the perfect anthropologist. His personal interests blinded him to areas that are inconceivably neglected. Polo traveled throughout the heart of China's tea-growing regions without making mention of the plant nor its uses. (Regardless of the fact that he traveled as a member of the Mongol occupation, it's astonishing, possibly indicative of his isolation from the indigenous "lower classes," that Polo could have been so oblivious to such a pervasive element of the native culture.) He was equally unaware of the development of printing technology in China, while at the same time proclaiming the presence of Prester John in the region, proving that Polo was still mired in myth. Polo also failed to make a single mention of the Great Wall, his most glaring omission of all. Mocked at home for his "exaggerations," Polo would have been held in even greater derision by his fellow Europeans had he described a great man-made fortification on a scale exponentially greater than anything Westerners could imagine. But legend has it that Polo assured those gathered around his deathbed that he had not told half of what he had seen.

Marco Polo died some time around 1324, but it is interesting to note we know very little about the years following his release from prison. His name can be found in official Venetian documents, and it's clear he maintained a profitable business. But his later years were probably quite calm compared to the excitement of his youth. He passed away with little fanfare, with little recognition given of his place in history and his own part in bringing that period to a close. Europe was reawakening to the presence of foreign lands and peoples, and Marco Polo had spurred it into action with his tales.

There are those who credit Marco Polo with altering history. Others suggest he was at least an active catalyst. "Marco Polo excelled all other known Christian travelers in his experience, in his product, and in his influence," writes historian Daniel Boorstin, who believes, "Never before or since has a single book brought so much authentic new information, or so widened the vistas for a continent." H. G. Wells simply credited *The Travels of Marco Polo* as leading "directly to the discovery of America." Polo went, he watched, and (eventually) he wrote it all down. His tales sparked the reawakening curiosity of the European mind, creating a smouldering flame that would ignite a full-fledged Renaissance several centuries later.

Marco Polo was by no means the first Westerner to have contact with the farthest Asian ports, and Niccolo and Maffeo may not have been the first European guests in Khan-balik. Throughout *The Travels*, Marco makes mention of a wide variety of foreign traders. Marco simply emerged as the best at letting others know of his exploits—he was the most widely read. A new era was dawning in Western civilization, and had a few lucky Venetians not blazed the way someone else would have come along in due time; Arabs and Mediterraneans were returning with reports of distant lands. Eventually one of these travelers would have recorded personal travels. Genghis Khan and his descendants are the creators of an era Marco Polo simply chronicled and in which he played some small role. The Mongol Empire would survive long enough for others to confirm what Polo had stated as fact, just long enough to plant a seed of imagination in the Western mind.

Before Marco, Niccolo, and Maffeo had even begun their journey back to Venice, a Franciscan friar, John of Monte Corvino, headed east as a representative of Pope Nicholas IV.

Monte Corvino traveled across Persia to the Persian Gulf and continued by water past India, through the Straits of Malacca, along the South China Sea, and finally into the Yellow Sea, reaching Khan-balik in 1294. He was allowed to construct a church directly across from The Great Khan's palace and managed to convert a large number of Chinese. The pope appointed the friar to the position of Archbishop of Cambaluc (Peking) in 1307 and later dispatched a number of subordinate bishops to his see.

One of the Archbishop's Franciscan visitors in China was Odoric of Pordenone, who set out to convert the continent, but estimated his final total at something closer to 20,000 conversions. He left an excellent record of his travels, reporting a number of things Marco Polo had failed to note, but is also remembered for the particularly taxing route he followed home. Pordenone traveled along the northern edge of the Himalaya Mountains before plunging down into the Hindu Kush range. He returned to the West in the year 1320, twelve years after having set out from Italy. It's probably no exaggeration to suggest it took every ounce of his dwindling energy to complete the journey, since he died shortly after dictating his adventures.

Only one other traveler from this era preserved a record of his adven-

For several centuries, world maps (such as the one shown, opposite page) owed an enormous debt to Marco Polo, and his story as related by Rustichelli. Subsequent travelers, even centuries later, were often surprised by the accuracy of Polo's descriptions and the breadth of his geographic understanding.

"Many cities did he visit, and many were the nation with whose manners and customs he was acquainted."
—Homer

tures comparable in scale to Marco Polo. He was a Moslem native of Tangier, known as Ibn Batuta, who set out on a pilgrimage in the 725th year of the Hejira. The Hejira was the flight of Muhammad to Medina and his subsequent establishment of Islam; in the same way that Christians measure time from the birth of Christ, Muslims employ this time as their point of reference. In this case, A.H. 725 corresponds to 1324. Along the way, Batuta encountered "one of the greatest saints in Alexandria," who suggests that Batuta visit his three brothers scattered among the farthest outposts of Islamic expansion. "I was astonished at what he said," reports Batuta, "and determined with

myself to visit those countries: nor did I give up my purpose till I had met all the three mentioned by him, and presented his compliments to them."

Batuta was by no means the first of his religion or race to reach most of the places he went, and his focus is frustratingly singular. *The Travels of Ibn Batuta* are myopically Moslem in their attention, chronicling the way fellow believers existed in foreign lands as opposed to the customs of the actual natives. In many ways, Ibn Batuta's book is similar to those of his contemporary Christian pilgrims on their way to their Holy Land. Dismissing most of the indigenous culture, they chronicle birthplaces, grave

"This may contribute but little towards impressing the reader with the greatness of his courage, his religious confidence, or his indefatigable [sic] perseverance, in overcoming the difficulties of passing deserts and of crossing mountains . . ."
—The Travels of Ibn Batuta

sites, and the miraculous venues of their respective faiths. Geographic information is scant and imprecise, social observation deemed unimportant. In fact, the pilgrimage itself, the ostensible reason for Batuta's departure from his home overlooking the Strait of Gibraltar, is hardly mentioned at all. Within two short sentences Batuta covers his visit to Mecca and quickly moves on to Medina.

The statistics regarding Sheik Ibn Batuta's journey are quite impressive. In just over thirty years he is estimated to have logged over 75,000 miles (120,000 kilometers), traveling through every Moslem country with the exception of portions of Asia Minor and western Russia. Batuta traveled extensively throughout Arabia toward the beginning of his wanderings and later expanded his treks to include China, India, Africa, and parts of Europe. Moving over mountain ranges and across seas, Ibn Batuta was relentless in his effort, if somewhat uncertain of his purpose.

Batuta's perseverance is particularly remarkable when one considers that he traveled during the time of the Black Death. Such historic facts occasionally emerge from his work and help us place it in time, but some of them stretch our criteria for objectivity. At one point, Ibn Batuta recounts a time "when the people were assembled for the purpose of prayer against the plague: which ceased on that very day." Perhaps Batuta's book would have been more fantastic had it been more descriptive. Instead it reads like a pilgrim's log, mired down in its emphasis on mosques and miracles. Nowhere near as colorful as Polo's "bestseller," Batuta's *Travels* weren't as informative or influential. Today, they provide bits of information and a sense of local color but fail to distinguish themselves as a literary work in the way that so many other chronicles of exploration have.

A final, brief mention should be made at this point of an Italian merchant who followed Marco Polo and

Ibn Batuta by a bit more than a century. Niccolo dei Conti was raised in Damascus and subsequently spent twenty-five years traveling throughout southern Asia. The precise information dei Conti provided cartographers was particularly helpful for the generation of explorers who rounded out the fifteenth century. Dei Conti appears to have adopted the ways of the peoples he traveled among, but made penance for his lapsed Christianity upon his arrival in Venice in 1444. Once again it was the Church that recorded this history and provided the framework from which the next generation would expand.

While Marco Polo (opposite page, above) was the most well-known traveler of his day, there were certainly others venturing into unknown lands at the same time. This Arabic map from the twelfth-century (opposite page, below) is stylistically different from western maps, but manages to convey the same essential information. The islands of Southeast Asia (above) were involved in a thriving trade as well, although it would be a few centuries before they became accessible to the west.

5

AROUND
& ACROSS

ere begins the period of greatest activity in the history of exploration and the widespread emergence of humanity's awareness of the planet. Far-reaching and well attended, this era of exploration, which encompassed the fifteenth and sixteenth centuries, accomplished the seemingly impossible and encountered the unimaginable. It mistook islands for continents, continents for islands, and North American "Indians" for Asians. And, to the ignorance of many involved, two new continents were discovered, and a third was rounded. In the early periods of discovery, only single journeys have survived to embody an entire movement, while the burst of activity that began with the Portuguese in the fifteenth century is filled with the names of the sailors and adventurers who swarmed the coasts of the New and Old Worlds. In an attempt to prevent the succeeding chapters from becoming little more than a catalog of names, a number of historic adventures must be overlooked. Like Homer, we focus on the spectacular while depriving others of their hard-earned place in history.

Europe emerged from a millenium of dormancy to reclaim control over itself, paving the way for a period of growth and relative enlightenment. (Keep in mind, however, that Portuguese expansion benefited from the oppression of the Spanish Inquisition and operated during its early stages under the guise of a sanctified crusade.) The seeds of Marco Polo were coming to flower in a renaissance, a rebirth, of Mediterranean Europe that eventually spread throughout the Continent. Seemingly unrelated endeavors led to mutual advances, so that the arts and sciences flourished alongside one another. Painting, sculpture, and architecture have received the most emphasis for that era, but impressive strides were also made in both abstract and applicable technologies. And while the elite were the direct beneficiaries of these discoveries, the rise in literacy and numeracy beyond the

circle of nobility and wealth were equally important.

It is impossible to say which advances were responsible for the burst of exploratory activity that marks this period of time. Proponents of each endeavor often come to the conclusion that theirs was the catalyst of the European reawakening, but to suggest that any one field's achievements singularly paved the way for the others would seem to be a great oversimplification. The reintroduction of Europe's own literary history from the Arabic in which it was preserved, had a hand in matters, as did great advances in astronomy, cartography, and cosmography. Journeys to the far end of the globe provided scientists with data allowing them to improve their navigational technology, which in turn allowed explorers to make more detailed records of their ensuing travels. Whether the rise in literacy produced more historical documentation as a by-product, or the need to record increasingly important and complicated information spurred the growth of literacy is impossible to determine.

Marco Polo's travels may have triggered Europe's renewed interest in travel. The need was felt in the royal houses to consolidate control over their kingdoms and to find exploitable foreign ports in order to maintain or develop affluence. The Portuguese were a unified nation throughout the fifteenth century, while the Mediterranean powers spent much of their time fighting the Moors and one another. The Spanish fought the Moors on their own soil up to the time of Columbus' 1492 departure date, while the Portuguese rid themselves of occupying forces before the end of the thirteenth century.

The remote Portuguese were forced to brave the difficult Atlantic waters, which had its obvious disadvantages, but made them better suited to the rigors of transoceanic exploration than the virtually landlocked Mediterranean maritime community. This gave the small, Atlantic coastal kingdom a head start on the competition when it became clear that their maritime trade was more profitable than anyone might have imagined. Eventually the Spanish, and subsequently the British and Dutch, surpassed the trailblazing Portuguese, but none could ever lay claim to their foresight.

The Portuguese fulfilled the inevitability of European expansion. They led the way for the nations of Europe in expansion and exploitation, establishing dominance over the new continents for centuries to come. The Portuguese were the logical manifestation of Europe's newfound energy, but they still needed the vision of a man who could serve as midwife to the birth of a global political community that has shaped the way nations and peoples of the world act toward one another to this day. That man had grand visions for the future, but could never have comprehended the long-term results of his actions. Even now it is impossible to understand the enormity of colonialism, imperialism, and racial and economic subjugation in the way we have come to see the past, the present, ourselves, and the world around us.

Henrique, Prince Henry the Navigator, provided Portugal with the vision that led the small nation to its pinnacle of global eminence over the course of the next century. With little apparent thought of—or desire for—ruling his father's kingdom, and with the idleness that often accompanies those not in the direct line of succession to the throne, Prince Henry developed a keen interest in the great continent that lay to the south. He wished to explore it, convert its infidels, and then finally to go around it in search of a direct water route to the riches of the East.

Prince Henry does not seem to have been motivated by personal political ambition, and his obligatory religious proclamations often sound rather perfunctory. Whatever his individual quirks—and those have been the subject of a good deal of debate—Henry

"This is the story of heroes who, leaving their native Portugal behind them, opened a way to Ceylon, and further, across seas no man had ever sailed before."
—Luis Vaz de Camóes

Prince Henry the Navigator, featured in a painting by Nuno Goncalves (opposite page), was the visionary who focused Portugal's, and subsequently the rest of Europe's, gaze toward the southern tip of Africa and the possibility of a direct maritime route to the Far East.

European explorers began to venture into all possible directions, reflected by this world map (below) created in 1502. The Portuguese development of Africa's west coast is indicated by the wealth of information provided for that region. Forays to the New World, many of which had just been completed by the time this map was compiled, were still quite sketchy in detail.

had a great personal curiosity. He perched himself at the southern tip of Portugal and orchestrated the opening movements in the renaissance of discovery. What Marco Polo had planted in the minds of Europeans, Henry the Navigator set into motion. Prince Henry concentrated on the expansion of the Portuguese maritime community, underwritten by the profits he had gained from trade along the Atlantic coast of Africa. Unfortunately, not all of Henry's expenses could be met personally, which meant that many of his endeavors were financed by his regal relatives. Some of Henry's contemporaries saw this as a wise in-

vestment in the future, while others claimed the Prince's frivolous pursuits were bankrupting the small nation.

Regardless of his motivation, it was Prince Henry, wrote one historian, "upon whose shoulders might worthily rest the arduous beginnings of continuous maritime discovery." He established a School of Navigators near Cape Saint Vincent and adopted a methodical, scientific approach toward discovering new sea routes and new lands. In his day, Prince Henry the Navigator was as useful for his recording of known routes as for the more daring, exploratory voyages he commissioned whose

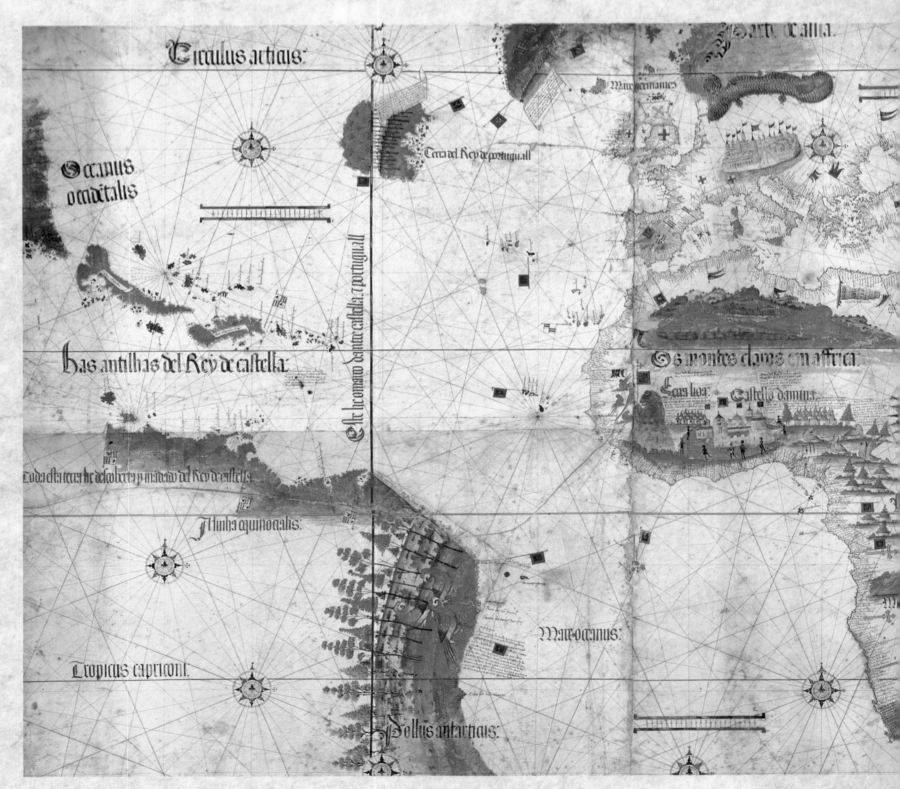

benefits were not as immediately tangible. Out of his academy came refinements upon the recently introduced *quadrant*, a device for measuring altitude, which had provided a useful alternative to the more delicate and complicated *astrolabe*. Henry's men also developed a ship that would serve as the prototype for several generations of vessels. A hybrid of Arab and Portuguese design, the *caravel* revolutionized voyages of discovery. Both its functional design and its peculiar combination of abilities established the caravel as the *modus operandi* for the remainder of sail-powered seafaring exploration.

The Portuguese, relatively free from internal strife and dependent upon trade for many of their staples, united to find access to those resources elsewhere. Spain's stranglehold on their interaction with continental Europe made it imperative for an independent Portugal to establish direct contact with other sources. The East beckoned, and the Portuguese felt that their naval superiority could be used to beat others to the fifteenth century's "Golden Fleece."

Along the way the Portuguese realized that some of those resources could be found much closer to home, from within the continent they were

looking to bypass. They were already establishing settlements among the Atlantic islands that had been rediscovered in the preceeding century—the Azores, Madeiras, and Canaries—and a slave trade was emerging along the Moroccan coast. Despite Prince Henry's personal vision, the Portuguese found themselves happily occupied with the business of exploiting the islands and coasts they had already discovered. With a wealth of untapped resources within reach, the Portuguese developed a barrier, based more on psychology than cartography, beyond which they seemed incapable of sailing.

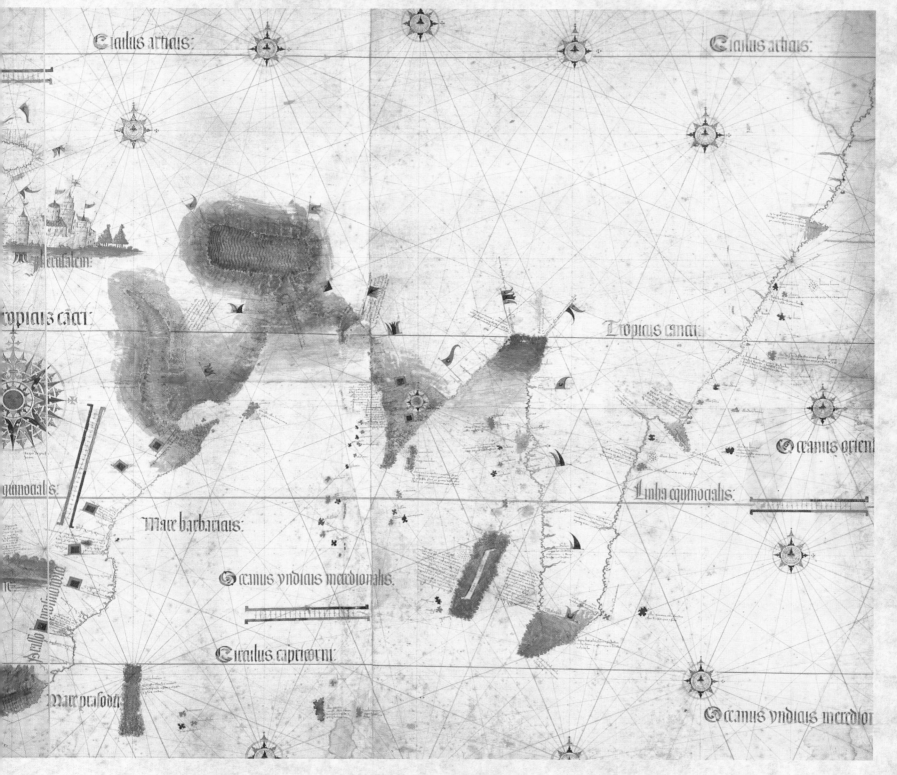

Over the course of time, Cape Bojador, just a couple of degrees below Gran Canaria Island, became established in the minds of sailors as an impassible marker to the end of the world as they knew it. Today the cape seems essentially unthreatening, though it's possible a few centuries have softened its reputedly menacing edges. In the fifteenth century, however, Prince Henry, despite all his enthusiasm, was unable to convince his captains to travel farther south than this bulge along the Atlantic coast. At least fifteen times the prince sent captains out with instructions to pass that strange barrier, and fifteen times they failed him. Some opted to tred the vaguely known shores of the eastern Atlantic islands, while others offered a variety of colorful excuses for their failure.

One of the later failures was made by a south Portuguese named Gil Eannes, who seems to have emerged from the lower nobility to a place in Henry's School of Navigation. Instead of rounding Cape Bojador, Eannes veered off to the Canaries, where he sacked a few villages and captured a few natives. Prince Henry patiently urged Eannes to try again, promising great rewards, and sent him back out, probably in 1434. This time, to the reported distress of his crew, Eannes mustered the courage to push beyond the Cape. They traveled a short distance past the dreaded promontory, gathering samples of dirt and fauna from the cape's far side as evidence that the world did not become a barren, boiling wasteland. The magnitude of Eannes' accomplishment has diminshed with time, but at the time, Prince Henry realized it was an important first step in the long journey eastward.

Eannes was well rewarded for his accomplishment, though its immediate financial benefits were apparently not enough to appease Henry's critics. During his own lifetime, Eannes' fame as an explorer was probably greater than that of most of his contemporaries. "Although the matter was a small one in itself," wrote Henry's biographer, Zurara, "yet on account of its daring it was reckoned great." Eannes repeated the voyage the next year, to prove it had been no fluke, and eventually approached the Tropic of Cancer.

Progress following Eannes was steady, but at a snail's pace. In the quarter century between Eannes' voyage and Henry's death, Portuguese sailors extended the African coast to Cape Palmas, at the western edge of what is today known as the Ivory Coast. The distance is a small fraction of what Henry had hoped to cover. Henry's death brought on a lull in Portuguese discovery and deprived the movement of an inspirational vision, leaving his unimaginative successors to reap the financial benefits of familiar, carefully plotted lands. A generation of Portuguese seems to have made no gains. They grew fat and content on their wealth, idly passing Henry's torch on to the next generation.

King John II, John the Perfect, renewed Portugal's exploratory energies with his accession to the throne in 1481. In that year he dispatched Diogo Cão (often spelled Cam) to venture farther south. Cão erected a pillar at the mouth of the Congo River and continued on a few degrees south to what he believed to be the southern tip of the continent. He returned to Portugal with the good news and a report of a Christian ruler far inland with whom the Portuguese could ally themselves. The Congo itself was thought to be the branch of a fabled Western Nile, which was believed to lead to the legendary Prester John. An alliance with such a powerful force could be as beneficial to Portugal as direct access to the spices of the East, and John pursued each with vigor. (The fact that Prester John was an essentially mythic creation in no way negates his role in history. The vision of a distant Christian monarch proved alluring and elusive to centuries of Europeans and had an effect upon many important decisions.)

In 1487, John the Perfect organized and dispatched two very different missions within months of one another. One would fulfill Henry the Navigator's prophecy; the other was a land-based trek of equally epic proportions. Pedro da Covilhã and Afonso da Paiva were briefed with all available information and sent out across the Mediterranean to find paths east to wealth and south to Prester John. The two separated at the Red Sea, with Covilhã proceeding eastward to India. He spent some time on the subcontinent before circling back to the western coast of Africa, traveling south into the Mozambique Channel.

In 1490, Covilhā made his second visit to Cairo, where he discovered his companion Paiva had disappeared during his search for Prester John in Ethiopia. John the Perfect bade Covilhā to take up Paiva's search, which he agreed to do with questionable enthusiasm.

Covilhā appears to have veered off to Mecca before heading south into Ethiopia and the realm of Alexander, "Lion of the Tribe of Judah and King of Kings." This Alexander was taken with his well-traveled visitor and thought better of letting him go. Covilhā never returned to Portugal, but eventually married an Ethiopian woman and raised a family, surviving several decades in his adopted home. Knowing he would be unable to present his information in person, Covilhā composed a very lengthy report to John II, which shaped the king's consequent actions. Unfortunately, Covilhā's letter has been lost to us, and all references are second-hand. Nonetheless, his story was impressive enough to have established the brave traveler as the Portuguese Marco Polo—as high a compliment as one could pay an overland journeyer.

The other weapon on John II's exploratory agenda was a voyage under

When Diogo Cāo found the southern tip of Africa, and planted a cross (left) at the farthest point of his second voyage, he was defining a new limit to the known world. One map (below), drawn before Columbus' journey, shows the extent of geographic understanding at that time. A Persian tapestry (opposite page), however, details the effects of Portuguese interaction with India just a century after their initial encounter.

When Christopher Columbus discovered the New World, he believed he had found a new route to the East. This painting by Jacopo Zucchi (below), entitled Allegory of the Discovery of America, *depicts some of the treasures found in the waters off of the coast of America.*

the command of Bartholomeu Dias, which hoped to expand upon Cão's accomplishments. Dias led his crew south along the familiar coasts of northern Africa, three ships passing well-established ports. (One of Dias' subordinate captains had accompanied Cão on his mission.) Along the way, Dias would release natives captured on a previous mission. These

men were supplied with small samples of the goods the Portuguese sought to trade and had been instructed to share this information with their peoples. (It is interesting to imagine what these repatriated Africans might have told their friends and families of their incredible kidnappings.)

As Dias' ships prepared to round Cape Palmas into the Gulf of Guinea

they probably swung out a bit too far to the west. There they encountered a relentless storm that blew them south for days, far from the mainland, into cold, unknown waters. Some of the crew resigned themselves to a sailor's death, but Dias remained calm. He turned his ships east, then north, and eventually encountered the mainland far from where he had left it.

Dias brought his ships to anchor in Mossel Bay on February 3, 1488. They rested for some time, restoring their battered craft and frazzled nerves. Dias directed his rejuvenated crew to proceed east, traveling another 300 or so miles (about 480 kilometers) to the site of modern-day South Africa's Port Elizabeth. By this point, Dias understood that his ships had indeed rounded the southern tip of the great African continent and that a steady route north would indeed bring him directly to the spice-laden islands of the East. Dias' crew, however, did not share his enthusiasm or his certainty. Even his direct subordinates seem to have favored turning around, which Dias finally did under protest. The primacy of having proven the route's feasibility, without actually completing it himself, served as Dias' bitter epitaph. He was lost at sea a dozen years later, rounding the very same Cape.

In December 1488, sixteen and a half months after setting sail, Dias' crew returned to Portugal. They confirmed the reality of a way around the great continent to John II in front of numerous interested parties, including Christopher Columbus. The Genoan had been lobbying his vision of a westerly route to the Indies, but Dias' great success traveling east was a severe setback for Columbus, who realized he would now have to look elsewhere for a monarchy willing to underwrite his efforts. The Portuguese, with a network of ports already in place along Africa's western coast, were now applying all their energies towards the rounding of that continent, and half-baked notions such as Columbus' were unnecessarily risky.

The Portuguese had advanced their cause one step at a time. With each careful move down the coast came advances in technology and capability, each step relying heavily on lessons learned during previous missions. They saved their greatest accolades for the individual who acted out the crowning achievement of these missions: a man named Vasco da Gama.

Dias, who had christened Africa's southernmost point the Cape of Storms on his return voyage, was miffed to discover that he would not lead the crowning mission. In fact, Dias would never lead another voyage, and he was lost at sea rounding the treacherous cape his king had optimistically rechristened the Cape of Good Hope. The first European to encounter the southern tip of Africa, Dias tried to warn others of the cape's dangers, but fell prey to them himself. By the time the writer Luis Vaz de Camões came to chronicle Gama's glorious accomplishment in *The Lusiads*, Dias' contributions were relegated to one single sentence. *The Lusiads* is a fascinating work written to praise Gama and several generations of Portuguese royalty. Camões patterned his work after Virgil's *Aeneid*—and thus it is quite similar to Homer's *Odyssey* as well—employing a similar cast of deities. The results are quite peculiar, since the Portuguese are portrayed as undertaking these missions in the name of Christianity while occasionally requesting the succor of ancient Greek deities. In an attempt to create a work even greater than those it imitated, Camões actually concocted a humorous hodgepodge of Greek heroes, bold Portuguese explorers, and a menagerie of sea serpents and nymphs. The fact that Dias' contributions to Portuguese exploration were summarized into one line of *The Lusiads* is important to keep in mind when considering the exclusivity of *The Odyssey* and *The Argonautica*. Had Camões' work remained longer in the oral domain, as its predecessors had, perhaps Dias, too, would have been lost to history, leaving a single

"At last the marvel has come to pass—land, land, and after we had almost giving up our belief in it."
—Fridtjof Nansen

individual to take credit for the accomplishments of many.

Vasco da Gama set out in July 1497, accompanied by Dias as far as the Cape Verde Islands, and rounded the stormy southern cape five months later. Beset with difficult conditions, contrary winds, and scurvy among the crew, Gama traveled as far north as the coast of Kenya before finding a native able and willing to guide him to India. That guide was an Arab by the name of Ibn Majid, who was said to know as much about the voyage to India as any man alive. In an ironic passing of the torch, the famed Moslem navigator passed his knowledge along to the man who signaled the onset of European hegemony in Asia. This was not readily apparent, however, since Gama's arrival in India was actually quite unspectacular. The trinkets that had fascinated coastal Africans were of little interest to the more sophisticated Moslem traders. Gama's time in the port of Calicut,

on the subcontinent's western coast, was tense and unprofitable, and he herded his remaining crew back to Lisbon in 1499. Fifty-five of the 170 original crew members survived, and only two of the four ships returned.

Yet Gama returned to Portugal a hero, honored by the new king and commissioned to undertake a second mission. In fact, Gama's voyage was considered so successful that he was asked to turn his experienced fleet over to Pedro Alvares Cabral. (Cabral's first voyage to circumnavigate Africa in 1500 involved such a wide sweep into the Atlantic—possibly in search of favorable currents, possibly in search of new islands, possibly on account of some very bad sailing—that he managed to discover Brazil in the process. Unaware of the fact that he had actually discovered an entire continent, Cabral believed it to be a large island. Despite his ignorance, Cabral became only the second captain to encounter South America.)

Columbus' third mission a few years earlier had included a visit to the continent's north coast, but he, too, failed to understand the significance of his actions. Cabral lingers in history as one of many early discoverers, but to his contemporaries he was the subject of a good deal of ridicule. In addition to losing four ships on his way to India—including one commanded by Bartolomeu Dias—Cabral managed to stir up a great deal of trouble upon finally arriving there, battling with its inhabitants and losing several more ships before returning home. Gama would not allow the next, most powerful mission to India to be led by such a bungler and set off himself on his second circumnavigation of Africa in February 1502.

While Gama's second voyage was as responsible for his acclaim as the first, it also establishes his place alongside the conquistadores for cold-blooded ruthlessness. The slaughter and mutilation of random victims encountered

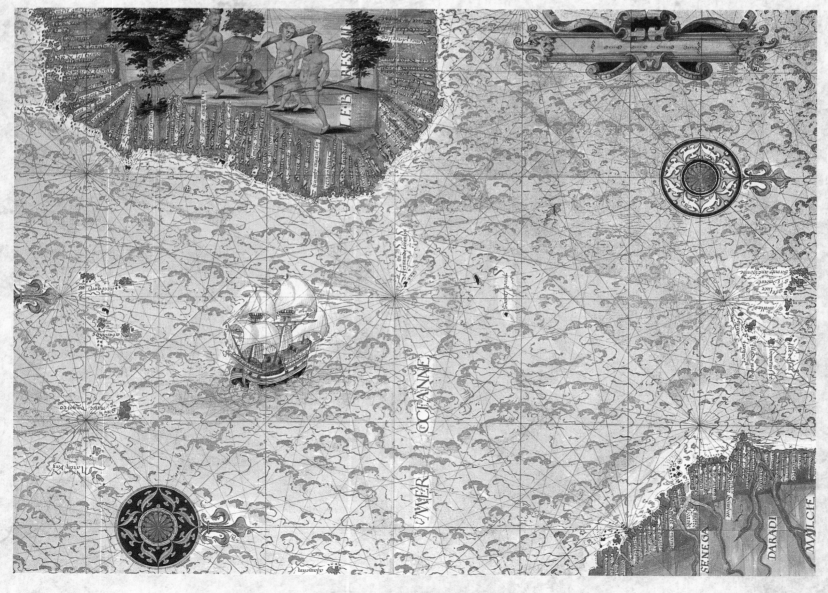

in the harbor of Calicut put a quick end to local resistance and established the first European fleet to be posted in Asian waters. Though Gama's ability to lead his crews through hardship and adversity was considerable, his murderous hand makes it difficult to glorify him in any way. The Portuguese had fulfilled the inspirational dreams of Henry the Navigator and nearly cornered the market on Eastern trade for decades to come. In the process, economic power began a move west that remains unchecked to this day. (Ironically, that westward movement will seem very close to having come full circle by the time this century is over, as the East becomes increasingly more economically prosperous and powerful.) The Portuguese ushered in nearly four centuries of European global domination with the requisite combination of adventure and oppression, a small sampling of what was to follow.

When Vasco da Gama set out for India, Christopher Columbus was undertaking his third trip to the Caribbean. Columbus had made a great leap into the unknown, whereas Gama was taking a route that had been well established by others. Columbus steered by his own reckoning, while Gama handed the navigation—once familiar waters were passed—to one of the most knowledgeable Arabs of his time. And yet, of these two, Gama was far and away the most celebrated explorer of the time. King Manuel I, successor to John II, would prove to be a successful ruler, and much of that reputation was established with the Portuguese lock on trade with India.

With the Portuguese proceeding swiftly on their own, Christopher Columbus came to realize he would have to look elsewhere for support. Columbus, present at Dias' triumphant return, had already presented his idea to Spain's Ferdinand and Isabella. Their advisers were equally unimpressed with the eccentric Genoan's theories. The Queen, though, was reputed to have been intrigued by Co-

lumbus, who seems to have been a very persuasive and intense individual. Upon his return to Spain, in the wake of his failure in Portugal, Columbus made the acquaintance of a number of influential merchants and friends of the court. Their support and the concern that the Portuguese were on the threshold of obtaining a great advantage over them, seem to have changed Ferdinand's and Isabella's minds.

However, neither of these facts support the idea that sea routes to the East were the primary concern of the Spanish throne. The Spaniards were nearing the final days of their eight-hundred-year struggle against the Moors, and the recapture of Granada was the focus of great attention. Before a complete victory, theories such as Columbus' seemed frivolous. (Historian Samuel Eliot Morison wrote: "It was as if a Polar explorer had tried to interest [United States President Abraham] Lincoln in the conquest of

A detail from Guillaume le Testu's Cosmographi Universale *(opposite page) displays the type of craft that sailed across the Atlantic. By the time this map was created in 1555, there were already many ships establishing trade between the New and Old Worlds. Unfortunately for the settlers, the natives they encountered were not as idyllic as those portrayed in this fanciful eighteenth-century painting (below). The improbable assortment of flora and fauna also seems to be a product of the artist's wishful thinking and imagination.*

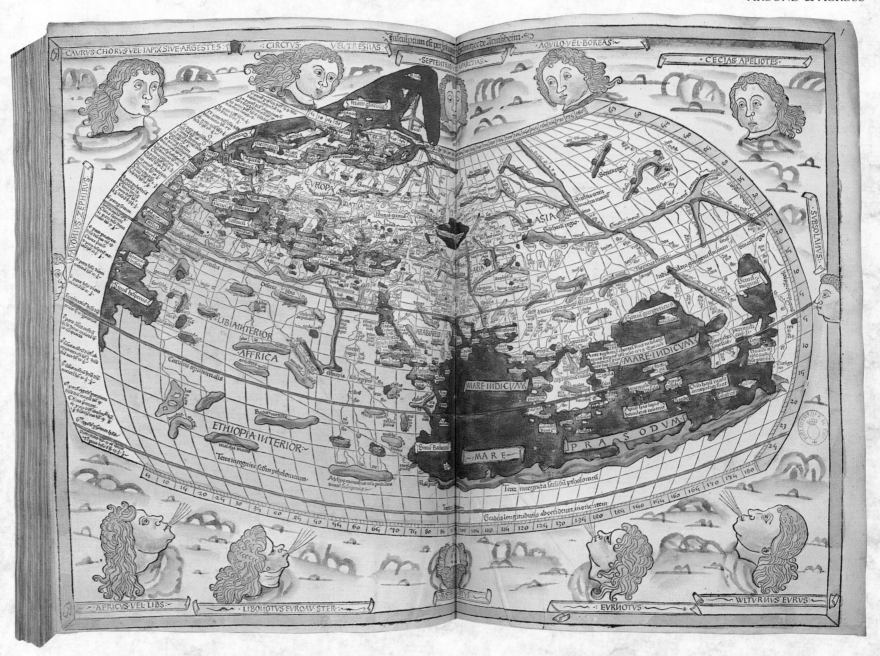

the Antarctic about the time of the Battle of Gettysburg.") Once Granada was returned to them and the Iberian peninsula was comfortably under Catholic control, such a mission seemed like a better idea.

On his second appeal to King Ferdinand and Queen Isabella—the verdict the first time around being that the mission was impossible and vain—Columbus actually received their financial support and royal blessings. After a decade of petitioning numerous European monarchies, Columbus received the underwriting he had dreamed about—yet he nearly threw it all away. In response to Isabella's support and Ferdinand's acquiescence, Columbus astonishingly made an additional series of demands of his benefactors. (Columbus sought enormous percentages of any wealth obtained and political control of any

lands he might discover.) These demands were far too strident and insolent for Ferdinand and Isabella to accept and resulted in his being driven from the court. Legend has it that Columbus was literally on the road out of town when a royal messenger brought Isabella's demand that he return to court.

The crown's trusted finance minister had come to Columbus' defense, arguing that his demands were in no way a danger to Ferdinand and Isabella. If Columbus were wrong about this western route, he would return— if he returned at all—in shame, and any titles or promises would be quickly forgotten. If, on the other hand, Columbus managed to establish a Spanish outpost in the East, his rewards would be a small price to pay compared to the wealth that would come flowing into the kingdom.

The artistic inclinations of cartographers manifested themselves in numerous ways. Some chose to portray the natural wonders and native inhabitants within their maps, such as Diego Homen's sixteenth-century perspective of South America (opposite page), *while others saved their fanciful touches for framing their information* (above).

We are provided with a number of contrasting portraits of Christopher Columbus, whose personal motivations are obscured in his own writings. It is safe to accept the contention that he was a very religious man, and he appears to have been able to cite biblical chapter and verse when it suited his needs. Some have argued that Columbus' conspicuous devotion may have been overcompensation for a Jewish heritage during a time of Christian zealotry. (Despite Ferdinand and Isabella's enlightened thinking in the area of exploration, it's important to remember that they were also the formulators of the Spanish Inquisition, which cast a pall over the peninsula for centuries; the Inquisition was operational in Spain until 1820.) Such devotion, whatever its motivation,

would surely have appealed to the religiously fanatical royal couple and served as a common ground in all of their correspondences.

At age forty-one, with three ships under his command, Christopher Columbus set sail from Cape Palos on the southeast corner of the Spanish coast. He sailed to the Canary Islands, where it was discovered that the *Niña* was damaged. Columbus suspected foul play, because some crew members were already wary of what lay ahead. Frustrated at the delay in departure, Columbus maintained a tight reign on his crew and finally sailed west on September 6, 1492.

It appears that each day at sea grew progressively more tense, with Columbus frequently on the verge of con-

fronting a mutiny. His crew wanted to turn around, while one of his captains, Martín Alonso Pinzón, was continually racing the *Pinta* ahead in hope of being the first to sight land. Pinzón, who had been instrumental in getting Columbus a second chance, and who owned two of the three ships on the voyage, appears to have had his own interests at heart. In his log, Columbus describes his concern with Pinzón's independent nature:

> I know that Martín Alonso cannot be trusted. He is a skilled mariner, but he wants the rewards and honors of this enterprise for himself. He is always running ahead of the fleet, seeking to be the first to sight land.

One month after leaving the Canaries, Columbus' men began to spot large flocks of birds. Their appearance was the first indication of land since they'd set out, and it provided a great boost to the crew's morale. In a few days there were still more birds, and then on October, 12, 1492, the lookout spotted land. Some maintain that Columbus set down near Guanahani in the Bahamas, though a lack of definitive proof will always allow for a variety of alternate suggestions. The actual sight is nearly irrelevant. The reality of land this far west was certainly confirmation of Columbus' theories, and the "Indies" were obviously just a few islands away. The Genoan captain had achieved his goal, and its attendant wealth was surely around the corner.

After encountering natives at their first landfall, which Columbus christened San Salvador, the ships ventured among the easternmost Caribbean islands. During this time Pinzón and the *Pinta* are reported to have disappeared for a time, reinvigorating Columbus' suspicions about him. He claimed to have been separated from the others by bad weather, though Pinzón has been suspected of striking off on his own in search of riches. Even now that his mission appeared successful, Columbus was still unsatisfied with the way events were unfolding. He had yet to find the spices and jewels he had come in search of and worried that others would wrest them from him when he did. The monomaniacal captain was more obsessed than ever with establishing his divine right to control the lands he so greatly misunderstood.

Columbus traveled among the Bahamian chain before making his way to Cuba, which he immediately mistook for China. Hispaniola (Haiti/Dominican Republic) was therefore perceived to be Chipangu (Japan), as Marco Polo himself had described it. While anchored off Hispaniola, the *Santa Maria* suffered severe damage, forcing the remaining two ships to take on as many of its crew members

as they could. Three months after arriving in the Caribbean, the *Niña* and the *Pinta* struggled home, having stranded a number of men from the disabled ship with promises of a hasty return. Columbus kept his word, embarking on his second voyage by September 1493, but the abandoned men had all fallen violently at the hands of the natives.

Columbus' subsequent journey to the Caribbean involved as much business as exploration, and history paints this as a difficult time for the visionary. As governor, he was inclined towards capital punishment and censorship. As a trickle of ships began to establish a route between Europe and the new settlements, word made its way back to Spain that Columbus

Christopher Columbus' coat of arms (opposite page) *reflects his accomplishments, yet does not touch upon their implications. Meanwhile, a symbolic depiction of the explorer's final moments* (below) *does not portray that he died a poor, broken man.*

> *"Columbus' greatest achievement was something he never imagined, a by-product of his purposes, a consequence of unexpected facts."*
> —Daniel Boorstin

had gotten out of hand. He returned to Spain to answer those charges (in the first ship constructed in the New World to make the voyage east) and appears to have cleared his name with the King and Queen. The third voyage, however, proved to be Columbus' most disgraceful, culminating with his return to Spain in chains on charges related to his abuse of power.

It is a testament to Columbus' personal persuasiveness that he was ever allowed to mount a fourth expedition. Unfortunately, the attempted "comeback" was as sad as that of a great boxer long past his prime. Columbus discovered Panama and Jamaica during the summer of 1502 but foundered along the coast of the latter. Co-

lumbus and his party were rescued, and eventually returned to Spain, the great captain's second embarrassing return. By this time Columbus' health was failing, physically and mentally, and he died within two years of his return.

Columbus was the first Renaissance-era European to encounter the New World, but he died believing he had simply discovered a route to the islands of the East. Despite four unsuccessful attempts at finding the Great Khan, Prester John, or anyone else he expected to encounter in the mysterious East, Columbus never abandoned the belief that he filled in the missing piece of the world map by connecting Europe and Asia with a

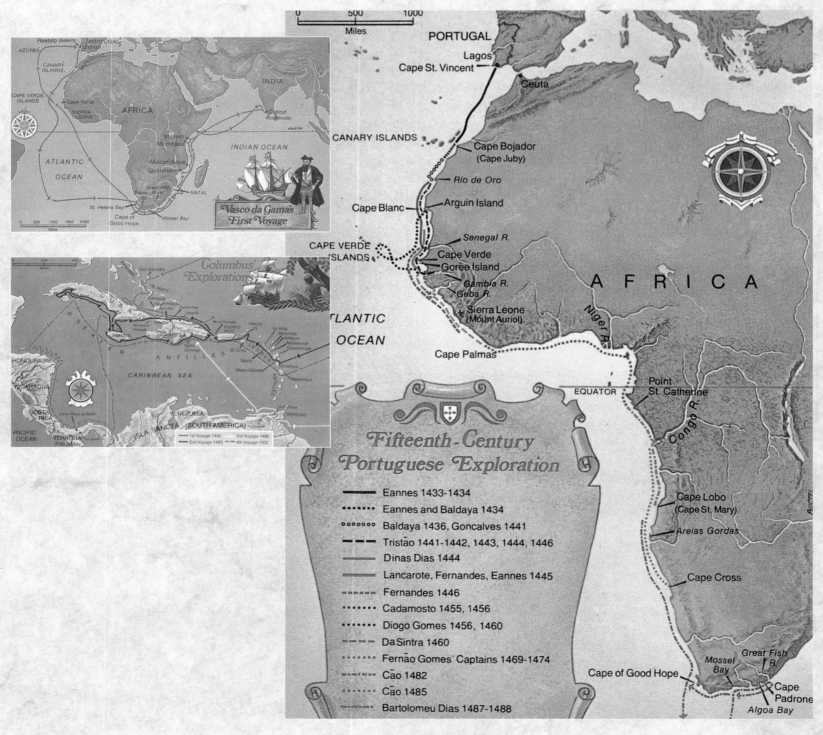

Vasco da Gama's First Voyage

Columbus' Explorations

1st Voyage 1492 3rd Voyage 1498
2nd Voyage 1493 4th Voyage 1502

Fifteenth-Century Portuguese Exploration

——— Eannes 1433-1434
••••••• Eannes and Baldaya 1434
ooooooo Baldaya 1436, Goncalves 1441
– – – Tristão 1441-1442, 1443, 1444, 1446
——— Dinas Dias 1444
——— Lancarote, Fernandes, Eannes 1445
- - - - Fernandes 1446
••••••• Cadamosto 1455, 1456
••••••• Diogo Gomes 1456, 1460
- - - - DaSintra 1460
••••••• Fernão Gomes' Captains 1469-1474
-•-•-• Cão 1482
••••••• Cão 1485
– – – Bartolomeu Dias 1487-1488

monthlong ocean voyage. When others proposed the possibility of Columbus' discovery representing a brand new landmass he argued against it vehemently, only acknowledging that perhaps the Asian islands were more extensive than he had imagined. Committed to a plotted line on a faulty map, Columbus remained adamant. He who is celebrated more than any other explorer in history went to his grave without the vaguest idea of where he had actually been.

Of course, there are a number of things for which Columbus deserves a great deal of credit. His lifetime at sea taught him a sailor's sixth sense, and his navigational instincts relied heavily on intuition. The routes Columbus took to the New World and back on his first voyage are almost exactly the same as those that are still employed to this day. He was an excellent ship captain despite possessing only the most rudimentary navigational skills. More often than not, Columbus' measurements and calculations were based on dead reckoning (the use of stationary or fixed objects as navigational aides), and a remarkably accurate one at that. (The ease with which Columbus returned to ports discovered on his first voyage is testament to his seafaring sense.)

In addition, Columbus' log of his experiences in the "Indies" is a descriptive, appreciative work, on a par with Marco Polo's. Though his interpersonal relations seem to have left something to be desired, the pious Columbus took great delight in the bounty of his god's handiwork. "I have never seen anything so beautiful," he writes upon discovering Cuba, continuing with an appreciative catalog of the flora and fauna he somehow managed to believe confirmed his contentions that these lands were Asian.

This was also the man who is believed to have stolen the credit, not to mention the lucrative reward and acclaim, for sighting land from one of his crewman. His estimates regarding the planet's circumference were way

off. (Columbus went by Ptolemy's thirteen-hundred-year-old miscalculations, which cut the globe by one-quarter.) Columbus' self-assuredness might have made it possible for him to have reached the New World, but made it unbearable for most to live under his rule. Like all driven souls, Columbus' convictions were responsible for the fire that fueled his ambitions. He believed in something, acted upon it, and succeeded at it. Perhaps it's better that Columbus died ignorant of what he had actually discovered. The truth would have only shattered the dream he had spent a lifetime pursuing.

———————————

Once the word of Columbus' discoveries got out, a flow of ships regularly made their way westward. For the next three-quarters of a century Europe sent its bravest, sometimes

This portrait of Columbus portrays the intensity of the man who died ignorant of how significant his discoveries were.

most reckless, captains to find a way through or around these interfering, still useless islands to the source of spice. Pepper was essential to making salted or spoiled meats palatable, and those farthest from the spice trade paid for it most dearly. John Cabot, a Genoan who was Columbus' contemporary, saw that Spain and Portugal were well established in their quests, and, therefore, not the best places to approach for sponsorship. England, however, was far removed from the spice trade and a bit chagrined at having turned Columbus' brother (lobbying on behalf of his sibling) away before Ferdinand and Isabella became receptive.

Henry VII leapt at the opportunity to sponsor Cabot's mission, particularly when it became clear that the Italian sailor would assemble his own fleet. While we are rather certain Cabot proceeded northwest past Iceland and Greenland to rediscover North America in 1497, we are left with no firsthand reports of his voyage. Even secondhand information is rather sketchy, and Cabot's coexploring son, Sebastian, further complicated matters in later writings by offering contradictory information. John Cabot probably visited Newfoundland, and possibly Nova Scotia, in his ship *Matthew* with a crew of eighteen. He returned to Bristol seventy-seven days after departing, with great enthusiasm for a quick return voyage.

The fact that Cabot had returned home empty-handed (even Columbus had managed to bring back a few natives), made it difficult for many to share his enthusiasm. But Cabot managed to assemble five ships and nearly two hundred men for a second voyage that departed from Bristol in 1498. This is where history and John Cabot part ways, and it's difficult to determine what might have happened. At least some of the original ships explored some part of the North American continent possibly as far south as Long Island or Chesapeake Bay. It's possible that the entire crew was lost,

101

but other pieces of the puzzle seem to indicate Cabot eventually returned to England. The pervasive uncertainty of anything regarding John Cabot has relegated him to an obscure place in history, despite his discoveries.

Cabot's observance of large schools of fish sounded interesting to the Portuguese, who organized a number of visits to the region. The Corte-Real brothers (Gaspar and Miguel) explored a great deal of North America's Atlantic coastline, where both were eventually lost. The Pinzón's, Martin Alonso and his brother, who had accompanied—and agitated—Columbus on his first voyage, each returned to the New World during the opening years of the sixteenth century. In fact, quite a few names begin to crop up around this time. Many have been lost to time, while one has attained a status no early explorer could ever have imagined.

Amerigo Vespucci, of Florence and later Venice, was a sailor for Spain and Portugal. He is probably the first man to have sailed along the coasts of North and South America, which he accomplished during four voyages west before 1505. Vespucci discovered Florida and large parts of Brazil. On his second mission he became the first European to sail south of the equator in the New World, as he sailed down the Argentine coast. Though his ships were in no condition to attempt it, Vespucci was convinced that farther south a passage did exist to the East, a passage that Magellan would employ nearly two decades later.

Though Vespucci's seafaring accomplishments are the equal of nearly any other explorer of the century, his understanding of where he had been exceeded all others. "The new regions which we found and explored," he wrote, "we may rightly call a new world." His letter to a friend after returning from his first voyage, later published as *Mundus Novus* (*The New World*), made it clear that Vespucci didn't think for a minute he had plied some shortcut to the East. While Co-

lumbus' estimation of the earth's circumference missed the mark by 6,000 miles (9,600 kilometers), Vespucci's calculations brought him to within 100 miles (160 kilometers). Such dimensions indicated a landmass of unimagined proportions.

The idea that these new discoveries represented a great new, unknown landmass had not occurred to most of Vespucci's contemporaries, and none who might have agreed proclaimed their convictions as strongly as did Vespucci. In speaking out, Vespucci unknowingly planted the seeds for the new lands to be called "America, after Amerigo, its discoverer, a man of great ability." A series of coincidences led to a few isolated references becoming the standardized name for these new lands. By 1538, cartography's household name, Mercator, had employed Vespucci's name for his maps, and by the turn of the next century the name was widely recognized.

Though Vespucci and Columbus were known to one another, and reported to be on rather friendly terms, it is ironic that later generations entered into a feud over their claims and accomplishments. Columbus' biographer-son was indignant that these new lands should be named for anyone but his father, and there seems to have been some mudslinging involved. Attempts to discredit Vespucci's accomplishments continued into the nineteenth century by a variety of indignant new American patriots who accepted the younger Columbus' disparaging remarks as fact. Nonetheless, Amerigo Vespucci's name has remained to figure prominently in history and in our own lives. Maps and newspapers print it daily, and millions speak the word with little thought of its origin. An entire hemisphere is labeled with his given name, yet Vespucci died without ever knowing of this legacy.

> *"It is lawful to call it a new world since, because none of these countries were known to our ancestors."*
> —Amerigo Vespucci

When the Cabot brothers embarked on their journey, the entire town of Bristol turned out to see them off (preceding pages). Ten years later, Amerigo Vespucci (opposite page, above) arrived in the New World, discovering large areas previously unknown. These lands later came to bear his name. This sixteenth-century map (below) depicts the flora and fauna encountered in these new lands.

6

DEFINING THE GLOBE

lthough it eventually became apparent that Columbus had discovered a whole new hemisphere, a single-minded Europe remained obsessed with establishing a route to the East. The wealth of available land for Europeans to settle was not a great lure early on. Land was still a very accessible commodity. Spices, however, were not. With a cheap labor force already in place, the East was a market ripe for exploitation. The profits were immediate, and cooperation was easily won or coerced. Easier access to these sources would deflate the ten-thousand-percent markups incurred by Europeans as the precious goods passed through twenty or more transactions.

Vespucci and others made strong arguments for the existence of an enormous landmass between the Atlantic Ocean and the Spice Islands. In the same way that the African coast interested some Portuguese while Prince Henry was hoping to reach India, these "Americas" certainly merited at least an investigation. Some foresaw potential wealth in these strange new discoveries, but many considered them as yet another obstacle on the road to the East.

There had to be a way around the Americas. Where it was, and how long it would take to round it, was anybody's guess. Perhaps it would be a matter of "simply" rounding a cape like Africa's stormy southernmost point, or maybe it would be long and imposing like the Arctic coast of Eurasia. Others wondered whether the new continents themselves might be conveniently crossed at some point, offering easy access to the Spice Islands.

The first European to know the answer was a colorful, storied adventurer by the name of Vasco Núñez de Balboa. He had initially settled in Hispaniola, where a combination of boredom and indebtedness are said to have prompted his stowing away aboard a ship headed west for the Isthmus of Panama. On the west coast of the

"Lasting fame is a fragile thing—it has often little to do with the magnitude of the achievement but rather with being fortunate enough to do the right thing at the right time—or to die in sufficiently romantic circumstances to capture the imagination of the public."
—Sir Edmund Hillary

Maps, such as this one of Santo Domingo (opposite page), *began to emerge from the New World as soon as settlers and captains had an opportunity to pool their information. As the occupation of these islands became more extensive, so did the maps.*

Gulf of Darien, where the northernmost Colombian territory abuts the nation of Panama, the first settlement planted on the North American continent was found in ruins.

The optimistic shipload of settlers was quite alarmed, and their commander was quickly deemed ineffectual. Balboa appears to have led the rebellious actions of the settlers and assumed command of the community. To confirm his authority he successfully petitioned Columbus' son, then presiding over the region from Santo Domingo. The deposed governors were resistant to this legitimization of Balboa and brought about their own deportation back to Spain by contesting his command.

Balboa was an adventurous man and was not likely to be content scratching out a living on some desolate foreign shore. In fact, many of Balboa's grandiose actions seem to indicate a flair for the dramatic and self-important. His ambitions were greater than those of sedentary perseverance. Certainly he saw that the local Indians produced food in abundance and possessed small quantities of worked gold. Balboa and the settlers, by nature an ambitious group, must have wondered how they could exploit these resources. Surely they were curious about the source of the natives' gold. In 1513, two years after King Ferdinand temporarily acknowledged his authority, Balboa organized a mission inland and headed south. Some say the mission went off in search of the gold, while others report that Balboa had heard from the local inhabitants of a great body of water nearby.

An enormous caravan set out from Darien, including hundreds of natives and quite a few of Balboa's men, possibly totaling two hundred. They hacked their way across the mountainous isthmus, through swamps and hostile territory. As late as the nineteenth century, ill-fated expeditions crossing the thin strip of land fell prey to yellow fever, poisonous snakes, and other unfamiliar hazards. Those expe-

ditions, however, did not have the sheer numbers of Balboa's troops, nor did they have a leader as ruthless. Balboa's heavy hand with the Indians was well known, and there's good reason to imagine he was a harsh taskmaster with his subordinates as well.

Balboa encountered primitive tribes along the way, which he dispatched with ease, and there are reports of his men setting their dogs on another tribe in which transvestism was practiced. (The Spanish were notorious for their use of canines in battle, setting the bred killers upon unsuspecting opponents.) Later, when guides informed Balboa that the great ocean could be spied from a nearby peak, the leader ascended it alone in order to lay claim to being the first European to set eyes upon it. Having done so, Balboa returned to his men and drew up a document notarizing the accomplishment. Throughout the journey the rebel leader showed a flair for the dramatic, and it is interesting to imagine such "official" proceedings taking place in the middle of a dense, inhospitable, mountainous forest far from any sign of civilization.

There was still some ground to be covered before reaching the coast, and even when they finally came upon it, Balboa and his men were a bit confused. A long expanse of shallow water greeted them, and it wasn't until the flood tide brought salt water rushing in that the Spaniards' oceanic suspicions were confirmed. When the magnitude of his discovery struck him, Balboa, we are told, resorted to one of his most grandiose gestures: He waded into the surf in full gear to plant the flag of his king and lay claim to "all that sea and the countries bordering on it." Later Balboa would take a ceremonial ride upon the new ocean to symbolize his dominion over it. (How unlike North America's Viking discoverer, Bjarni Herjolfsson, who never even set foot on the land he had stumbled upon.)

The earliest historians of the New World, at least one of whom—

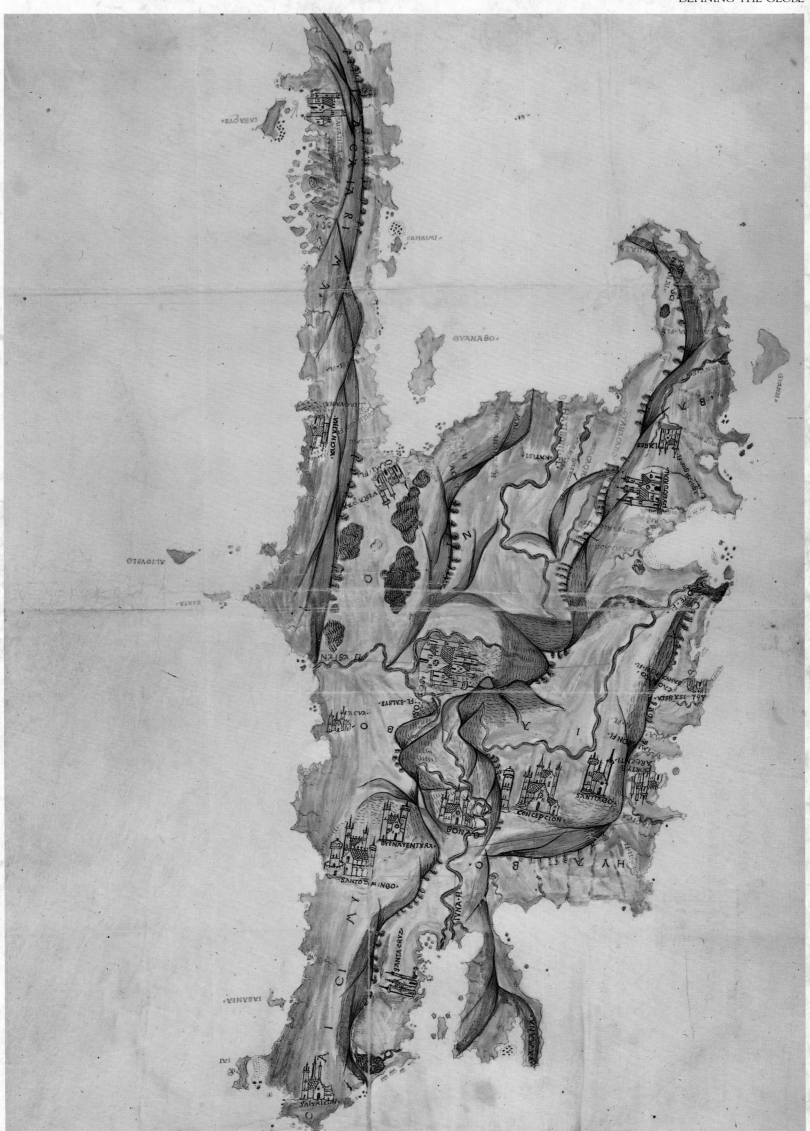

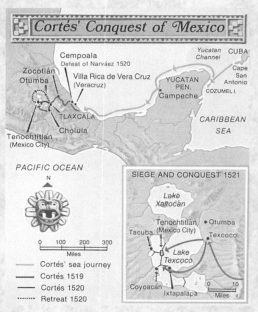

Cortés' Conquest of Mexico

natives provided the Spaniards with quantities of pearls and gold, which would certainly go a long way toward subsidizing Balboa's plans for a shipyard on the opposite side of the isthmus. The news would also have pleased the king greatly, though, to Balboa's misfortune, the news did not arrive quickly enough. The officer Balboa had originally ousted had returned to Spain and given a detailed—if partial—report of the insurrection. This led to the appointment of a new commander, who was sent to replace the fugitive upstart, overturning the younger Columbus' earlier decision.

In 1517, while he worked to ready another expedition for the great Southern Sea, Balboa was taken into custody by the new appointee. The explorer was summarily convicted and beheaded long before his supporters could rally to his defense. The fact that the new commander was backed by twenty ships and fifteen hundred men seems to indicate any resistance Balboa's faithful might have mustered would have been futile.

The new regime was heavy-handed in its dealings with the natives, which apparently served to galvanize their opposition. Gold was the objective, and within a decade its murderous pursuit wreaked havoc upon the civilizations of Central and Southern America. Balboa would surely have committed genocide as his Spanish successors, had he been in a similar situation, but his brief moment in history is primarily focused on his discovery of the Pacific Ocean. Like Columbus, Balboa did not understand the implications of his discovery. This does not, however, diminish the accomplishment. A European had found a western edge of the New World and seen an enormous ocean, setting the stage for someone else to determine how large that ocean was.

Balboa's short time in the New World occurred during a period of great exploratory activity. Columbus, Vespucci, the Pinzón brothers, the

Oviedo—knew Balboa personally, have painted a dramatic picture of his discovery of the "Southern Sea." They were intrigued by its dimensions and wondered where such a body of water would sit in relation to the East. Balboa himself began considering the feasibility of constructing ships on this new shore and completing the westerly route to the Spice Islands. He was one of the few. Those who were barely managing to survive on the new continents rarely had sufficient resources to mount such ambitious projects. Only Balboa, and to a certain extent Cortés, whose westward glance was quickly distracted by the glitter of gold, seem to have maintained an interest in the East after having become involved in the politics and profiteering of the New World.

On the way back to Darien, Balboa and his men encountered yet another tribe of Indians. These intimidated

Cabots, and the Corte-Real brothers were all traveling back and forth across the Atlantic; Ponce de León, who had accompanied Columbus on his second voyage to the New World, searched for a fountain and discovered parts of Florida instead; and a young Cortés was taking the first step toward the annihilation of the Aztecs. At the same time, there was a great deal of European activity in the East, where the Portuguese were rapidly expanding. Having charted most of the Asian coast along the Indian Ocean and the Bay of Bengal, the Portuguese began poking through the Malay Archipelago toward the western fringes of the Pacific Ocean.

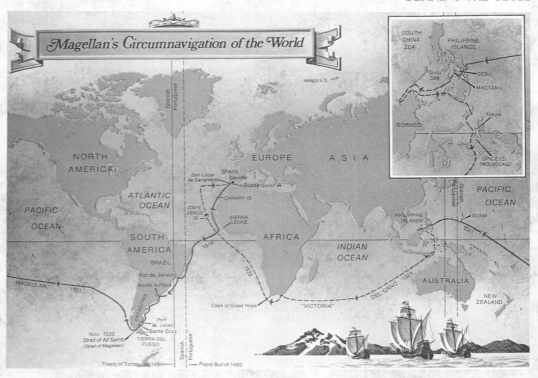

Hernan Cortés (opposite page) *was a ruthless man who all but annihilated the civilizations already in existence in Mexico upon his arrival there in 1519. Ferdinand Magellan* (left), *the first man to circumnavigate the globe, could also be a cruel leader, yet he only turned to violence as a last resort.*

Ferdinand Magellan connected a series of known entities in his circumnavigation. World maps, such as this one (below), relied upon the information assembled by Magellan and his predecessors, none of whom had managed to shed much light on the northwestern coast of the New World.

Ferdinand Magellan was captain of a caravel on one Portuguese mission among the Spice Islands, the first such post he had received. It was another step up for the ambitious young man, who had worked his way through the ranks without the help of patronage or favoritism. Magellan, already a veteran of several bloody Moslem battles, seems to have opted for exploration over the messy business of looting and pillaging. (Some credit Magellan's shift to his witness of the decimation of Goa in India, where Alfonso d'Albuquerque brought Portuguese might down upon the port city with bloody finality. Magellan did not share in the profits of the looting, which may indicate his refusal to participate in its sacking.)

Magellan had been a well-rewarded, oft-injured, loyal servant of Portugal's John II, but was strongly disliked by the king's successor, Manuel the Fortunate. Manuel may have had the good luck to have sponsored da Gama's mission, but he wanted no part of anything Magellan had to offer. The two are known to have come into conflict while the young Magellan served as a page to the royal court. Manuel's obvious disdain for the sailor, and his general lack of interest in navigation, paved the way for the final encounter that goaded Magellan into history.

Like so many historic figures, Magellan was forced out of retirement on account of financial difficulties. The sizable fortune he had accumulated in the East had been swindled, and Magellan "reenlisted" to fight the Moors in Morocco. There he received a crippling wound, followed by allegations of malfeasance. Magellan was eventually cleared of the charges, but his good name was smeared, and the king's pleasure with the turn of events was obvious to all. Magellan continuously petitioned the throne for a greater stipend or command of a vessel to return to the East, but neither

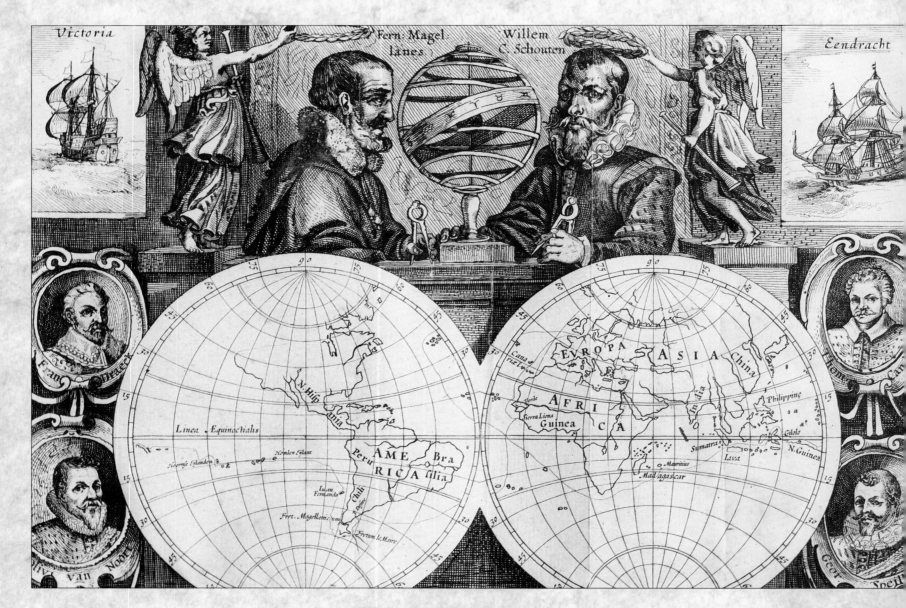

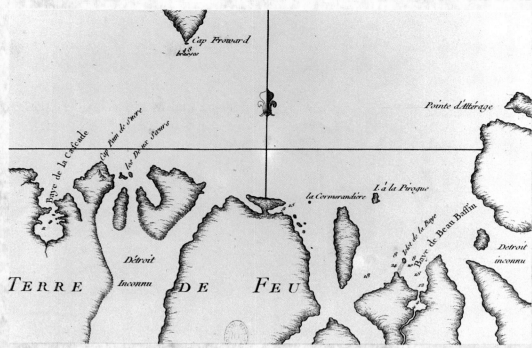

was forthcoming. His final request was met with derision and dismissal. Magellan was free to go elsewhere.

Embarrassed and enraged, Magellan was a sailor without a flag, harboring a vendetta against his homeland. Around this time, with a streak of uncharacteristic good luck, Magellan seems to have encountered a number of crucial allies. Some were Portuguese colleagues distressed with the king's treatment of a friend; others were wealthy Spaniards looking for access to the spiceries of the East. But the only person who could put Magellan in a position to seek his revenge was Spain's young King Charles I, grandson of Ferdinand and Isabella.

The meeting between the weathered sailor and the seventeen-year-old boy-king was apparently a great success, since Charles granted a commission on the spot. Magellan would command again—on a voyage no one had yet dared. He would head west, round the Americas to the south, and cross Balboa's Southern Sea to head for the East. In the process, Magellan hoped to prove to King Charles that the Spice Islands lay within the Spanish half of the globe as apportioned in a treaty it had signed with Portugal, which conveniently laid claim to the other half. Here, more than anywhere else, was Manuel susceptible to Magellan's retribution.

Unfortunately, Charles' enthusiasm for Magellan did not spread to many of his subjects, some of whom suspected the Portuguese expatriate's motives. As if the ambitious journey itself weren't enough of a challenge, Magellan's former countrymen worked to hinder his preparations every step of the way, fearful that he would lead the Spanish to infiltrate their profitable discoveries. For more than a year Magellan oversaw the repairs to the five ships he would command and the laying in of provisions for the journey. He was finally leading a mission, and tried hard to keep an eye on all aspects of the preparations.

As Magellan's was a royal commission, it was subject to the vicissitudes

and political infighting of all such court projects. As captain-general he was quickly surrounded by an assortment of scheming Spanish appointees. Before his ships had departed from Tenerife in the Canary Islands (a familiar refueling stop for transatlantic voyages) he received word from back home in Portugal that a number of Spanish captains under his command had assured their friends they would take control of the mission. Magellan's own life, they warned him, was in great jeopardy.

With this information, Magellan adopted a conciliatory air of resignation and acceptance toward the Spaniards' daring insubordinations. He maintained that demeanor until their leader overstepped his bounds and proclaimed his mutinous ideas in the presence of many witnesses. The disarmingly meek Magellan leapt quickly into action, had the ringleader put in chains, and reestablished his authority for the time being. All of this took place before the ships had even crossed the Atlantic.

When the coast of South America appeared on the horizon, Magellan quickly veered south to avoid any lands already claimed by the Portuguese. Nearing the Tropic of Capricorn, Magellan spied the southernmost point of Portuguese expansion, as described to him before his expatriation. Apparently in control of his ex-

Above: *Although Magellan successfully navigated the strait that bears his name, the many bays that littered the waters made navigation very difficult.*

pedition, convinced "el paso" to the Indies was just ahead, Magellan was certain his promises to Charles were about to be fulfilled. Once again, Magellan's fate was less than he had hoped for—and more than he could imagine.

It had not occurred to Europeans that this southern landmass of the Americas might extend much farther south than the African continent. Lingering concepts of symmetry were applied to unknown lands (leading to the concept of *Terra Australius*), but no one could have envisioned "el paso" situated 1,000 miles (1,609 kilometers) farther south than the Cape of Good Hope. When Magellan's crews rounded Cabo Frio and sailed into the harbor of modern Rio de Janeiro, he assured them their route west was nearby. None realized how far away they still were from their goal, nor the mutinous events the delay would incite.

As Magellan's entourage made its way south, the onset of winter was apparent. The coastline became increasingly barren and the men became increasingly uneasy. They hoped Magellan would allow them to return north for the winter, back to the lush, friendly villages they had visited on the outward journey. (Magellan's first encounter with American natives was an interesting lesson in diplomacy. He allowed his men to barter for the natives' women—even developed an efficient schedule leaving the men enough time for their sexual pursuits to ensure they would still be willing to do the work needed on board—yet refrained from any of the wanton destruction and abuse that most other expeditions perpetrated upon their unsuspecting hosts. When Magellan felt moved to action he could be quite merciless; he was not, however, prone to unnecessary displays of aggression.) Magellan, however, had no intention

of retreating north. In addition to offering a bleak prospect for the winter itself, this confirmed for many uninformed crew members the idea that this was not going to be any "ordinary" New World expedition.

The combination of animosities, hardships, vendettas, and tensions eventually erupted into a conflict that pitted three ships against Magellan's *Trinidad* and one other ally. The insurrectionists may have been politically adept, but they had little battlefield experience and appear to have had little support among the skilled crew. The wily Magellan, however, veteran of a number of bloody skirmishes, acted decisively. In less than a day, one of the captains was dead, and the two others were in chains. After a five-day trial, Magellan meted out a bloody sentence. One of the captains was beheaded, and then— along with the one killed during the take-over—drawn and quartered, their

FERDINAN. MAGALA.

remains hung from gibbets as a warning. Cartagena, the ringleader who Magellan had already handled leniently on the trip across the Atlantic, was marooned at their winter base in San Julian along with a lay-priest coconspirator. (Ironically, Francis Drake, the next circumnavigator, would drop anchor in the same port for the same reason—the execution of another mutineer.)

Upon resuming a southerly heading, the crew soon spotted some natives of great size, whom they termed *Patagonians* (derived from Spanish for their large size, with particular reference to their enormous feet). A bungled attempt at bringing two Patagonians back to Spain resulted in hostilities between the visitors and natives, which forced Magellan to move on. He dispatched the *Santiago* to find a new base of operations, which was subsequently wrecked in a violent storm. Two of the *Santiago*'s crewmen

made an impressive journey overland back to San Julian, leading to the rescue of those stranded down the coast. Eventually, the remaining four ships were ready to travel again, and Magellan directed them south, where they encountered storms like the one that had brought an end to the *Santiago*.

During one of these fierce storms, two of Magellan's ships were driven out of sight as each battled for survival. When it grew light the next day a lookout spied smoke across a promontory, and the four ships were eventually reunited. The men celebrated on the decks of the two strayed ships: They had discovered a passage connecting the Atlantic Ocean and Balboa's Southern Sea. Magellan's "el paso" had been found.

It took all of Magellan's navigational savvy to steer through the strait that came to bear his name. For more than a month his ships snaked

A detail of Magellan's great voyage (below) *shows the strait through which he rounded South America. Yet, Magellan's accomplishment was still likely to conjure up images of fabulous creatures and improbable occurrences* (opposite page).

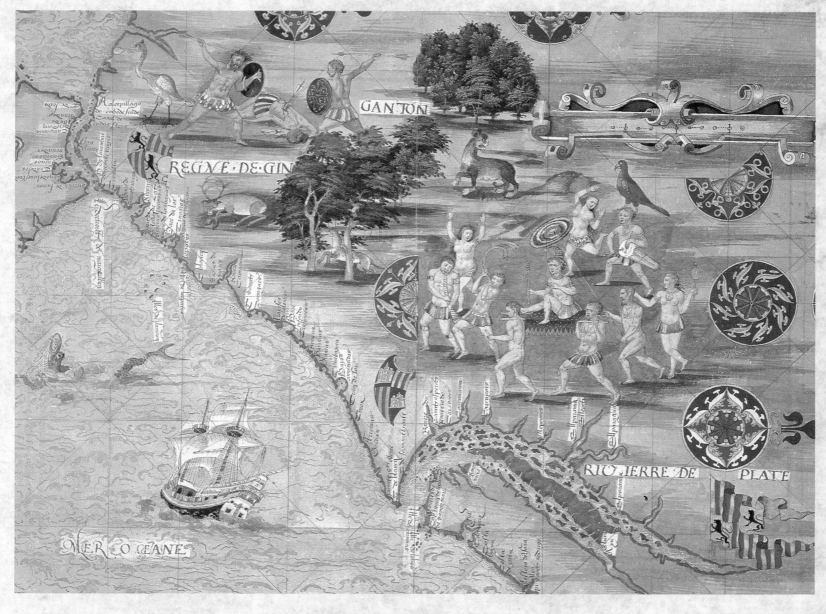

past unknown islands, steep cliffs, and treacherous currents. Magellan managed to lead the way, but he failed to see all four remaining ships through. The *San Antonio*, whose captain was one of Magellan's more prominent antagonists, disappeared during a short excursion and quickly hightailed it back to Europe. As the fleet entered the vast, unknown ocean, they were three in number.

The *San Antonio*'s departure set the stage for the tragedy that would befall the crew on its interminable crossing of the Pacific. The largest of the original five ships, the *San Antonio* carried a disproportionately large amount of the fleet's stores. Had Magellan been familiar with the great ocean he was embarking upon he could easily have replenished his supplies along the way. Instead he encountered one small island in the Tuamotu chain on the very edge of the archipelagos of the great ocean, his men already on the verge of starvation and weakened by malnutrition and scurvy. Christened Saint Paul's, the island offered brief respite. Magellan and his men departed from Saint Paul's Island on January 28, 1521; they were undernourished and understocked. It would be well over a month before they encountered an island with food and water, a few weeks longer before they could recuperate away from inhospitable natives. Nearly twenty men died of scurvy along the way, and the entire crew suffered from some form of malnutrition. The ragged, ravaged fleet stayed some time on Guam and then moved on to the Philippines.

Had Magellan headed due west, as opposed to the west-northwest route he took, he would have snaked through the hearts of Polynesia and Micronesia. Had he been a mere 20 or so miles (about 32 kilometers) farther south than he'd been at any point along the way, he would have skirted their northern fringes. Instead, he led his three impoverished charges into the desolate corridor of the south central Pacific, where that great ocean seemed to merit its name. (We now know the Pacific to be a particularly stormy ocean. Magellan named it during a period of uncharacteristic calm.)

Upon reaching the Philippines it became readily apparent to Magellan and his crew that they had arrived at the very edge of "the Indies." Some suggest that Magellan had visited the Philippines during his days in the Portuguese navy. This could account for his insistence on remaining there while all others urged that they move on to the spiceries as soon as possible. Instead Magellan remained, becoming increasingly involved in regional affairs. At Samar, the first Philippine island he encountered, Magellan arranged a grand Catholic mass for all the natives to watch. The request of their raja and his family to be baptized, and subsequently an enormous number of Filipinos as well, inspired the religious captain and may have even stirred a zealotry that bordered on hysteria. The sheer number of people who came to accept Magellan's savior seem to have made the few that did not all the more bothersome. (The Philippine conversion was a remarkable event, establishing it as the only predominantly Christian Asian nation to this day.) For reasons too complex to understand through the second- and thirdhand reports of others, Magellan engaged himself in a relatively petty local squabble with a few tribes who refused to acknowledge his god; he was killed in the process.

Magellan's death could have been avoided in any number of ways. His own foresight could easily have prevented it, and a helping hand as he literally battled to survive may also have saved him. Instead, Magellan and a band of about sixty untrained men stumbled into an ambush where they were outnumbered fifty-to-one. It is a testament to Magellan's fighting acumen (or perhaps to history's embellishing hand), that he is said to have held out with his back to the surf for an hour before being slain. Only then did boats arrive to rescue a handful of survivors, including Magel-

Pizarro's Expeditions to Peru

lan's lifelong slave and another man whose chronicle of the entire voyage is our only firsthand account. The slave, a Malay whom Magellan had acquired nearly twenty years earlier, revenged his master's death by arranging an ambush of the senior members of the Spanish command. Their slaughter spurred the fleet's long overdue departure for the Spice Islands.

By this time little more than one hundred men remained, an insufficient number to pilot three ships. As a result, the new commander ordered the torching of the weakest vessel, the *Concepción*, which he first loaded full of Magellan's voluminous papers. The Spanish captain, wary of what would happen if the true events of the mission were revealed, burnt Magellan's thoughts and feelings out of the pages of history.

Three years after five strong ships sailed out along the Mediterranean to round the globe, one rickety, undercrewed vessel returned. Juan Sebastian del Cano captained *Victoria* into safe harbor with enough valuable spice to ensure the mission would turn a profit. Cano and fewer than twenty other survivors attested to the fact that they had indeed circled the world. The Indies could be reached by going west, but the condition of the pitiful few that returned indicated it was not an easy route. Half a century passed before another captain would set out with Magellan's ambition.

It remained for a Venetian by the name of Antonio Pigafetta, one of few survivors of the journey, to chronicle it. In his diaries, Pigafetta proves to be a curious, observant writer and our best source of enlightenment on the enigmatic Magellan. Some historians include Magellan alongside the Spanish butchers of Central and South America, pointing to the swift and bloody punishments he often doled out. Others, however, defend him as a man who only turned to violence as a last resort, but then engaged in it with great ferocity. Pigafetta seems to have had a great deal of admiration for Magellan and paints a very flattering portrait of the man. The Venetian offered the following epitaph about him:

> He was always the most constant in greatest adversity. He endured hunger better than all the rest, and more accurately than any man in the world he understood dead reckoning and celestial navigation. And that this was the truth appeared evident, since no other had so much talent, nor the ardor to learn how to go around the world, as he almost did.

It is a matter of some debate, but despite the fact that Magellan did not survive to complete the voyage, he may have literally circumnavigated the globe nonetheless. A voyage during his captaincy in the Portuguese navy among the Moluccas may actually have brought Magellan to a point farther east than his landfall in the Philippines. The details, however, are irrelevant. Magellan crossed the vast Pacific Ocean and established a basis for all future measurements of the earth itself. He defined the blank spots that subsequent explorers would attempt to fill in. For all intents and purposes, Magellan had circled the planet.

The rape of the civilized Americas deflected some of the westward interest in the Spice Islands. Reports of an abundance of gold were coming with increasing frequency, and the Spaniards invested their energies in the decimation of the Incas, Aztecs, and,

later, Mayans. Cortés learned of Mexican gold and laid waste to the Aztec capital the same spring Magellan met his end in the Philippines. The next year Pascual de Andagoya heard rumors of a wealthy civilization atop the Andes as he plotted South America's Pacific coast. Years later, Francisco Pizarro helped destroy an Incan society as complex as any contemporary European nation in terms of political, social, and religious organization. Pizarro had accompanied Balboa on his journey across the Panamanian isthmus before descending into South America in search of wealthy king-

Francisco Pizarro (above) was one of several brothers who hacked their way through the jungles and tribes of Central and South America. The most successful of the lot, Francisco traveled south along the Andes and uncovered the riches of the Incas.

> "... you may be sure that we shall obey you, and hold you as the representative of this great lord of whom you speak, and that in this there will be no lack or deception, and throughout the whole country you may command at your will, because you will be obeyed, and recognized, and all we possess is at your disposal."
> —Montezuma to Cortes

Jacques Cartier (opposite page) was an extraordinary navigator who safely piloted his ships through scores of unfamiliar harbors and miles of new coastline. Unfortunately, Cartier was not quite as good at establishing settlements, since his attempt at doing so along the St. Lawrence River (his arrival there depicted above) resulted in a hasty return to Europe at the end of a long, cold winter.

doms. He arrived to wring the final riches out of a decimated civilization.

The Spanish discovered most of the central-latitude Americas. They reached up into the Great Plains Basin of North America and down the length of South America. They stumbled upon the natural wonders of an unknown continent and managed at times to show a genuine appreciation for their discoveries. But the Spanish "exploration" of the New World was a grizzly, genocidal affair. To credit them for their discoveries is akin to being thankful for advances in surgical technology derived from battlefield triage. Francisco Vásquez de Coronado's discovery of the American Southwest—more extensive than the travels of the more famous conquistadores—was considered useless because it resulted in no profit. Coronado traveled north along the Gulf of California in 1540, was abandoned by his support crews, and eventually went beyond the Arkansas River before struggling back to Mexico empty-handed. Hernando de Soto's exploratory successes throughout the 1520s in Central America earned him the governorship of Cuba and the right to explore Florida. His subsequent adventures throughout the Americas left him penniless and dead alongside the Mississippi River.

Of all the Spanish voyages of discovery, none were as fascinating as the one led by Francisco de Orellana. Dispatched by one of the Pizzaro brothers

(five would follow half brother Francisco to the New World), whose caravan had become mired down in the rain forests of eastern Peru, Orellana set off down the Napo River in search of food and help. It is uncertain whether Orellana and his men could not return or simply chose not to. The sixty men climbed aboard a quickly fashioned raft and were carried the length of the small tributary that fed into one of the greatest rivers in the world, the Amazon. When it became clear that their makeshift transportation was not up to the demands of the great river, they stopped and constructed a better craft.

Orellana and his men traveled the breadth of a continent, through the largest rain forest in the world, to an unknown destination. For the better part of a year they snaked through South America, before washing out into the Atlantic Ocean. They made repairs and alterations to their ship, and subsequently proceeded to sail north along the coast of Brazil up into the Caribbean. Seventeen months after parting ways with Pizarro (who had long since made his own way back to safety), Orellana was back in Spain, chronicling his journey and gaining a governorship. His return eventually led to another fiasco resulting in Orellana's death.

To the north, France would initiate its own era of exploration headed by Jacques Cartier. Born the year before

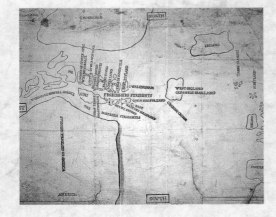

Sir Francis Drake (above) circumnavigated the globe (opposite page, above) and distinguished himself as a successful military strategist as well. His attack of the Cape Verde Islands five years after his circumnavigation is an example of his aggression (opposite page, below), and the temper of the times.

Columbus set sail for the Indies, Cartier was an excellent navigator, pilot, and seaman. He made three voyages to the New World (from 1534 to 1542) without losing a ship. He entered at least fifty unknown harbors without a mishap and lost remarkably few men. In the course of those voyages he explored the majority of southeast Canada, establishing the first European settlement at Quebec and traveling on to Montreal. But Cartier was no Erik the Red. In fact, he was at least partially responsible for diminishing French interest in the New World for the succeeding half century. The severity of the winter Cartier and his men experienced along the Saint Lawrence River dampened whatever enthusiasm they might have had for further exploration or settlement, and their hasty return the moment the ice melted resulted in a thawing of French interest in exploration.

The British, also, were increasingly interested in the Americas and were the first to make an effort at finding a passage to the East. A Yorkshire pirate by the name of Martin Frobisher was inspired by the concept that North America was in fact the lost island of Atlantis and therefore easily circumnavigated. When he encountered a bay along the southern portion of Baffin Island he convinced himself that it would lead to the Northwest Passage, and returned to England with the good news and a few hunks of iron pyrite. The aptly named *fool's gold* led Frobisher on two successive wild-goose chases in pursuit of North American gold. The Englishman carted hundreds of tons of useless soil across the Atlantic certain it would yield enormous wealth. His endeavors bankrupted his investors and must have been rather embarrassing, yet Frobisher was eventually appointed vice admiral in the Queen's navy, knighted, and oversaw the journeys of his successor.

Francis Drake was even more of a pirate than Frobisher—and proved himself to be a very capable one at that. In 1577, Drake took his "privateering commission" to sea in an attempt to undermine Spanish hegemony in the New World. He raided vessels and settlements, Spanish or Portuguese, while sailing the east and west coasts of South America and then traveled as far north as Vancouver. The cold weather convinced Drake to retreat south before heading out across the Pacific.

Already filled with the booty of his privateering, Drake's ship was loaded to the brim with spices in the Moluccas and sailed around Africa's southern cape. All the other ships that had initially accompanied Drake's flagship had turned back or perished, leaving Drake to return to England alone. The first Englishman to circumnavigate the globe was also the first commander to complete the journey, but Drake's accomplishments were more important politically than geographically. Drake's mission was to destroy the Spanish empire; he deemed his discoveries secondary in importance. After helping to dismantle the Spanish Armada in 1588, Drake returned to the New World, where he caught a fever in the West Indies and died. The Spanish domination of the Americas was on the decline, and the nations of northern Europe were beginning to assert themselves.

Like the English, the Dutch were also late arrivals to the Indies, but quickly established their maritime presence. They became familiar with the route around the Cape of Good Hope and wondered whether there might be another way to the East. Toward that end, Willem Barents set out in 1594 to find a northeast passage across the top of Europe and Asia to reach the Indies; unfortunately, he died in the process. The survivors of his journey, however, became the first Europeans to winter in the Arctic, and their experiences set the stage for three centuries of polar exploration. They passed the long arctic night in an improvised house and returned in open boats along the sea that now bears Barents' name. (A Dutch captain named Jacob van Heemskerck

Another British pirate, Martin Frobisher, sought natural riches in the northern reaches of North America, and believed (as indicated by a contemporary map, opposite page, below) that he had discovered a northwest passage to the East. Frobisher's geographic assumptions were incorrect, as was his belief that the "fool's gold" he brought back to England had any real value.

119

was the actual commander of Barents' ship and the man who brought the survivors across hundreds of miles of arctic waters. The journey was one of the bravest in exploratory history, equal to Sir Ernest Henry Shackleton's perilous odyssey amid the icy waters above Antarctica at the beginning of the twentieth century.)

By the turn of the seventeenth century, the French were reinvestigating the New World via Samuel de Champlain, and the English and Dutch were sending Henry Hudson out into arctic seas. Champlain enjoyed friendly relations with the natives along the Saint Lawrence River and established trading posts where his predecessor, Cartier, had failed. Hudson searched northwest and northeast of Europe in three missions, with most of his discoveries taking place in North America. The river in New York State and the great bay in Canada that bear his name today attest to his perseverance. So do the mutinous actions of Hudson's crew, who left the explorer, his son, and a handful of faithful crewmen adrift in that bay.

After a long, hazardous winter, Hudson's refusal to return to Europe resulted in his abandonment on the bay during the spring of 1611. There was little question that the returning crewmen had revolted, but the information they provided was considered too valuable to jeopardize by punishing their mutinous actions. (In fact, Robert Bylot, who took command of Hudson's mission, would later be employed by William Baffin in his search for the Northwest Passage.) Soon after, British colonists began settling in the New World, and trade with them became an important part of the British economy. As the century progressed, the French also staked a claim to portions of the New World through Jean Nicolet, René-Robert La Salle, and Louis Jolliet.

Iberian navigators dominated the seas during the sixteenth century. They circled the globe and lay claim to all of South and Central America.

In the New World, the emphasis was on profit, and westward exploration was almost nonexistent. In 1567, a Spanish captain named Alvavode Mendaña was one of the few to set out across the Pacific from Peru. He ended up discovering the Solomon Islands near New Guinea, but generated little enthusiasm for a second voyage. In fact, it took nearly thirty years for Mendaña to put together another fleet, which proved incapable of relocating his original discovery. The captain died along the way, and his successor, Pedro de Quiros, organized a return voyage after leading Mendaña's survivors back to Peru.

Quiros' second journey across the Pacific was a muddled, ill-fated affair that nearly resulted in mutiny. The captain just missed discovering New Zealand before turning back, while his companion ship sought refuge in the Philippines. That vessel, commanded by Luis de Torres, passed between the southern shore of New Guinea and the Cape York Peninsula in 1607. If Torres even spotted the promontory—and there is no record of his having done so—he probably would not have realized it represented the fabled Terra Australius. That strait now bears his name, but it would take another generation to understand its importance.

Toward the very end of the sixteenth century, the Dutch emerged as the new leaders in maritime exploration. After freeing themselves from Spanish rule, they quickly established a base of operations in the Indies. The Dutch East India Company "liberated" many of the Spice Islands from Portuguese, Spanish, and British control, conveniently setting up Dutch merchants in their place. Their first coincided with the beginning of the seventeenth century, by which time the Dutch were familiar with most of Indonesia. In 1605 a Dutchman named Willem Jansz (or Janszoon), took command of a small *pinnace* (a small boat carried by larger ships for tending missions) and set out along the southern coast of New Guinea.

He overshot the strait Torres had discovered and sailed down into the Gulf of Carpentaria along Australia's northern coast. The land was barren and the few natives extremely hostile. After losing nine of his men in battle, Jansz quickly returned to safer, more familiar harbors.

A number of similar excursions brought about a consensus among the Dutch that the land south of New Guinea was of little interest. Their next encounters provided similar results. As Dutch navigators learned

Matflo Delgo

to swing wide around the Cape of Good Hope into the south Indian Ocean, they were increasingly likely to drift east. In 1616, Dirk Hartog encountered Australia's northwest cape and reported, "Nothing of importance has been discovered on this exploratory voyage." (His reaction is similar to the nonplussed Vikings who first came upon the cold, barren islands of the North Atlantic.)

The Dutch were quite aware of a landmass to the south of them, but had little enthusiasm for learning

more about it. What they knew was bad, and the profitable Moluccas were enough to keep them busy. Not until 1642 was an expedition dispatched with the intention of mapping "the remaining unknown part of the terrestrial globe." Abel Tasman commanded a voyage that managed to miss most of Australia but discovered the island that bears his name (Tasmania), as well as the Fiji and New Zealand islands. His gaps of understanding were great, and somewhat complicated by a follow-up voyage two

From North to South, the limits of the known world were slowly expanding. While William Barents (below) ventured North for the first Arctic winter in 1594, others were still seeking Terra Australius (following page), which remained a mystery until James Cook's enlightening expedition in the late eighteenth century.

years later. Between the two expeditions Tasman eventually formed a picture of Terra Australius that incorporated western New Guinea, western Australia, southern Tasmania, and the eastern coasts of New Zealand. While many of his assumptions were unfounded and his failure to take notice of such bodies of water as the Tasman Sea and Cook and Torres straits were disturbing, Tasman still managed to delineate a landmass much smaller than the theorists had predicted.

The mid-seventeenth to the mid-eighteenth centuries marks a lull in oceanic exploration and an end to the greatest burst of discovery in recorded history. The age of discovery would give way to a more scientific brand of exploration. Nations were occupied in cataloging all that they had claimed. Once all of the desirable land had been charted, it remained for hardy, curious souls to seek out the unknown for rewards less tangible than gold or spice. One of the few names that stands out between the time of Tasman's journeys and the burst of French and English exploration in the middle of the eighteenth century is representative of this transition period. William Dampier was an English buccaneer who doubled as an amateur explorer. He discovered a handful of islands in the Coral Sea, followed much of the Australian coast already visited by the Dutch, and took copious notes on his travels.

The days of blundering along foreign shores were numbered. Now that the rough outlines had been established, exploration would take on an increasingly refined touch. Military and naval men and scientists began to figure more prominently in this phase of discovery as exploration became less profitable. Businessmen now knew where to concentrate their efforts, leaving the art of exploration to governments, hobbyists, and adventurers. Surely the next generation of explorers kept a keen eye for potential profits, but their greatest achievements were a bit more abstract.

7

THE PACIFIC CENTURY

he early eighteenth century marked a period of transition. The first generation of European expansionist countries—Portugal, Spain, and Holland—were struggling to maintain the large chunks they had optimistically bitten off. Their successors, particularly the French and English, were still familiarizing themselves with established sea routes. As the concept of colonization became more popular—or more necessary as the number of oppressed and dispossessed grew—the wealth of land came under renewed and intensified scrutiny. Settlers, not discoverers, were crossing familiar routes to other worlds.

Europeans of this era were comparable to the unambitious Portuguese, who had sat back and reaped the rewards of Prince Henry's efforts. In both cases, the visionaries opened up more new lands than their contemporaries could handle, and the backlog occupied a generation or two of explorers. France and England were content to concentrate on the colonization of profitable ports primarily occupied with the slave trade. The land the Dutch had encountered, even if it was Terra Australius, was barren and sparsely populated. Such lands, devoid of an exploitable work force, were of little interest to merchants.

A number of Frenchmen had exhibited an interest in maritime exploration throughout the early eighteenth century, but were unable to convince those in power to organize such expeditions. (Perhaps the problem was that its proponents were politicians and not captains capable of personal action.) French lore spoke of a windswept mission back in 1503 that had revealed a great landmass whose exact location the crew could not pinpoint afterward. A lame attempt in 1739 at relocating this land instead resulted in the discovery of Bouvet Island, one of the most remote islands in the southern Atlantic, which its discoverer proclaimed the legendary Australius.

The French might have organized other voyages had they not been otherwise occupied by a protracted conflict with the British. In North America, they battled under the guise of the French and Indian wars, while in Europe the two nations chose opposite sides in the Seven Years' War. The fact that England got the better of France in these exchanges is, not coincidently, reflected in the British domination of North America and its ascendancy in the South Pacific.

The British found the time and manpower to support exploratory efforts. The British Navy underwrote one such expedition in search of unknown continents led by Commodore John Byron, who departed from England in 1764 bound for the lower Pacific via Cape Horn. He visited a number of islands but turned up nothing along the lines of Terra Australius. Within two months of returning to England, his ship, the *Dolphin*,

was refitted and sent out under the command of Samuel Wallis. A second ship, the *Swallow*, accompanied Wallis, with Philip Carteret at its helm. The two were separated soon after rounding the tip of South America and made their separate ways across the Pacific during the summer of 1767. They hopped from island group to island group, across the archipelagoes that dotted the unfamiliar ocean. Both were pushed north by the natural forces that prevented all transpacific westward voyages from stumbling upon Australia. Ever since the time of Mendaña and Quiros, captains inevitably found themselves drifting northwest toward the coast of New Guinea instead of the fabled land they sought.

There would be little to distinguish Wallis from this new generation of explorers were it not for the discovery of one particular island along the way. The *Dolphin*'s encounter with Tahiti,

Encounters between Europeans and natives of the idyllic South Pacific, as represented to the public by artists such as Paul Gauguin (below), were probably a lot closer to the less artistic drawing (opposite page) of Bougainville's men in pursuit of an indigenous craft.

and the subsequent reports of it created a European yearning for the idyllic South Pacific, establishing him as the discoverer of paradise. Had he not found Tahiti, many other tropical islands could have provided the same fantasies, and someone besides Wallis could have been the recipient of great accolades. But as the British, and subsequently the French, made the small island a metaphor for all that was natural and unspoiled, Tahiti's fate was sealed. As a result, Wallis' name remains forever linked with the beauty and vulnerability of the South Pacific and its fall from innocence.

Though the British presence in the South Pacific was, and would continue to be, dominant, a number of Frenchmen were also discovering the secrets of the enormous ocean. The most prominent captain of this era was Louis Antoine de Bougainville, a well-schooled military man whose resentment toward the British led him into history. As a member of the vanquished French forces in Quebec, Bougainville had a personal score to settle with the British. A member of the French embassy in London, he kept alert for ways to exact his revenge. Ironically, Bougainville's method was suggested to him while reading the published writings of a British captain who had circumnavigated the globe in 1744. That commander had pointed out the potential strategic importance of the Falkland Islands located off the southern tip of South America, from which the nearby Strait of Magellan could be easily patrolled. The British had already laid claim to that territory, but they'd done little to settle the islands. Meanwhile, the Spanish naturally assumed it was part and parcel of the continent they had claimed centuries earlier.

Bougainville gathered a shipful of displaced French Canadians willing to attempt settling the Falklands (and irritating the British) and sailed in 1763. Shortly after the captain's return to France, Louis XV decided to relinquish the islands to the Spanish,

whose claim he chose to honor over that of the British. Louis XV took pleasure in denying the British, as symbolic as the action may have seemed. (In retrospect, however, the argument seems less frivolous when one is reminded of the number of lives lost in a twentieth-century skirmish between the British and the Argentines—Spain's heirs to the Falklands—over the same desolate islands.)

In return for "handing over" his settlement, Bougainville was outfitted with a new ship and commissioned to lead another expedition. This time the Frenchman rounded South America and headed west, finally determining the location of Terra Australius. Like all those that preceded him, Bougainville never saw Australia's east coast, though he came closer than any previous explorer. He encountered the Great Barrier Reef and, low on supplies and enthusiasm, turned north. Bougainville eventually rounded New Guinea, having little faith in the existence of the Torres Strait some spoke of, entered the well-plied waters of the spiceries, and returned to France.

For merely having come close to Australia and having discovered a handful of islands (such as Pitcairn Island, the Louisiade Archipelago, and members of the Solomon chain Quiros which had misplotted more than a century earlier), Bougainville

would probably have gone down as a peripheral name in the history of discovery. He has remained conspicuous, however, on account of some of the events and effects of his mission. The first was his idyllic encounter with the natives of Tahiti, whose charms were greater than the captain could resist. Bougainville rhapsodized extensively about this paradise and brought back to France a Tahitian of noble birth. (This coincided with the popularity of philosopher Jean-Jacques Rousseau's version of "the noble savage" and cemented Tahiti's place in Europe's romanticization of primitive simplicity. The native, Aoutourou, died on the way back to Tahiti from a Western disease against which he had no immunities. The metaphor was not lost on the French, who continued their colonizing ways nonetheless.)

As the first Frenchman to circumnavigate the globe, Bougainville was sure to have retained a place in French history, but one of his passengers occupies a different place in the history of "firsts." That crew member, whose soft features, shy disposition, and lack of enthusiasm for the women of Tahiti were the subject of a good deal of speculation, was eventually revealed to be a woman. Bougainville's sole official response to the revelation was to grant the crew woman her own quarters. Jean Baré, therefore, is believed to have been the first woman to circumnavigate the globe.

"There was one supreme man in that ship. We knew that he was the lord by his perfect, gentlemanly and noble demeanor. He seldom spoke, but some of the goblins spoke much. But this man did not utter many words: All that he did was to handle our mats and hold our mere (spears) and (clubs) and touch the hair of our heads. He was a very good man, and came to us—the children—and patted our cheeks, and gently touched the hair of our heads."

—Te Horete Te Taniwha

A year after Bougainville's men had bid their wistful farewell to Tahiti, another ship approached the island. Flying the British flag, it pulled into a harbor slightly down the coast from where the Frenchman had taken up temporary residence and was quickly met by enthusiastic natives. Ostensibly, Captain James Cook had led his ship to Tahiti to establish a makeshift observatory for viewing a transit of Venus across the Sun. This infrequent event (in which a planet can be observed passing between the Earth and the solar photosphere) would allow scientists to calculate the distance between the Earth, the Sun, and Venus, and, therefore, to arrive at the basic dimensions of the Solar System. While this was certainly one of the missions of Cook's expedition, it was by no means the only one, and probably not even the primary one. Cook's objective was Terra Australius, and the right man was in the process of arriving at the right time.

It's interesting to note that the astronomical aim of Cook's stop in Tahiti was a relatively sophisticated one, reflective of great advances made in that field as well. This is an excellent example of the interaction between apparently unrelated endeavors, but has its ironic side as well. The fact that human understanding had advanced to the point where it was able to determine the grand scale of outer space while it was still unaware of the geography of its own planet seems quite contradictory. That such astronomical sophistication could be responsible for an old-fashioned vessel's sailing in search of an elusive continent raises an number of humorous paradoxes.

Captain James Cook worked his way off a Yorkshire farm to an appointment in the Royal Navy. Like Magellan, Cook rose through the ranks despite his status as a commoner, with no influential members of court lobbying on his behalf. He became known for his abilities as a navigator and a pilot and excelled when his intelligence, intuition, and initiative came to be appreciated. Cook survived an extended apprenticeship—constrained by a mandatory service requirement—and appears to have made the best of it. He was awarded command of the *Endeavour*, entrusted with a crew of ninety-four, and appointed official astronomer for the expedition.

The crew and cargo were unlike those of any mission to have preceded it. A generation of British explorers, captains, heroes, and villains learned their craft during Cook's three expeditions. The first mission's naturalist and botanist would both contribute enormous amounts of information to the study of natural history, while a number of officers would later lead historic journeys of their own. The ships were customized to accommodate an enormous amount of scientific equipment, preventing the mission from becoming a quest for a hold full of spice or gold. This was a scientific expedition, unlike the swashbuckling exploits of earlier "explorers." A new era was beginning, in which scientific curiosity took the place of mercantile greed. James Cook ushered in a new generation of inquiry and documentation, more civilized if equally devastating in the long run.

After visiting Wallis' justly fabled Tahiti, Cook passed through the So-

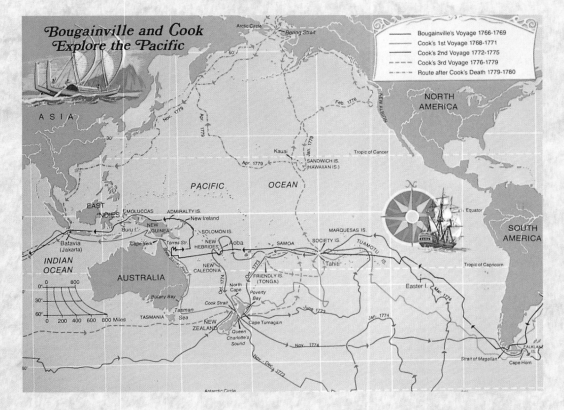

Bougainville and Cook Explore the Pacific

Bougainville's Voyage 1766-1769
Cook's 1st Voyage 1768-1771
Cook's 2nd Voyage 1772-1775
Cook's 3rd Voyage 1776-1779
Route after Cook's Death 1779-1780

ciety Islands before dropping down into the vast, unknown regions of the southwest Pacific. More than forty degrees below the equator, he began a looping westward course that eventually brought him to the coast of New Zealand, which Tasman believed to be the eastern edge of Terra Australius. However, Cook discovered otherwise, proving Tasman's discovery comprised, in fact, two separate islands. Initially, Cook had several menacing encounters with the islands' Maori natives, but relations improved once the ship began following the coast in a northern direction. The *Endeavour* followed a rough figure eight around the islands and established for the first time their sovereignty from Terra Australius. Slowly but surely, the mythic continent was being chopped down in size.

The *Endeavour* took a westward heading out of New Zealand, with Cook hoping to expand upon the work Tasman had begun more than a century before. It took less than a month to cross the Tasman Sea, at which point a sharp-eyed crewman spied the southeast corner of Australia below modern-day Sydney. The *Endeavour* traveled north along the uninviting coast and eventually came to rest in a safe harbor with uncharacteristically abundant flora and fauna. Cook christened the anchorage Botany Bay in honor of the great scientific benefits derived from its discov-

ery. It is just another example of Cook's omnipresence that nearly all the histories of eighteenth-century sciences, and a few that weren't even recognized as sciences yet, eventually invoke his name as a reference during the course of their narratives.

Cook piloted his fragile ship north, unknowingly entering the Capricorn Channel, between the continent and the Great Barrier Reef. The treacherous reef that had deterred Bougainville's advance would present the British captain with his greatest challenge. (Of course there was no way Cook would have heard the details of the Frenchman's journey before his own departure, especially since the two sat on opposite sides in a long history of nationalistic animosities. Cook's own apprenticeship included a role in the defeat of the French— including Bougainville—in Canada on the banks of the Saint Lawrence River.) Along the way Cook nearly lost the *Endeavour* to the reef, but his calm attention to the perilous situation allowed him to salvage the damaged ship and guide it into a nearby river for repairs. From there Cook continued north to Cape York Peninsula and passed through the Torres Strait. Before heading into the more familiar waters of the Arafura Sea, Cook laid claim to the eastern portion of New Holland. He christened it New Wales and established the basis for the island's eventual colonization.

Natives of New Zealand (above, top) grew accustomed to the influx of foreigners; Bougainville, however (above), missed the islands on his way towards the Australian barrier reef.

While the claim's long-term effects were the greatest of all his discoveries, Cook thought little of it. The fact that he never returned to the treacherous coast—although he made repeated visits to the more hospitable ports of New Zealand and Tahiti—is reflective of his lack of enthusiasm for the harsh land. "Was it not for the pleasure which naturally results to a man from being the first discoverer," Cook wrote at the time, "even was it nothing more than sands and shoals, this service would be insufferable."

By the time the *Endeavour* limped into the busy port of Batavia (now called Djakarta) for repairs, Cook's list of accomplishments was extremely impressive. While his geographic discoveries might have been important to the heads of state, his dietary experiments made him the savior of many a seaman. His insistence on certain levels of personal hygiene and sanitary quarters were stricter than any sailor had ever been expected to meet, yet these rules assisted in his efforts at maintaining a healthy crew. Though a British physician had discovered the efficacy of citrus juices in combating scurvy in 1753, his deductions were not widely known. Cook, however, experimented with a variety of antiscorbutics (foods and liquids capable of preventing scurvy), stocking large supplies of sauerkraut, concentrated broths and jellies, and citrus extracts. When his ships had been long at sea, natural antiscorbutics (by far the most valuable) were made the first priority following landfall. Once an island was deemed safe or uninhabited, its vegetables and fruits were often more essential than whatever local game might be found.

Unfortunately, Cook's prophylactic measures had no defense against malaria and dysentery, both of which ran rampant in Batavia. After having accomplished one of the greatest voyages in exploratory history—comparable to Magellan's, Drake's, and others'—without losing a single man to disease, Cook would watch at least thirty of his men succumb. Traveling

across the Indian Ocean and up the coast of Africa, his previously healthy crew struggled to bring the *Endeavour* home. Upon its return, Cook's own accomplishments soon took a backseat to those of the scientists he had brought along. Naturalist Joseph Banks and Swedish botanist Daniel Solander were public heroes (Banks was later knighted), while Cook received a promotion and a quiet year at home with his family while planning his next, and greatest, mission.

Almost a year to the day after he had returned to England, Commander Cook set out on his second expedition in the newly built *Resolution*. Cook headed south this time, passing the Cape of Good Hope before meandering down toward the Antarctic Circle, which he crossed on January 17, 1773. The man whose name has become synonymous with the South Pacific's tropical paradises became the first European to steer into the cold clime of Antarctica. He pushed toward the pole through ice floes and light packs and eventually came within 75 miles (120 kilometers)

of the continental coast before retreating to the northeast. Shortly thereafter, Cook lost touch with his companion ship, the *Adventure*, and consequently plotted a course for New Zealand, where the two captains had agreed upon earlier to meet under such circumstances.

Cook ran east, parallel to the Antarctic Circle, through uncharted waters around sixty degrees south before calling in at New Zealand during the spring of 1773. There he found the *Adventure* recovering from the three long months the ship had gone (without sighting land) in the fierce polar waters. Cook gave the crews time to replenish their stores and themselves before resuming the expedition. This time the objective was to describe a tight circle through the South Pacific northeast of New Zealand in order to explore the only remaining temperate, uncharted regions that might still contain a landmass worthy of the legendary Terra Australius.

The New Wales Cook had discovered on his first voyage was nothing like the theorists had imagined, causing some to assume that the fabled continent still existed elsewhere. Cook was intent on laying any myths to rest once and for all and replacing them with geographic fact. As Polynesia revealed itself to be a scattered series of islands and the southernmost portions of Micronesia proved to be more of the same, Cook was able to safely conclude that there was no continent hidden among these small tufts of land. It was, instead, scattered with chains of tropical paradises on the threshold of a fatal encounter, islands thrown into turmoil by the arrival of these strange white men.

The *Resolution* and the *Adventure* were separated again on their return to New Zealand. The latter's captain was an able man but did not embody the ship's name and returned quickly to England. Cook put in among the Maoris once again and readied his ship for another season in the high, Antarctic latitudes. This journey would take the *Resolution* southeast and then zigzag back and forth across the Antarctic Circle. Conditions allowed them to push farther south than they had on the first leg of the journey, though they were even farther away from the continental shelf in these longitudes. The ship meandered across the desolate southeast corner of the Pacific, and Cook became convinced in the process that the possibility of another Terra Australius was nonexistent. "The greatest part of this Southern Continent," Cook wrote with great prescience, "supposing there is one, must lay within the Polar Circle where the sea is so pestered with ice, that the land is thereby inaccessible."

Although his mission was essentially accomplished, Cook decided to continue exploring the South Pacific. He visited previously sighted islands about which little was known, revisited old ports of call, and discovered a

Cook's travels throughout the Southern Hemisphere were largely responsible for most of the information contained within eighteenth-century maps of the region (such as this one, below). Along the way, Cook's crew established steady trade with New Zealand's Maori natives, shown here (opposite page) bartering a lobster with one of the Endeavour's crewmen.

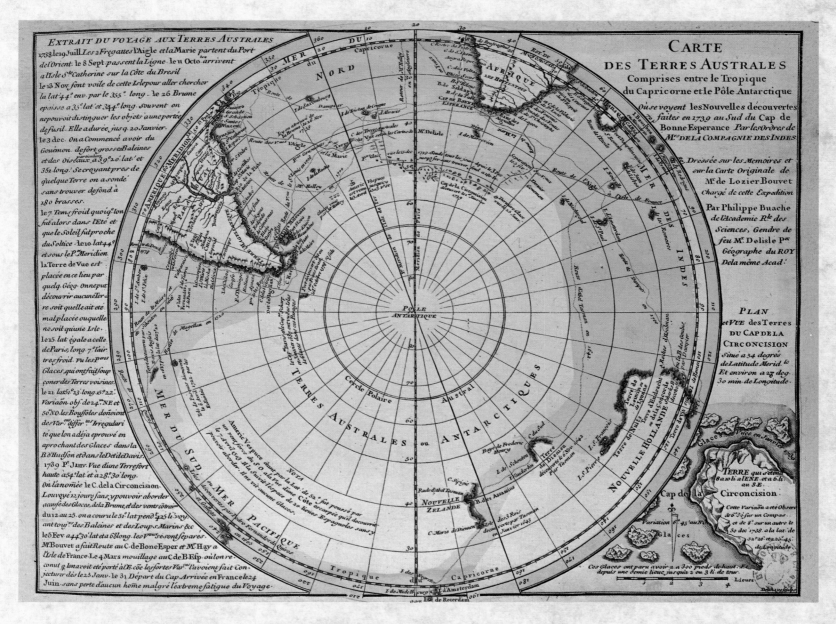

few new bits of land as well. Remarkably, one of those discoveries, New Caledonia, the fourth-largest island in the South Pacific, had previously managed to go undetected by Cook himself or any of his European predecessors. (The New Caledonians were singular in Cook's experiences as an impressively hospitable people who were poor, yet did not steal from the ship, and whose women would have nothing to do with the sailors.) In the course of his travels throughout the Pacific, Cook reinforced his belief that there were no more continents, but grew certain that there were many islands still to be claimed for king and country.

On his final journey home from New Zealand, Cook rounded Cape Horn, explored the southern Atlantic for two months, and put in at the Cape of Good Hope. He returned to England on July 30, 1775, after slightly more than three years at sea. Though usually more modest in his writings, Cook summarized his second voyage this way:

> I had now made the circuit of the South Ocean in a high latitude and transversed it in such a manner as to leave not the least room for the possibility of there being such a continent, unless near the pole and out of the reach of navigation. By twice visiting the Pacific tropical sea, I had not only settled the situation of some old discoveries but made there many new ones and left, I conceive, very little more to be done even in that part. Thus I flatter myself that the intention of the voyage has in every respect been fully answered, the Southern Hemisphere sufficiently explored, and a final end put to the searching after a Southern Continent, which has at times engrossed the attention of some of the maritime powers for near two centuries past and geographers of all ages.

Cook was celebrated as a hero upon his return and promised a comfortable and profitable position, if he so desired. In the meantime, the *Resolu-*

tion would be refitted for arctic sailing in answer to renewed British interest in discovering a Northwest Passage. Whether by force, coercion, or mutual agreement, Cook was named to lead the expedition and set sail twelve months from the time of his return.

Cook turned out to be poorly prepared, ill-tempered, and ill-fated. He was no longer an implacable, inspirational leader of men. Instead, Cook became inconsistent, subject to fits of rage and violent action, often followed by personal recrimination. The pillar of stability Cook's men had come to expect was gone, and as a result his third mission became the kind of bungled, poorly executed affair that is usually forgotten when recounting the grand moments of exploration. Some attribute the change in Cook's personality to physical problems, while others suggest a variety of psychological causes. No one has managed to provide a definitive answer.

Two ships, Cook's *Resolution* and the *Discovery*, rounded the Cape of Good Hope, cruised the southern Indian Ocean beneath Australia, and returned to the familiar shores of New Zealand. Cook remained only two weeks before setting out for Tahiti. Along the way he called in among the Tonga and Society islands, during which time his uncharacteristic behavior toward the natives and his own crew was increasingly apparent.

Conflicts over petty thievery, the rationing of spirits, and Cook's attempt to prevent venereal sailors from further infecting the native women created tensions that were not reported on the first two voyages.

Cook grew distressingly familiar with the routine of his encounters with natives. He watched them prostitute their women and trade their most valuable possessions for the trinkets and nails the Europeans offered in trade. Some islands were tainted in a single visit, while others resisted longer. In the end, however, Cook knew the results:

> Such are the consequences of a commerce with Europeans and what is more to our shame, civilized Christians. We debauch their morals... and we introduce among them wants and perhaps diseases which they never before knew and which serves only to disturb what happy tranquility they and their forefathers had enjoyed. If anyone denies the truth of this assertion, let him tell me what the natives of the whole extent of America have gained by the commerce they have had with Europeans.

In Tahiti, Cook meted out harsh punishments to native thiefs, mutilating some and personally leading a search-and-destroy mission through one village to find a stolen goat. He departed after a stormy four-month stay and set his ships on a northeast course. Equally uncharacteristic were reports that the curious Cook had demurred from exploring islands spoken about by natives. The normally inquisitive commander, already behind schedule, steered for the west coast of North America instead; once there, he worked his way toward the Arctic Circle and the strait Bering had discovered fifty years earlier. Along the way, however, Cook encountered a whole new chain of islands and promptly named them after the Earl that had helped him obtain command of this mission. The Sandwich Islands, now known as the Hawaiian Islands, were alluring, but Cook felt the need to move along quickly in order to approach the Arctic during a period of favorable weather conditions.

Along the coast of Oregon, Washington, and British Columbia, Cook and his men came into contact with a whole new group of indigenous tribes. For his exploration of this coast and the Bering and Chukchi Seas alone, Cook would have staked a claim in

the history books. His ships slipped around the Aleutian Islands, through the Bering Strait, and beyond the Arctic Circle. He touched down upon the North American and Asian coasts and attempted to probe farther north, but met with ice no ship of that era could have withstood.

Cook's orders were to winter upon the Kamchatka Peninsula on the western Bering Sea, but he chose to return to the Sandwich Islands instead. This, too, was uncharacteristic, if understandable, and would seal the captain's fate. His initial return to Hawaii was celebrated as the coming of a god. Cook was deified upon his arrival, but the natives began to grow suspicious with the passage of time. Cook wisely realized he should depart as quickly as possible, before matters got out of hand. He did, in fact, bid farewell to Hawaii, but was forced to return when the *Resolution* became incapacitated; one of many such incidents throughout the third voyage.

The Europeans' humiliating return, particularly in light of their initial reception, began on a bad note and de-

From the tropical shores of Tahiti (opposite page) to the Arctic waters between Asia and North America, outlined by an eighteenth-century map of the territory (below), Cook's journeys ran the gamut of environments. None who followed the British captain ever managed to incorporate such a wide variety of climates into their list of discoveries.

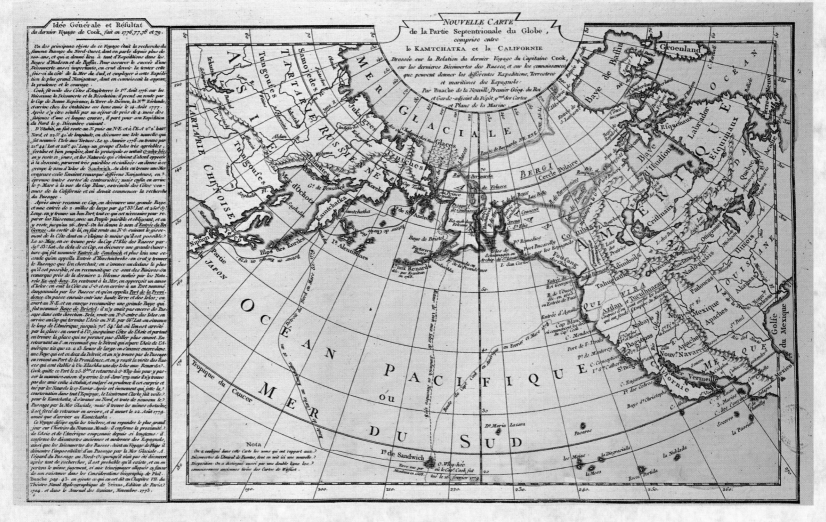

teriorated from there. When informed that a piece of valuable equipment was missing Cook became enraged and went ashore to take a local chieftain hostage for its return. The ploy had worked for the Englishman in the past but proved to be his undoing this time. A crowd surrounded the handful of foreigners along the shore, and the ensuing scenario bears a strong resemblance to Magellan's final moments. Some sailors escaped to the ship, while Cook and four others did not. The captain was literally butchered by his attackers, his remains returned shortly thereafter as an act of contrition.

Charles Clerke, who sailed on all three of Cook's Pacific expeditions after having served under Commodore John Byron before that, assumed command of the expedition, and made a noble effort at completing its objectives. In the process, however, Clerke succumbed to the tuberculosis that had plagued him throughout the voyage, and his successors agreed on returning to England as soon as possible. Word of Cook's death had already reached home—Clerke having passed it along to the Russians at Kamchatka—but the British public was too concerned with their upstart North American colonies to appreciate Cook's accomplishments. His peers, however, understood that no one like him had come before them and that no one like him might ever come again. His discoveries were so numerous that succeeding missions simply hoped to find the few small scraps of land he might have overlooked. There was little talk of disproving Cook's assertions or improving upon them; only to seek out "the lands that had escaped the vigilance of Cook."

The tributes, eulogies, epitaphs, and honors bestowed upon Cook's name are countless. At the time he was credited with having "fixed the bounds of the habitable earth, as well as those of the navigable ocean." Today, there are few historians who do not concur with the justice of Cook's lofty standing. He has come to represent the final glorious chapter in the age of discovery, while ushering in an era of curiosity and specialization. Cook's successors were all specialists, adding details to the maps of specific continents. In some ways, Cook may well have been one of the last Renaissance men, capable of advancing understanding in a wide range of fields. It is little exaggeration to suggest that Cook was all of the following: navigator, pilot, officer, diplomat, astronomer, anthropologist, nutritionist, geographer, cartographer, ethnologist, linguist, artist, soldier, adventurer, and author.

James Cook visited both the Arctic and Antarctic circles. He discovered islands in the Atlantic, Pacific, and Indian oceans. He gave shape to the last-known continent, proved the existence of gaps between Asia and North America and the islands of New Zealand, and traveled twice around the world, top to bottom. His name was eventually bestowed on antipodean straits, an arctic inlet, and islands in Antarctica and the South Pacific. Cook helped to eradicate the scourge of scurvy, calculate the sizes of the planets, and plot the archipelagoes of the Pacific. He opened up British trade with cultures across the globe, consequently bringing them to the attention of Western civilization (for good or bad). He claimed a great deal of territory for England that has remained aligned with the crown to this

day. He gave shape to world atlases, as well as having advanced the careers of a generation of successors. Some became instrumental in the machinations of the Royal Society (such as Sir Joseph Banks), while others would make discoveries (George Vancouver) or be subject to mutiny (William Bligh).

For the most part (or at least during the first two voyages), it can be safely said that Cook earned the respect of his men, the natives he met, and the people back home. As time progressed, however, Cook became increasingly distressed by the evidence of the European contamination of the natives. Morally and physically the results were apparent, and there is ev-

idence that Cook began to question his deeds. His noble actions were having disastrous consequences, and attempts to correct the situation only managed to make things worse.

Time, and perhaps the odds, caught up with James Cook in his fiftieth year. The greatest explorer of them all was not immune to the uncertainties of foreign relations and lost his life in the kind of situation from which he had emerged successfully many times in the past. But the natives of Hawaii struck Cook down—and with him an era. Cook had all but settled the major questions of coastal cartography. Now it remained for other brave, adventurous explorers to fill in the blank spots.

In this painting (below), Pacific natives pay "Divine Honor" to Captain Cook and his fellow officers. A short time later, a similar collection of islanders killed the Englishman in a petty squabble over the theft of livestock. Cook's bloody end came at the hands of the very same people who had once deified him. By the end of the eighteenth century, maps (such as the one on the following pages) chronicled the end of the world as men had known it, and the beginning of a global awareness unimagined by earlier generations.

A MONSEIGN
Par son très-humble, très-
H

GLOBE TERRESTRE ET AQUATIQUE EN DEUX PLANS—HEMISPHERES ;
L'EAU, SUIVANT LES RELATIONS LES PLUS NOUVELLES. Par le Sᵗ. SANSON, Geographe Ordinaire du Roy . 1719.

S. Iacobus

8

DESERTS, JUNGLES, FROZEN TUNDRA

ames Cook accomplished a great deal during the course of his travels, but he also made it clear how much more there was to explore. The Australian continent was an enormous unknown, and the English who settled there remained confined to the Botany Bay region and Tasmania for thirty years around the beginning of the nineteenth century. Africa's interior remained a mystery, the Americas were still hiding enormous tracts of untainted lands, and the poles were completely unknown. The century following Cook was by far the most active, if dispersed, period of discovery and exploration. Each region possesses its own heroes, its own adventurous tales, and its own unfortunate victims.

At this point an emphasis on chronology gives way to a regional focus. During the eighteenth and nineteenth centuries it became necessary to separate the landmasses and study their explorations individually. It was no longer feasible for single journeys to contribute to the understanding of more than one continent's geography. The difficult work of filling in the remaining, isolated gaps would be as treacherous and hard to achieve as any of the great Renaissance voyages.

The smaller the uncharted space on a map, the more hazardous it was likely to be. As fewer and fewer places remained unknown, the desire to explore them merely for the sake of having done so became a motivating factor when none other surfaced. With the possible exception of the Irish anchorites, there are few instances of exploration being undertaken for its own sake. Certainly, such travelers as Marco Polo and Ibn-Batuta were touched with a spirit of wanderlust, but the benefits of their trips were rather tangible and their destinations comparably habitable. Those who hacked their way through practically impenetrable jungles or trekked across flat, desolate plains offered little more than information, much of which served to heighten the sense of

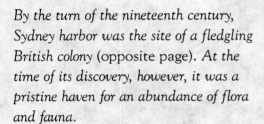

"Though there is a grim picture put before you, yet I would not have you daunted."
—Malcolm Fraser

By the turn of the nineteenth century, Sydney harbor was the site of a fledgling British colony (opposite page). *At the time of its discovery, however, it was a pristine haven for an abundance of flora and fauna.*

barren isolation or impenetrable treacherousness that had prevented others from undertaking the journey any earlier.

This generation of explorers quickly disembarked from the ships that had played an important role in the previous era and set out across the land. Some traveled alone or in small groups. Others organized huge caravans to support their expeditions. It all depended upon the terrain, the climate, the local inhabitants, and the inclinations of the explorer. These factors changed from continent to continent, and often within continents. They accounted for a colorful, diverse period of exploration, during which time atlases began to look closer to their present state.

In the aftermath of Cook's discovery of Australia's west coast, England developed a particular interest in the barren continent. There was, of course, the chance that its interior might contain more hospitable—or profitable—regions, and the last thing the British wanted was to see another nation, particularly France, beat them to the unveiling. In addition, some made modest proposals that the continent's vast tracts of land could house the overcrowded "undesirables" of the urban lower classes, the unplanned product of England's Industrial Revolution. In order to solidify their claim on Terra Australius, the English wanted to map the forbidding land as soon as possible.

George Bass was one of the first to expand upon Cook's sketchy information, making three separate journeys along Australia's western and southern coasts between 1795 and 1799. Bass first explored the region south of the area that is now Sydney, but his most famous discovery was the existence of a strait between the continent and the shores that Tasman had touched upon and christened Van Diemen's Land. The island came to be known as Tasmania, while the

strait came to bear its discoverer's name. Bass made a second voyage to circumnavigate Tasmania counter-clockwise, to confirm its complete independence from the mainland and even sailed up the Derwent River toward the island's center. On each of his missions, Bass was accompanied by a gifted young man named Matthew Flinders, a protégé of Banks' who had also spent a great deal of time under the command of another Cook alumnus, William Bligh. At the age of twenty-seven, having already become familiar with the Pacific environs, Flinders was given command of a weathered vessel and charged with the circumnavigation of Australia.

There were still many questions about the shape and size of this new land, including suspicions that New Holland and New Wales were divided by inland seas and great rivers. Flinders set out to answer these questions and came up with the idea of naming the single entity he circled, Australia, after the famed Terra Australius. He began at Dirk Hartog Island, off the western coast and traveled south and then east. Along the familiar coast Flinders refined his maps, then rounded Cape York into the Gulf of Carpentaria and the Arafura Sea.

Flinders' ship, the *Investigator*, was in particularly bad condition by the time he reached the continent's northwest coast. With an emphasis on survival, the young captain gave up mapping the coast and decided to head home. Along the way, he chose to stop for repairs at the island of Mauritius, unaware of the fact that his countrymen had gone to war with the French, who controlled the island. Flinders was imprisoned there for more than six years, effectively putting an end to his role in the history of exploration.

Despite, or perhaps on account of, the information Flinders was eventually able to bring back to England, the British occupation of Australia remained limited to the southeast coast for several decades, settling what is today Sydney. The residents of modern-day Sydney continued to probe in-

land, hampered by the Blue Mountains behind them, part of the Great Dividing Range. In 1813, Gregory Blaxland crossed the Blue Mountains with a small expedition, and subsequently fought his way through dense brush to a lush valley capable of supporting a settlement. Freed convicts and adventurous settlers made their way there and continued extending those boundaries. One of the first priorities, it appears, was to connect the people in the Sydney area with those that had taken up residence along the gulfs and bays of southeast Australia. By 1824, an expedition set out to determine the feasibility of a land route between the two areas so that livestock might be herded between them.

Hamilton Hume, a man who had already spent a good deal of time learning about life in the bush, looked to undertake such a journey, but was unable to finance it personally. To rectify that situation, he took on a wealthy backer, William Hilton Hovell, who insisted on accompanying the expedition. They crossed numerous inland rivers along the way, which Hume erroneously interpreted as confirmation of the existence of a tremendous inland sea occupying the center of the Australian continent. Equally incorrect was Hume and Hovell's assumption that they had reached their destination, today's modern-day Adelaide. Instead the two emerged near what is now Melbourne on the north coast of the Bass Strait. (In later years a well-publicized squabble developed between the two men regarding their responsibility for the mission and its misconceptions.)

Hume's next traveling partner was another key figure in Australia's early history, Charles Sturt. In 1828, the two led a party of twelve that scoured the interior of New South Wales and discovered the Darling River in the process. Sturt returned the next year to travel along and upon the Darling and a handful of other large rivers in the area. He was swept from one to another, encountering a number of previously undiscovered lakes along the way. Sturt and his men were forced to row upriver against the Darling to make their return, and the effort drained the explorer's energies for some time to follow.

The next burst of activity in Australian exploration came during the 1840s, at which time the western and southern portions of the continent were crossed and skirted. Edward Eyre, who believed the area north of Adelaide was surrounded by a ring of impenetrable lakes, set out in 1841 to cross the Nullarbor Plain to King George Sound. His epic journey along the inhospitable coast of the Great Australian Bight was a marvelous tale of survival as well as a stern warning that the vast, hostile Australian deserts were not to be taken casually. Three of Eyre's companions perished along the way—one at the hands of the other two—while Eyre and a native companion barely emerged with their own lives. (Eyre rose to prominence afterward, and was eventually made governor of Jamaica. His handling of a minor riot that escalated into a bloody massacre resulted in dismissal, though his role in the incident is unclear.)

The first Australian settlements, particularly those established inland, were always close to life-sustaining waterways (above). The British attempted to bring their ways of life to the hostile continent "down under," and met with varying degrees of success. Expeditions into the interior of the continent, such as the one led by Captain John Stuart (following pages), generated a great deal of interest in hopes of finding a portion of the unknown land that might sustain them better, if not actually uncovering great wealth in the process.

Sturt returned to action around this time, having recovered from temporary blindness. He paired up with a newcomer to Australian exploration, John Stuart, to lead an expedition north from Adelaide in search of the hypothesized inland sea. Instead they encountered a handful of new rivers, barely missed discovering the largest of the inland lakes, and came upon the southern fringe of the Simpson Desert. In 1845, they returned home, having come up painfully short in their attempt to reach the continent's geographic center. (The party was believed to have been within 150 inhospitable miles [250 kilometers] of their destination.) Like Eyre, however, they were successful in determining that Australia's interior had little to offer potential settlers.

At the same time, Ludwig Leichardt was wandering about the north-

west corner of Australia. His first journey out of Brisbane was moderately successful, though his second proved ridiculously ambitious. Leichhardt's attempt at exploring three of Australia's four coasts in the year 1846 was prematurely undertaken, ill-conceived, and over before it ever really got started. Unfortunately, this did not deter Leichhardt from trying an even more ambitious journey two years later. This time he attempted to cross the continent from east to west. Leichhardt disappeared in the process and was never heard from again.

The exploration of Australia was confused by a number of factors. The "discoveries" of ex-convicts and independent explorers were often ignored, but were later claimed by government expeditions. The strict separation of classes worked its way into all matters, and the process of exploration

The first objective was a south-to-north crossing of eastern Australia, for which a handsome reward was posted. An official expedition was organized, and an ex-patriated Irish policeman by the name of Robert Burke was chosen as its leader. This selection, and its consequences, bears a striking resemblance to the course of events involving Robert Scott's fated Antarctic expedition a few decades later. Burke knew little of the art of bushwhacking and not much more about handling men. He disdained indigenous adaptations and made deadly mistakes with rations and support arrangements.

Only one man returned from Burke's push to the Gulf of Carpentaria—Phillip King, a governor's son, who was discovered by a rescue party in the care of aborigines who had found him near death. Eventually King reported how he and Burke had come within a short distance of the gulf before encountering the impenetrable marshes and swamps of the Barkly Tableland. The return journey was torturous and underprovisioned, resulting in the deaths of Burke and the others. Thus, the honor of successfully completing the south-to-north crossing fell to another, but Burke's name has occupied a prominent place in Australian lore ever since. In the same way that Robert Scott's blunders were forgiven, many Australian's chose to concentrate only on Burke's valiant effort.

John Stuart made several attempts at the south-to-north crossing before finally succeeding in 1862, reaching what is now called Darwin and establishing the route for the telegraph line that brought Adelaide and southern Australia into contact with the world. To the east of that line the Pacific coast and interior was known and fairly well settled. To the west, however, were enormous deserts and a distant coast. In addition, the line represented the earliest link across a continent in which large tracts of uninhabitable, uninviting land separated establishments from one another.

was no exception. As a result, English officers often usurped the credit for a find, further alienating the "lower" classes. In addition, the simple fact was that much of this new continent was uninhabitable by European standards. The British were contemptuous of the primitive aborigines and had little inclination toward settling the vast tracts of barren land their adventurous explorers described.

Throughout the 1850s Augustus and Frank Gregory covered enormous expanses of western and northern Australia. Augustus, the elder of the two brothers, spent most of his time in the northern quadrant, covering ground between Brisbane and the Gulf of Carpentaria, as well as venturing south into the central wastelands. Frank might not have logged as much distance as his brother, but did manage to spot a few habitable inland

sites around western Australia. The Gregorys, whose travels actually began in 1846, remained active into the 1860s. Their expeditions were relatively uneventful but still managed to provide a good deal of information for the next generation of Australians.

By the 1860s, all of Australia's present-day capitals had been established, as well as a number of smaller enclaves. There was, however, little interaction taking place between the settlements that did not rely upon harbor-to-harbor maritime communication. Technology and population growth were catching up with distant Australia, and the time was coming to connect the scattered towns by railway, road, and cable. The politicians and the businessmen (the terms were often interchangable) wanted to see this accomplished and were accumulating the funds to bring it about.

The remainder of Australia's exploration consisted of mapping the remaining desolate wastelands. Colonel Egerton Warburton followed the telegraph line halfway north before turning west. He skirted the northern edge of the Great Sandy Desert under conditions that did little to inspire imitators. Warburton occupies a place in history as the first to travel overland to Australia's Indian Ocean shores, but the expedition was a disaster. Upon his return, Warburton managed to assure his fellow colonists that they wanted little to do with these parched lands.

A contemporary of Warburton's, John Forrest, emerges as one of the most accomplished and consistent explorers in Australia's short history. Forrest led three expeditions across vast acreage of harsh terrain. His first mission was to track the route Leichardt had taken more than twenty years earlier. Despite vague rumors among the aborigines that Leichardt was alive, no traces of him were found, and the mission marks Forrest's only "failure." He returned to Perth before undertaking his second, and most famous, expedition.

In 1870, Forrest set out to retrace Eyre's steps along the Great Australian Bight. Forrest's expedition was better provisioned and supported than his predecessor's torturous journey had been. This gave him the opportunity to explore the region in greater detail, as well as reconnoiter a safe harbor that had been founded halfway along the bight. Forrest covered the distance in less than half the time it had taken Eyre and his Australian companion.

Forrest's third and final adventure was his most dangerous, traveling east across the continent through the Gibson Desert. The accomplished bushwhacker was forced to rely on all of his resources in order to eventually reach Lake Eyre and float downriver. Forrest spilled out near Adelaide and into a prominent place in Australian history. The explorer was the first premier of western Australia and would become the first Australian statesman to enter the peerage.

Ernest Giles and William Gosse made extensive treks throughout the continent during the 1870s as well. The former named the Gibson Desert for a partner who was lost there,

while the latter failed in his east-west mission, but gained attention for discovering Ayers Rock in the process. The final burst of transcontinental activity came in 1896 when two separate missions by Lawrence Wells and David Carnegie crossed western Australia south to north. Both clarified the enormity of the Gibson and Great Sandy deserts, and helped fix the boundaries of habitable Australia. Five years later, at the turn of the twentieth century, England granted Australia commonwealth status.

Africa was never "discovered." Like Europe and Asia, it was always *there*. Traders, colonists, and support bases were established along its periphery ever since men were able to cross the Mediterranean Sea in boats or travel overland through the Middle East. Yet Africa's interior remained a great mystery. Despite Portuguese way stations dating back to the fifteenth century, the Dutch settlement of the southern tip, and the Arab infiltration of the east coast, the center of the "Dark Continent" remained veiled

by thick, forbidding jungles guarded by frequently hostile natives, and crisscrossed by a complex assortment of lakes and rivers.

Africa's European exploration was mostly a case of white men learning what the natives had already known. (This was true to an even greater extent than in Australia and the New World, where the concepts of regional geography were generally unfamiliar to natives.) For every coastal settlement planted along the outskirts of Africa, all the way back to the earliest seafarers blown south across the Mediterranean, there are stories of adventurous souls venturing inland in search of essentials, valuables, and desirables. Queen Hatshepsut's nearly prehistoric expedition, the Carthaginians' methodical expansion, and ancient Rome's flirtation with the northern edges of the Sahara are all examples of the kind of superficial probes made by the earliest visitors. Thus, the intrepid white men who ventured into the "heart of darkness" traveled well-worn paths established by merchants and slave traders.

The modern era of African exploration was also very regionalized in nature. There is not enough room here to recite the scores of names of hardy travelers who expanded the African horizon from each of their respective coastal perches over the course of a few millenia. Their information was cumulatively extensive, but added very little to the mysteries of the continent's interior. In the heady days following Cook, groups of explorers united to seek out the dwindling number of geographic mysteries still unsolved. Fortunately for them, but unfortunately for most Africans, their interest coincided with a shift in political attention, since the colonies of the New World were growing increasingly independent and the imperialistic powers of Europe had to look elsewhere for profit and political intrigue.

While early African explorers laid the groundwork, the beginning of the modern era began to take shape when the Portuguese all but abandoned Af-

rica for their interest in the Indies. The Spanish inherited their African ports, reaped the rewards, and gradually faded out of the picture as the Dutch began to establish a presence centered around Cape Town. In 1613, a Spanish Jesuit, Pedro Paez, became the first European to encounter Lake Tana, the source of the Blue Nile (which along with the White Nile, combined to form the Nile itself—the source of life for one of the oldest centers of civilization). The relationship was not understood, however, until James Bruce determined this in 1768. To the south, toward the end of the 1770s, the Dutch discovered the Orange River. Between these two regions, the atlases could offer little information. The curious and the greedy were anxious to fill in the blanks.

Sir Joseph Banks, knighted following his days with Cook, was a prominent member of England's Royal Geographic Society, and a cofounder of the African Association. That organization had underwritten three disastrous expeditions in search of the Niger River before being approached by a Scottish surgeon willing to make another attempt. Mungo Park sailed from Portsmouth harbor in the spring of 1795 for the Niger River by way of Gambia. He was to determine the direction the river ran and find its terminus. Along the way, the association hoped Park might visit the area's major cities as well.

Park's trek was remarkable, one of the few in the exploration of Africa who relied on the knowledge of a few, rather than enormous, enslaved entourages. He began with a small group and watched it whittle away as he passed through the kingdoms of western Africa. The remaining party was taxed and robbed until they were reduced to the clothes on their backs. The treachery of a handful, however, was equaled by the kindness of the majority, and Park's later best-selling reminiscences display a great deal of warmth for most of the Africans he encountered. He reserved his racial

"The view of this extensive city, the numerous canoes upon the river, the crowded population, and the cultivated state of the surrounding countryside, formed altogether a prospect of civilization and magnificence which I little expected to find in the bosom of Africa."
—Mungo Park

Europeans looked to the south for land, resources, and slave labor. The fact that African civilizations (such as the one depicted opposite page, along the Congo River) operated independently of them was perceived as irrelevant, to be squashed as quickly, and as ruthlessly, as possible.

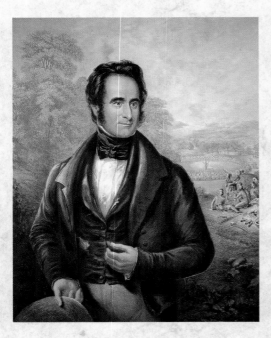

David Livingstone (above, top), *began his African explorations in the shadow of Robert Moffat* (above, bottom), *who had traveled across much of southern Africa. In his boat* Ma Robert (opposite page), *Livingstone headed north and never turned back, spending the remainder of his days in the central regions of the mysterious continent.*

disdain for the Moors, who held him captive during his journey for several months before he managed to escape. Unfortunately, like most of his contemporaries, Park usually relied on sweeping racist generalizations when discussing the natives, pro or con. And while the Scotsman felt slavery was an evil, he still believed that it was best for the African people, whom he deemed incapable of managing their own affairs.

Park eventually reached the Niger River near Ségou, but explored less than 100 miles (160 kilometers), of the river before accepting that he was not equipped for the task. He retreated along the Niger back to Bamako, capital of modern-day Mali, and then headed due west overland. The return journey was as eventful and hazardous as the trip out, and the assistance of an African slave trader was necessary for Park to cover the final distance to the Atlantic coast. The explorer's return to England was feted by its sponsors and marveled at by the public. Park's *Travels in the Interior Districts of Africa* was a sensation on the order of Marco Polo's *Travels*, and the Scotsman does much to merit the comparison. His style is informative and even, while his actual adventures were far more harrowing. Both Park and Polo ushered in new perceptions of the far corners of the earth while still relying on contemporary misconceptions and prejudices to do so.

Eight years after his initial acclaim, Mungo Park returned to Africa for the second and last time. On this occasion, he was encumbered by an unwieldy entourage totally inappropriate for the mission at hand. The hardships mounted, and Park's luck is thought to have run out near Nigeria's Kainji Lake. He may have been killed by hostile natives or drowned in the Bussa Rapids while trying to escape them. Much like Francisco de Orellana's ill-advised return to the Amazon, Park's reprise cost him his life; but, in typical British fashion, it elevated his place in history. Park's first journey is often perceived as the

beginning of modern African exploration and the second as a chilling portent of all too many that would follow.

Until the 1820s, most post-Park exploration was confined to the southernmost portions of the continent. Missionaries such as John Campbell and Robert Moffat roamed the Veldt to unfamiliar rivers and mountains, while a pair of adventurous Portuguese crossed west to east from the southern Atlantic to the Mozambique Channel. Pedra Baptista and Amaro José snaked back and forth across the fifteenth degree of latitude south of the equator; but their journey, hazardous as it may have been, does not seem to have sparked much interest in the region.

Europe remained particularly interested in northern Africa during the early decades of the nineteenth century, developing a fascination with fabled Moslem forbidden cities. Alexander Laing, a Scotsman, reached Tombouctou (the modern spelling nowhere near as lyrical as its original anglicization—Timbuktu) in 1825, but was murdered within days of his departure. René-Auguste Caillié was renowned for returning from that Moslem stronghold safely, while the rest of his extensive travels throughout northwestern Africa remain largely unheralded.

In 1822, a group of Englishmen organized an expedition that came to be known as the Bornu Mission, named after a region in the Sudan they hoped to reach. Despite a great number of delays and infighting among the leaders, Hugh Clapperton, the leader of the mission, became the first European to discover Lake Chad. In the process he buried one colleague and spent most of his time separated from the purported leader of the expedition. A naval lieutenant, Clapperton's perseverence was remarkable, though it should be noted his adventures were supported by the backbreaking work of hundreds of natives. Few Europeans followed Park's lead on his first, successful journey. Ironically, most seem to have opted for the cumbersome burdens that doomed his second expedition instead.

Clapperton returned to Africa on a second mission, this time in the company of Richard Lander. The two headed north from the coast along the Gulf of Guinea (more specifically, the Bight of Benin), and met up with the Niger near the Bussa Rapids, which had claimed Park. The intention was for Clapperton and Lander to explore the region north of the Niger and then follow that river to its mouth. Unfortunately, Clapperton died while in Sokoto, and Lander decided to return home.

Just three years after his original partner's death, Lander came back to Africa with his brother John to complete the first mission's goals. The brothers traveled overland to Bussa, explored upstream for a short distance, and then let the river carry them along. They emerged out of the Niger Delta in November of 1830, finally completing a chapter that had begun thirty-five years earlier with Park. Unfortunately, Richard Lander made the same fatal mistake as Park and returned once too often. He met his death on his third visit to the Niger. As exciting as African travel must have been, it was equally deadly.

―――――――――

During the 1840s, a number of Europeans began to expand on the still-limited knowledge of African geography. Some, like Heinrich Barth, began to answer the smaller, unresolved questions regarding western Africa, while others were taking the first tentative steps toward the center of the continent. Two German explorers, Johannes Rebmann and Johann Krapf, set out for the interior in 1848. Unlike most of their predecessors, however, they headed inland from Africa's eastern shores along the Indian Ocean. (Original forays into the continent's interior usually began along Africa's western coastline.) Rebmann became the first European to sight Mount Kilimanjaro, while Krapf laid claim to Mount Kenya. Their reports of vast lakes were treated with skepti-

cism, even derision, upon their return, but were later credited with having inspired a future generation of explorers to investigate the region.

But the greatest of all explorers throughout this era was a Scottish missionary who came north through the Kalahari Desert. David Livingstone had hoped for an assignment in the Orient, but ended up in Africa when England entered into the Opium War with China in 1839. Instead, Livingstone served under Robert Moffatt in South Africa, bristling under his and all subsequent authority. The Scotsman bided his time for a while under Moffatt's control before crossing the Kalahari Desert and making his first expedition, accompanied and underwritten by a European big game hunter, to Lake Ngami.

After making several relatively short trips throughout the region, Livingstone sent his wife and children back to England and set out to prove that the Zambezi River, which he had encountered on a previous trip, was a viable means of crossing Africa. Livingstone had hoped that a convenient water passage through the continent would spur trade with the natives, replacing slavery by providing economic alternatives. The missionary's eloquent firsthand reports on the prevalent horrors of enslavement were a rallying point for the growing aboli-

tionist movement. Some of Livingstone's geographic assumptions proved incorrect, but the acclaim back home was becoming tremendous nonetheless. (Though often referred to as a missionary, Livingstone failed to convert any Africans he encountered during his expeditions. The Scotsman believed that their religions were much better for their way of life.)

David Livingstone was an adventurous, religious man, who wrote eloquently on the state of affairs in Africa and the effects of European encroachment. He was a voice coming out of equatorial Africa against the slave trade, and his dispatches and journals are testament to his concern. A burst of exploratory activity was going on at this time, and its implications for the future of many unsuspecting tribes were alarming. Livingstone recognized this and warned those that would listen. Despite his final misconceptions about the Nile's true source, Livingstone's career was distinguished by its humane attitude toward, and dealings with, the people of Africa. Over the course of three decades, Livingstone explored a wide variety of regions. He traveled along the Zambezi River and discovered Victoria Falls in the process. He was led to Lakes Tanganyika and Nyasa and discovered the source of the Congo River as well.

Livingstone's later expeditions were undertaken in response to the reports of contemporaries claiming to have assembled the final pieces of the Nile puzzle. And while this inevitable discovery seems to blend in with the litany of lakes and rivers that fill the pages of Africa's histories, no geographical question had eluded cartographers and theorists for so long. Ever since Herodotus had reported the great river taking a sharp turn toward the west two millenia earlier, the question remained the subject of much debate. Lake Tana fed the Blue Nile, and perhaps this relatively small body would be the only specific headstream, but the answer was by no means settled.

In 1857, Richard Burton, a well-traveled British linguist and scholar, was named to head an expedition in search of the source of the White Nile. (He had been given a similar assignment six years earlier, at which time an injury and the Crimean War put matters on hold.) Burton had spent a great deal of time among Arabs, including clandestine visits to such "forbidden cities" as Mecca and Harar, and shared their disdain for Africans. Burton was equally ill-disposed toward his assigned partner for the expedition, a proper Victorian named John Speke.

Burton and Speke squabbled a great deal, and their mission was essentially a failure. The two were sick most of the time, carried by natives for much of the way, and utterly disheartened when they learned that the body of water they had reached, the Sea of Ujiji (now known as Lake Tanganyika), was not the Nile source they sought. Burton wanted no more of central Africa and made for the continent's eastern coast with haste. He returned to the Arabs, whom he preferred. Speke, however, driven by his own ambitions and a desire to accomplish something that had eluded Burton, veered north on the return trip.

John Speke suffered great hardship on the second leg of his journey, before finally emerging onto the southern shore of Lake Victoria in 1858. He made no attempt to circle the enormous lake, the second-largest such freshwater body in the world, and never spotted its outlet to the Nile. Nonetheless, Speke proclaimed his discovery of the Nile's source with great certainty; a conviction that seemed to grow more intense as others became increasingly skeptical. Burton entered the fray against Speke as well, and the insulted explorer mounted yet another expedition to prove his assertions once and for all.

In 1860 Speke set out from Zanzibar, reaching Lake Victoria the next

year. He and his companions, and the scores of enslaved attendants that accompanied them, encountered a series of capricious monarchs, one of whom held them for some time as de facto prisoners. Speke was eventually taken to the lake's northern end, but his passage was through mountains and not along Victoria's coast. He was subsequently free to travel northward, during which time he crossed the Nile but again chose not to follow alongside it. Toward the very end of his expedition, Speke was met by a couple who had been dispatched by the regional administrator and provided them with the information that served to shape their own destinies.

Samuel Baker was an adventurous, colorful soul who comes closest to embodying the romanticized notion of African explorers created by the entertainment industries of later generations. He was accompanied by Florence Ninian von Sass on all of his expeditions, which included an incredible series of close calls and wonderous discoveries. The two first set out on a painstaking voyage up the Nile, meticulously tracking its tributaries. After encountering Speke and accepting his word for the White Nile's origin, they veered west instead and discovered Lake Albert.

Baker's reception by his British countrymen was icy, particularly on account of his scandalous relationship with Sass, which was not "legitimized" by marriage until long after they had returned from their travels. As a result of his homeland's indifference, Baker eventually came to serve under the Ottoman Viceroy of Egypt, for whom he annexed a great deal of territory and from whom he received a prestigious posting. It should be noted that during this tenure, Baker played a substantial role in eliminating slave trade in the region, a decade after America's Civil War. Though the moral stance Baker espoused at the time seems rather obvious today, it is important to realize how many of his and Livingstone's contemporaries consorted with slave traders.

Light was finally falling onto the Dark Continent, and though many nooks and crannies remained in the shade, a rough sketch was beginning to form. Germans such as Friedrich Rohlfs and Gustav Nachtigal spent the 1860s traveling throughout Northern Africa, and Georg Schweinfurt became the first to explore both the Nile and Congo River systems during the same expedition. David Livingstone remained active—and occasionally out of contact. After a particularly long period of silence, some European and American papers reported his demise. Eventually, however, letters from the Scotsman emerged, and his popularity reached new heights. Unlike so many of the other African explorers, Livingstone was a proper role model, operating under a true Christian morality. This helped elevate him above some of his less savory peers. Livingstone's flawless reputation allowed "polite company" to embrace him wholeheartedly.

The fascination with Livingstone eventually resulted in one New York newspaper publisher's dispatching his most flamboyant writer to track down the elusive explorer, even though three previous attempts by various adventurers during the early 1870s had met with failure. Nonetheless, Henry Morton Stanley set out to "rescue" the man in 1873. He crossed between Lakes Victoria and Nyasa through modern Tanzania, struggling all the way, until meeting up with Livingstone in Ujiji on Lake Tanganyika. Stanley's fine detective work and perseverence had paid off.

Stanley uttered his famous line of supposition to a sickly Livingstone, who readily accepted the former's medicines and supplies while resisting his entreaties to return with him to "civilization." The two men, apparent opposites who got along quite well nonetheless, remained together for a few months. They explored the lake region until Stanley returned to file his story and Livingstone resumed his travels. Within months, however, the Scottish missionary fell ill once again.

Samuel Baker and his companion Ninian von Sass (conspicuously absent from the watercolor on the opposite page) traveled throughout northern Africa for geographic knowledge as well as the adventure of it all. Henry Morton Stanley (left) made his travels for the fame and wealth it would bring him. In the process, Stanley illuminated many of the dark recesses that had made Africa (as depicted in a sixteenth-century map, following pages) a truly dark continent.

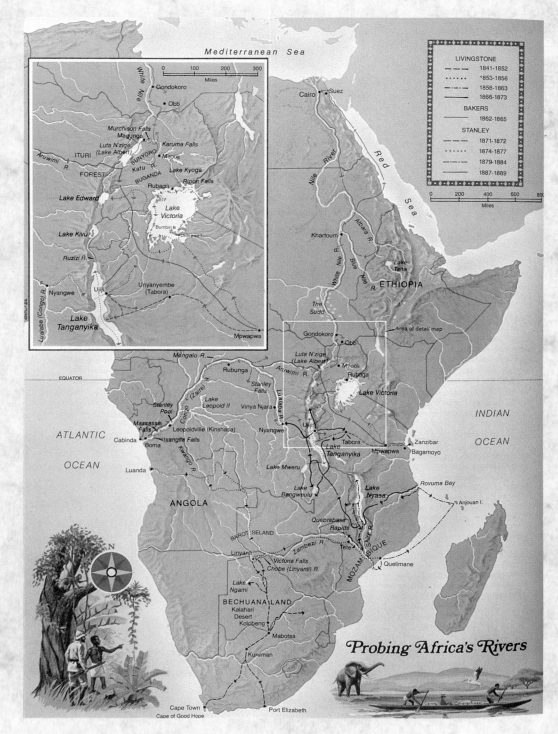

Probing Africa's Rivers

Depictions of Stanley's famous encounter with Livingstone (above) had often relied more heavily on fiction than fact. The meeting was, in fact, a low key affair later glorified by the press. Stanley's flair for the dramatic may have led him to strike poses such as the one seen on the opposite page, though it's more likely they were imaginative renderings performed by those who had never actually met the man.

> " . . . he was the hero of the lads of my generation; his name was a trumpet-call; his mere existence stirred us as a child is stirred by a fairy-tale."
> —Jacob Wassermann

David Livingstone succumbed to the jungle on May 3, 1873.

The torch Livingstone carried was passed on to the flamboyant Stanley, whose second and third missions answered the final major questions of African geography. The well-traveled, multifaceted adventurer seemed to have inherited Livingstone's fascination with Africa and its people. Certainly the acclaim it brought him was greater than anything else he had experienced. Yet, while the general public embraced Stanley on account of his dispatches from Livingstone's camp, it would take another, more impressive journey to gain him the acceptance of the elitist exploratory community.

Stanley's second mission was intended to provide the definitive answer to the question of the Nile's source once and for all. He vindicated John Speke, more than ten years after Speke's death, and established the fact that Lake Tanganyika (which he circumnavigated) was not connected to the Nile. With the support of hundreds of slaves, whom Stanley is reported to have ruled with an oppressive hand, he crossed overland to the Congo, which he then rode out to the

Atlantic. The mission crossed the Congo Free State (now the Republic of Zaire), battling nature and natives along the way. Stanley's eloquent style brought readers around the world a glimpse of interior Africa and reduced the remaining dark spots into smaller, diminishing shadows.

A decade after completing his second expedition, Stanley set out for central Africa one last time. His purported mission was the rescue of Eduard Schnitzer, a self-styled German renegade who had adopted the name Emin Pasha while serving as an official of the Egyptian government. The Pasha was eventually appointed governor of Egypt's central African holdings, but quickly fell into conflict with the Mahdi, a Moslem revolutionary whose title reflected his belief that he was a "divine guide." Mahdi's European contemporaries labeled him "one of the most dangerous fanatics who had ever troubled the peace of mankind," but today he might be thought of as simply a religious fundamentalist attempting to overthrow colonialist oppression.

Stanley used the Pasha's plight as an excuse to enter the region and establish trading relations for England with local rulers. He approached the interior from the Atlantic coast and followed the Congo into the Aruwimi toward Lake Albert and the Pasha's remote base. (Stanley's expedition was the first to span the continent from east to west across the Congo.) Those who appointed Stanley to lead this mission had been concerned about his potential treatment of the seven hundred men under his command, and it appears that their fears were well founded. The journey was an incredible strain on the support crew in bondage, but Stanley eventually reached the Emin Pasha, whose desire to be "rescued" was on a par with Livingstone's. Stanley did not get along as well with the Pasha as he had with Livingstone, and there seems to have been a good amount of conflict between the two.

Eventually, the combined forces of the two charismatic men set out from Lake Albert, discovering the Semliki River and the Ruwenzori mountain range (believed to have been the basis for Ptolemy's Mountains of the Moon) on their passage south of Lake Victoria. The party's arrival at Bagamayo, on the Tanzanian coast across from Zanzibar, was celebrated by German supporters of the Pasha, who was seriously injured (accidentally) during the festivities. Of the ten thousand followers the Pasha and Stanley had led away from Lake Albert, just a few hundred eventually completed the journey to Cairo. Some turned back, others were captured, and the remainder died in transit. A lucky few managed to depart with Stanley.

The Emin Pasha returned to central Africa, initially with the support of the German government. When he continued to disregard their orders and operate under his own set of guidelines, the Germans were forced to disavow their association with him. The Pasha pushed on anyway, returning to his original base on Lake Albert. Those who were still there no longer recognized his authority, so he continued west. Somewhere south of the Congo's Stanley Falls, the Emin

Pasha was murdered in his sleep by Arab slave traders. The circumstances surrounding the attack have never been clear.

Between Henry Stanley and the Emin Pasha the central regions of the once-dark continent were being illuminated. The two shed light on the Nile-Congo watershed, and wandered from desert fringes to tropical rain forests. Throughout the decades that followed, a wide variety of traders and adventurers crossed these same paths and expanded upon them. The map-

ping of Africa was by no means complete, but cartographers had much more information at their disposal.

In 1887 Samuel Teleki went about exploring eastern equatorial Africa. Teleki climbed Mount Kilimanjaro and then discovered Lake Rudolf and the Omo River that flowed from it. He added a handful of other minor discoveries to the maps of the region, but was actually just one of scores of men involved in such pursuits. The late nineteenth century was a period of European expansion and occupa-

" ... we were never weary of admiring, at night, the beauty of the southern sky, which, as we advanced to the south, opened new constellations to our view."
—Baron Alexander von Humboldt

Baron Alexander von Humboldt was one of the last great renaissance men, whose pursuits involved nearly all fields of scientific endeavour understood at that time, and a few that had yet to be understood. This 1806 portrait (opposite page) *shows Humboldt at work on his botanical classifications.*

tion throughout Africa. By 1912, only Egypt, Ethiopia, and Liberia had any semblance of self-government. Colonialism was at its peak, and the Dark Continent was perceived by its northern neighbors as land and labor for the taking.

A handful of names emerge from the final years of African exploration, although their occupations became increasingly difficult to define. Some were strictly profiteers looking to legitimize their reputations by passing along information obtained from natives. Others, such as Mary Kingsley, more appropriately fall under the category of anthropology and ethnography. Charles Doughty spent a few years among the Bedouins during the 1870s, and their grudging acceptance of this avowed Christian is one of the first examples of that culture's peaceful coexistence with outsiders. Doughty was barred from Mecca, but his glimpse into this heretofore mysterious society created a great deal of interest back home in England.

The subsequent history of Africa is one of subjugation and revolt; a trend that has sadly continued to the present time. The concept of Africa as a place with a wealth of raw materials and valuable ores to be exploited has remained in the minds of many governments and corporations throughout the twentieth century. While many European explorers are still celebrated by their fellow countrymen, they are viewed in a different light by those suffering from the consequences of their actions. The bravery of the men and women who ventured into the forbidding jungles and explored the treacherous waterways of Africa is unquestionable. Their motives, unfortunately, were not always as admirable.

Across the Atlantic, South America, nearly half the size of Africa, had already been fairly well explored. The dense jungles of the tropical rain forests had been somewhat defined, and

the grasslands of the northeast were familiar to settlers as well. The mountainous Andes were depicted by rough sketches, and the only area that had yet to be cursorily explored was the inhospitable region still known as Patagonia.

Francisco de Orellana had followed the length of the Amazon during the 1540s. North of that great river the early Spanish settlers and conquistadores had managed to assemble a pretty clear picture of the region's coastlines and major waterways. Tributaries were followed into the Amazon, and settlements along the continent's northern coast sprouted up, dependent at first upon the Caribbean link to the Old World. The wet, menacing jungles deterred any further expansion, and offered little more to be explored but the rivers that ran through them.

The first of the great South American scientist/explorers was a Prussian (there being no unified Germany yet) adventurer, Baron Alexander von Humboldt. As a young man, Humboldt had developed an impressively broad-based curriculum for himself that took him in and out of a number of universities, institutes, and apprenticeships. After being freed from familial obligations by the death of a manipulative mother, and subsidized by the inheritance that accompanied it, Humboldt decided it was time to take his learning into the field. He traveled to Paris in 1796, hooked up with a botanist named Aimé Bonpland, and the two set about determining where they should apply their learning.

Their initial destination was Mexico, but an outbreak of typhoid on the voyage west convinced Humboldt to disembark in Venezuela. The result was a lengthy stay along the coastal settlements before following the Orinoco River, northernmost South America's principal waterway, to its source. Along the way, Humboldt and Bonpland "discovered" the Casiquiare River, a natural canal that linked the Orinoco to the upper reaches of the

Negro River, which itself flowed into the Amazon. (Humboldt is often credited with the river's discovery, but the information appears to have been general knowledge among Spanish settlers who had little desire to ascertain its accuracy.) Following their stay in the tropical rain forests of southern Venezuela, the traveling companions proceeded on to Cuba and Mexico, both of which they mapped with unprecedented accuracy.

Humboldt also paid a visit to the Andes (in 1801), where he collected more specimens, monitored meteorological conditions, and marveled at a multitude of native species. And while the Prussian adventurer's intellect would be celebrated forever after, his physical prowess should not be underestimated. During his visit to the Andes, Humboldt climbed Mount Chimborazo, a peak that stood more than 20,000 feet (6,100 meters) above sea level. At that time, Alexander von Humboldt was further distinguished for having scaled the greatest height of any Westerner. No European had ever climbed that high, though it would be foolish to think that natives among the Himalayas, if not the Andes, had not exceeded this accomplishment.

Throughout his travels Humboldt kept impressively busy. He studied the wreckage of the decimated Native American civilizations and shed light upon them for Europeans who had considered these unfortunate victims as primitive and "unsophisticated." He envisioned the construction of a canal across the Panamanian isthmus and suggested a route nearly identical to the one that would be decided upon a century later. Following his distasteful introduction to the Venezuelan slave markets, Humboldt became an early, prominent supporter of the abolitionist movement almost seventy years before the North American states went to war over this issue. In the sciences he developed the concepts of isothermal mapping and plant geography.

Humboldt spent his entire life associating with a wide variety of the most important contemporary figures of their respective fields. He worked alongside the founders of geology and was active in the discussion of botany, astronomy, oceanography, and anthropology. His writings on biology were treasured by Charles Darwin, who brought Humboldt's works along for reference on his famous *Beagle* expedition. Humboldt met a "who's who" of famous eighteenth- and nineteenth-century figures during the course of his lifetime, including Louis Antoine de Bougainville, André-Marie Ampére, Samuel Morse, Louis Agassiz, Carl Gauss, Johann Goethe, Ralph Waldo Emerson, and Thomas Jefferson.

The majority of Humboldt's life was essentially devoted to chronicling his five years of travel. At the request of the Czar of Russia who underwrote an expedition through Siberia to the Chinese frontier, he made one last journey at the advanced age of sixty. Humboldt returned safely and spent another quarter of a century assembling the known facts of his day and being recognized as a patriarch of the European scientific community. The learned Baron von Humboldt died in 1859, at the age of ninety.

The other notable names from this era of South American exploration are also more prominent for their roles in other endeavours than exploration. The voyage of the British naval ship *Beagle* from 1832 to 1835, under the commander of Captain Robert FitzRoy, was intended to be a global circumnavigation with an emphasis on the mapping of the coasts of Patagonia and Tierra del Fuego. The expedition, however, would have quickly fallen into the depths of historical obscurity were it not for the presence of a seasick young scientist. Charles Darwin, incapacitated whenever his ship left port, spent his time on land examining a wide range of species. He relied on the observations made throughout Patagonia, and later at the Galapagos Islands, for the development of his influential theory of natural selection.

A British entomologist, Alfred Wallace, visited South America from 1848 to 1852. He and Darwin simultaneously published their evolutionist theories in 1858. Wallace followed the Amazon with Henry Bates, another adventurous scientist who spent a total of ten years traveling throughout the region and collecting thousands of specimens. Wallace also spent a few years traveling with his brother, Herbert, from a base camp they established with a British botanist, Richard Spruce, at the confluence of the Amazon and Tapajós rivers. From there they made trips throughout the north central portion of the continent, adding to our geographic understanding of South America while cataloging its wildlife.

Much of North America had also been discovered by the first generation of New World explorers. Spaniards had wandered across large portions of its southern regions throughout the sixteenth century, during which time Hernando de Soto traveled up into the lower reaches of the Blue Ridge mountains. Francisco Vásquez de Coronado's simultaneous wanderings had taken him into the heart of the Great Plains and throughout the American Southwest; John Cabot, Sir Francis Drake, Henry Hudson, and others reintroduced the eastern coast of the North American continent to Europe, paving the way for the late-seventeenth-century travels of Frenchman Louis Joliet, and his countryman Robert La Salle a few years later. Drake had sketched the western coast as well, towards which the Spanish had expanded from their Central American strongholds.

The remaining mysteries were mostly to be found in the northwest corner of the North American continent. Throughout the eighteenth century, rugged trappers and traders were pushing west, moving farther away from Quebec and Montreal, while the British and French fought it out, once again, for control of the North American fur trade. England's victory resulted in a monopoly being granted to the Hudson Bay Company, an organization charged with the profitable task of establishing trade with the natives and burdened with the responsibility of discovering a Northwest Passage once and for all.

For nearly a century the Hudson Bay Company brought England a great deal of wealth, but failed to accomplish its exploratory goals. Pressure from home instigated a renewed interest in the elusive passage, and one fur trader, Anthony Henday, was

dispatched to the northwest in 1754. He crossed the Saskatchewan and North Saskatchewan rivers, explored Lake Winnipeg, and spent time among the Blackfoot Indians. Henday was followed by Samuel Hearne in 1769, who also wandered at random about the rivers of central Canada. Hearne sought a river that would carry him to the Pacific, but wound up near Aberdeen Lake instead. The trapper's route home circled west to the Great Slave Lake and Slave River, Lake Athabasca, and eventually the town of Churchill on the western shores of Hudson Bay.

Along the western coast, one of Cook's students, George Vancouver, was mapping the Pacific Northwest. The boundaries were taking shape, from the Alaskan peninsulas to the tip of Baja California just below the Tropic of Cancer. But the interior of northern North America, the cold Laurentian Plateau with its coniferous forests and subarctic tundra, remained unexplored. If it possessed furry animals in abundance or contained a waterway across the continent, the rewards would be enormous.

Maps from the seventeenth (opposite page) and eighteenth (below) centuries show the enormous strides taken in Western civilizations' understanding of the world they inhabited. Even so, regions such as the North Pacific remained blank, what little information cartographers had at their disposal was often vague and contradictory.

Before an enormous influx of immigrants made land the most valued commodity, North America's wildlife held that unfortunate distinction.

The trappers and traders along the frontier were certainly the most knowledgeable of the region's geography. Unfortunately, though, these men were not inclined to recount their journeys with the detail and insight for which their ship-bound predecessors and contemporaries are noted. Even those diaries that have survived are a far cry from the entertaining hand of Stanley or the informed curiosity of Humboldt. The result is a jumbled hodgepodge of dead-reckoning estimations and confused chronologies. Credit for discovering lakes and rivers was frequently conflicting, with men such as Peter Pond and Charles Isham claiming the same accomplishments, rendering each a minor footnote in the history of Canadian exploration.

The man who has best come to represent the accomplishments of this period of exploration, the first to cross the Americas north of Mexico, was Alexander Mackenzie. He was born

on the northernmost of Scotland's Hebrides Islands and toiled in the New World as a nominally successful, industrious young merchant. Mackenzie was appointed to the North West Company's Athabasca District (the region surrounding the lake of the same name) as part of the reorganized organization's attempt at breaking the Hudson Bay Company's monopoly. In 1789 Mackenzie set out from Lake Athabasca for the Great Slave Lake. There he discovered a large river spilling out of the lake's southwest corner and followed it in hope of reaching the Pacific. Mackenzie rode the river that is now named after him into a bay that was also given his name. Unfortunately, the bay sits along the southern edge of the Beaufort Sea, north of the Arctic Circle, a long way from the navigable waters of the Pacific Mackenzie sought.

Alexander Mackenzie returned east and resumed his travels in 1792, following the Peace River back to its source opposite the Omineca Mountains in the northern Rockies. After a torturous mountain crossing of the Continental Divide, Mackenzie

picked up an unknown river, which he initially mistook for the Columbia, which was actually far to the south. When it became apparent it wasn't the Columbia and a quick route to the western ocean, Mackenzie headed west over land. He eventually came upon the Bella Coola River, which took him to the Pacific coast north of Vancouver. Mackenzie's acclaim eventually led to his election to the Canadian assembly and subsequent knighthood. His name is found all over the farthest reaches of Canada to this day, and the account of his journey and his failure to find a northwest river passage resulted in others being forced to search further north for the answer. Simon Fraser followed Mackenzie's route from Lake Athabasca in 1805, traveling along the Peace River before veering off to the waterway that would eventually come to bear his name. Fraser, like Mackenzie before him, originally thought he was following the Columbia River, but realized his error by the time he washed out into the Pacific.

David Thompson was another fur trader who wandered across North

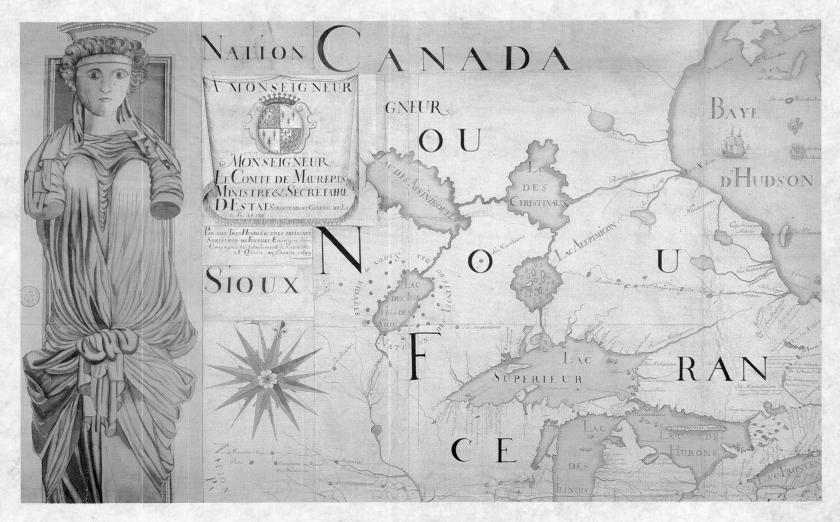

America. For more than twenty years (from 1790 until 1811), he covered ground from the Great Lakes to the Pacific Ocean. Thompson began in the employ of the Hudson Bay Company but eventually went into business for himself. He explored the farthest reaches of the Northwest Territories, as well as the upper regions of the Mississippi and Missouri rivers. From the Columbia River to the Hudson, Thompson demonstrated that it was possible to travel by boat across the continent with only small stretches of overland travel required.

It was becoming clear that the northern region of the continent had little to offer the average individual. The Laurentian Plateau had been explored and found wanting, while the center of North America remained known to its native population only. The explorers who established friendly relations with the natives they encountered were those that survived. And the smartest trappers knew to rely on the knowledge of local inhabitants.

In American lore, the most famous of Indian guides was the one who led Meriwether Lewis and William Clark through their fledgling nation's brand new acquisition, the Louisiana Purchase. Sacajawea (and her French-Canadian husband, conveniently omitted from many romanticized accounts of the voyage) helped Thomas Jefferson's hand-picked explorer tour the enormous parcel of land he had just purchased. In fact, Meriwether Lewis, a childhood companion of Jefferson's, had waited patiently in Saint Louis for several months until the transaction between nations had been formally completed.

Two weeks after the ink dried, on May 14, 1803, Lewis and Clark set out along the Missouri River. Lewis attended to the discovering, while Clark, an army officer, oversaw the expedition. They reached the territory of the Mandan Indians, in the area around modern-day Bismarck, North Dakota, by the winter of 1804 and stayed there until spring. When the

Missouri River veered suddenly east near the Bitterroot Range of the Rocky Mountains they abandoned it and headed west.

Lewis and Clark received a great deal of hospitality at this point from the Shoshone Indians, Sacajawea's relatives. They were fed, sheltered, and provided with a great deal of regional geographic information. After their lengthy overland passage, they were pleased to find themselves alongside the Snake River, running west. Lewis reported being certain this waterway would lead them to the continent's "far" shores when a Shoshone host offered him roasted Pacific salmon. In November of 1805, Lewis and Clark emerged from the Columbia River into the Pacific Ocean. They split up, and separately explored the rich Oregon Country, then jointly claimed by England, Spain, Russia, and the United States. (France had only relinquished its claim as part of the Louisiana Purchase.)

Before Lewis and Clark had even returned to St. Louis, others were following their trail. Expansion into these newly explored areas was inevitable, and their expedition, officially known as the Corps of Discovery, provided a wealth of basic information upon which their successors could elaborate. The Corps had managed to define an area of land greater in size than the young United States that had just acquired it. In appreciation for their efforts, Clark was appointed governor of the Missouri Territory, while Lewis was given the same title to the upper half of the Louisiana Territory. In St. Louis, Meriwether Lewis became mired in the responsibilities of his position and was apparently overwhelmed. Administration, it would appear, proved more hazardous to Lewis' health than exploration, and he died under mysterious circumstances on his way to Washington, D.C. to answer accusations made against him regarding his administration of the territories.

While Lewis was completing his mission and putting an end to his ex-

"I now laid myself down on some willow boughs to a comfortable night rest, and felt indeed as if I was fully repaid for the toil and pain of the day, so much will a good shelter, a dry bed, and comfortable supper revive the spirits of the waryed, wet and hungry traveler."
—Meriwether Lewis

While trappers and traders shed light on the lands north of the Great Lakes (opposite page), Meriwether Lewis (above) led a company across the central portions of North America, helping to establish the boundaries that have since come to form the United States. Unfortunately, Lewis' skills as an explorer were far greater than his political acumen, and his return to civilization marked the beginning of a long, sad decline.

ploratory career, a number of his contemporaries were beginning to visit the last major portions of unmapped terrain. On the journey back from the Pacific, Lewis encountered two men who had already set out to follow his trail. One of Clark's charges, John Colter, requested his leave from the Corps in order to join these men, with whom he would report on the natural wonders that have since been incorporated into Yellowstone National Park, the very first of its kind.

Zebulon Pike, an army officer, was also an active explorer during the first decade of the nineteenth century. In 1805, Pike was dispatched to determine the source of the Mississippi. The unstated motive for the mission, however, was to send a message to the British in Canada that any land south of their present settlements was considered American territory. Pike returned to report an incorrect source for the Mississippi, but was rewarded with another mission anyway; this one throughout the American Southwest. Aside from discovering the peak that has immortalized him, Pike was even less successful on this expedition, which resulted in his temporary

incarceration by the Spanish in Mexico. Pike created a number of misconceptions about the western territories that would go unclarified for several decades, but his writing inspired others to follow in his path, and he became one of many voices that culminated in Horace Greeley's entreaty for all to head west.

The young American government encouraged the settlement of its recent acquisitions. Land was there for the taking (the resistance of the Indians having become increasingly symbolic), and the crowded Easterners were excited by the prospect of expansion. Initially, military expeditions were sent west, often escorted by trappers. The men who earned their living off of the land were rugged, solitary, self-reliant individuals, their existences nomadic. In pursuit of pelts, these mountain men uncovered the wonders of an entire continent.

Peter Ogden was one adventurous mountain man, a fur trader who roamed across large expanses of western America. He was the first to travel north to south across the length of the country's western region, discovering a number of lakes and rivers in

the process. Ogden was also the first to chart and explore the eastern face of the Sierra Nevadas along the Great Basin. He was the kind of tough, rugged individual that could be found throughout most of what now constitutes the midwestern and western United States. But of all the mountain men with an inclination toward sharing their geographic discoveries with those east of the Mississippi, none rose to the mythologized heights of Jedediah Smith.

Smith was a well-educated Easterner who headed west to earn a fortune in beaver skins. His journals feature tales of peril, including a grizzly attack that nearly took his life. Smith managed to maintain good relations with the Indians (with one fatal exception) and took a personal interest in their cultures. From the early 1820s until his death in 1831, Jedediah Smith collected scattered bits of geographic information and assembled them into a more coherent picture. Expanding upon Robert Stuart's discovery of the South Pass in southwest Wyoming (in connection with Wilson Hunt's 1811 expedition to the Columbia River for New York merchant John Jacob Astor, who hoped to establish a trading post west of the Rockies), Smith paved the way for that gap's use by the men who later established the Oregon Trail.

Smith covered the length and breadth of the Great Basin and was one of the first white men to see the Great Salt Lake. In 1826 he crossed the Rocky Mountains, the Mojave Desert, and the Sierra Nevadas, to become the first man to travel overland to California. Smith's arrival in California was disconcerting to the Mexicans there, who realized that the mountainous border they had expected to protect them from their expansionist neighbors was crumbling. The local authorities held Smith in custody for a while, but finally allowed him to make arrangements for his return, establishing himself as the first to travel north through California to the Oregon Territory.

Crossing North America

The man who did so much to focus attention on the American West was killed on his return journey along the Santa Fe Trail. Jedediah Smith was murdered by Comanches at the age of thirty-three, but his place was already being taken by scores of new white men. They infiltrated the hidden valleys and passes of the West, and connected the far shores of North America. They pushed the continent's natives into consistently smaller, more impoverished reservations, claiming the remainder of the land for themselves and those like them.

There are many individuals responsible for filling in the details on the maps that had been drawn up, but the concept of discovery was becoming less meaningful in America during the middle of the nineteenth century. Most areas that had not yet received at least a cursory glance were assumed to be harsh and unyielding. The few exceptions were those expeditions, often sponsored by the military, sent to explore the continent's uncharted natural wonders. Major John Wesley Powell's detailed exploration of the canyons of the Colorado River illuminated just a small portion of the North American map, but that area has received a great number of visitors ever since.

The man who is often credited with having closed out the era of America's self-discovery was another colorful officer, John Charles Frémont. In 1838, as a member of the United States Army Corps of Topographical Engineers, Frémont set out to explore the Mississippi and Missouri rivers. In 1841 he charted the Des Moines River, and the next year he crossed the central plains to dispel rumors of a vast desert in the area. As Frémont's accomplishments grew, so did his reputation.

By the time Frémont set out for California in 1843 he was no longer as concerned with being a meticulous surveyor. Instead, he became involved in attempts to free California from Mexican rule. Although he traveled frequently over the course of the next

decade, Frémont's motives were now political and occasionally even military. He always made detailed notes of the geographic features he encountered along the way, but his focus had shifted. After a stint as governor of the newly liberated California, Frémont undertook an unsuccessful bid for the presidency in 1856 and was later appointed governor of the Arizona Territory. Like many of his contemporaries and predecessors, Frémont was an explorer with other goals in mind. Together these men and women pieced together the various parts of the terrain that was eventually assembled into the United States and opened the lines of communication that made it all possible. Any subsequent alterations to the maps of North America were more likely to be political than geographic.

John Charles Frémont (above) *signals the end of America's initial burst of exploration. His transformation from explorer and adventurer to soldier and politician was a smooth one, representative of the changing concerns of a growing nation.*

9

A CENTURY ON ICE

hile most explorers were mapping the habitable portions of the globe, a different group was involved in the examination of the earth's polar regions. Initially, their efforts were a continuation of Europe's search for passages across the top of Asia and the Americas. When it became rather clear that such routes, if they did actually exist, would never be as commercially viable as those in warmer climes, the pursuit took on a more scientific and nationalistic demeanor, leading to the creation of some of the most recent and best-documented expeditions. In the process, they introduced some of the greatest heroes in the history of discovery. (Perhaps their chronological proximity has exaggerated their greatness, and time will judge them a mere postscript to the golden age of exploration. In the meantime, however, men such as James Clark Ross and Fridtjof Nansen rival the most admirable discoverers of any other era.) On the fringe of the greatest advancements in the recording of historic events, men like Nansen and Sir Ernest Henry Shackleton are primitively preserved for posterity in comparison to those of the late twentieth century whose every movement and utterance are captured and cataloged. But compared to the vague sketches of the earliest adventurers, these men emerge as three-dimensional, identifiable personalities.

Passages to the northeast and northwest had been probed since the sixteenth century. In 1553, Hugh Willoughby led an ill-fated British expedition northeast, which cost him his life but led to his second-in-command Richard Chancellor's encounter with the little-known people of Muscovy. Several centuries of business trade was established with this contact, but little was accomplished in terms of expanding Europe's geographic knowledge of the region. Toward the end of the sixteenth century, Willem Barents, a Dutchman, probed the sea that now bears his name, reaching the islands of

Novaya Zemlya. One of Barents' partners had actually begun to investigate the Kara Sea before the entire mission was repelled by the perilous ice that heralded the onset of winter. Barents' second expedition reached farther east and resulted in his crew's spending the winter of 1597 farther north than any Europeans had ever dared before. Miraculously, most of the expedition survived the endless night, but Barents was dreadfully weak with the coming spring and died during the journey south.

Henry Hudson's unfortunate encounters in the upper reaches of North America and Martin Frobisher's subsequent foolishness did little to inspire others to visit the Canadian Arctic. John Davis led three efficient expeditions to the Arctic region during the 1580s, but made it rather clear that the icy waters of the Northwest Territories had little to profit even the most adventurous trader. William Baffin ventured far north along Greenland and Ellesmere

Island but failed to recognize one of the sounds he discovered as a gateway to the Northwest Passage. After Baffin's 1615 expedition, the cumulative effect of these four Englishmen's unrewarded efforts meant that there was little attempt made at probing this region. When the Hudson Bay Company reinvigorated the search during the mid-eighteenth century, it hoped to find a continuous waterway across the lakes and rivers of northern Canada rather than hazarding the arctic waters to the north. Samuel Hearne and Alexander Mackenzie made it clear that the mainland held no secret passages, so the search, increasingly impractical, moved north.

It wasn't until a decade or so before Hearne had reopened the exploration of the Northwest Territory that anyone could be certain there was even an outlet between Asia and North America to make either of the two—overland or by sea—passages viable. Ivanov Deshnef had led a Russian expedition through the strait between

Initially, Willem Barents' crew managed well in the Arctic conditions, as illustrated by their industrious activities (opposite page). *Once their ship was crushed by ice flows, however, Barents' men were forced to construct a shelter* (below) *and wait out the seemingly eternal Arctic night.*

Alaska and the Anadyr Plateau in 1648, but his reports were considered suspect and generally ignored. Not until Vitus Jonassen Bering made the same crossing in 1729, out of sight of the American mainland, did some begin to believe in its existence. Certainly by the time Captain James Cook led his final mission into the region, most believed it to be the far side, and therefore the goal, of each of the passages. The search was begun anew, taken up by a nation with a great deal of manpower to spare.

The defeat of Napoleon at Waterloo was a great moment for the British. After the triumph, the common foot soldiers returned to their families and their livelihoods. Among the officers, however, there appears to have been an inclination to stay in the military. This surplus of able-bodied men sought ways to advance themselves now that battlefield promotions were becoming harder to come by. The enormous navy England had assembled was left idle, and a number of ambitious individuals hoped that journeys of discovery, usually in conjunction with the Royal Geographic Society, might distinguish them during peacetime. And nowhere was the British military's presence felt so strongly as along the polar icecaps.

The conditions for the renewal of arctic exploration were ripe when a period of cyclic warmth spurred reports of ice-free waters. William Scoresby, a whaling captain, amateur scientist, and friend of Sir Joseph Banks, produced a pamphlet detailing recent conditions and inspiring the creation of a two-part undertaking. One expedition, led by Captain David Buchan, headed north from England, passing between Greenland and Spitzbergen with the intention of crossing the Arctic Ocean to the Bering Strait. Buchan was instructed to pass as close to the North Pole as possible, but never managed to get much farther than Spitzbergen. In fact, Buchan's mission was essentially a failure and is primarily remembered for two reasons: the results of its companion expedition and the presence of Buchan's second-in-command, a lieutenant by the name of John Franklin, who would figure prominently in the exploration of the Northwest Passage several decades later.

The second half of England's plan was a complementary expedition led by John Ross in search of a Northwest Passage across the top of the North American continent. Ross rediscovered the islands and inlets that Baffin had charted centuries earlier. He sailed through the Davis Strait into Baffin Bay and came upon a succession of sounds Baffin had named for his benefactors. The Smith and Jones sounds were quickly determined to be

> *"Soon the ice began to drive together one upon the other with greater force than before and to crash against the shippe with a boystrous south-by-west wind and a greate snowe, so that the whole shippe was borne up and inclosed and squeezed, whereat all that was in it began to crack as if about to burst into 100 peaces, which was most fearfull both to see and heare, and made all ye haire of our heads to rise upright with feare. And after this the shippe (by the ice on both sides being joined underneath her) was driven so upright as if she had been lifty with a wrench or vice."*
> —Gerrit de Veer

landlocked to the west, and Ross was certain he saw a chain of mountains at the far end of the third, Lancaster Sound. In fact, Ross was so certain of their existence that he named them the Croker Mountains and then turned back. Ross' second-in-command, William Parry, trailing behind in another ship, did not see the mountains and felt certain the sound would lead them farther west. He retreated unwillingly; and he later lobbied for a return expedition the moment he was back in England.

John Ross' failure to fully explore Lancaster Sound, and Parry's arguments for having done so, put Ross in a bad light with Sir John Barrow, secretary to the admiralty. During his forty year tenure, Barrow was one of the most influential figures in British polar exploration, a strong proponent

of the English prerogative to the uninhabited world. Barrow listened carefully to Parry and outfitted him for an expedition. Parry's expedition was operated in conjunction with John Franklin once again, who would travel overland through the Northwest Territories in search of a route along its arctic coastline.

Parry departed in 1819 with two ships and quickly made his way back to Baffin Bay. There he entered Lancaster Sound and stood alongside his men anxiously keeping watch for Ross' "Croker Mountains." Parry was a mere twenty-nine years old, and his crew equally young. They were energetic and enthusiastic, and it is fitting that they should mark the beginning of a new era in man's deciphering of the Northwest Passage. Further and further they sailed into the sound,

John Ross (right) was entrusted with the exploration of the Canadian Arctic and the search for the Northwest Passage in 1818. William Parry (above), who served under Ross, disputed his conclusions. Parry returned within a year and proved that Ross's conclusions were wrong.

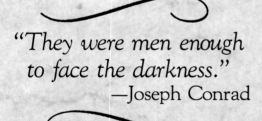

"They were men enough to face the darkness."
—Joseph Conrad

long past the coordinates where Ross predicted they would encounter land, and then spilled out into Viscount Melville Sound.

The two ships didn't get much farther before encountering a horizon full of ice, which rapidly enveloped them and drove them into the safe harbor in which they spent their first arctic winter. Parry's failure to break through the barrier the next summer (a mere 100 miles [160 kilometers] from open waters to the west)—where he still estimated the ice walls in front of him to stand 50 feet (approximately 17 meters) high—permanently shifted the focus of those who sought the Northwest Passage southward, below Victoria Island. His return was greeted with acclaim, rewards, and vindication for having questioned Ross's assumptions.

Unfortunately, John Franklin's half of the expedition was not nearly as successful as Parry's and proved to be considerably more hazardous. Whereas Parry demanded military officiousness and certain levels of personal hygiene from his crew, much like James Cook had from his men, Franklin stumbled along with an incompatible assortment of natives, French Canadian traders, and military personnel. Eleven men died along the trails Alexander Mackenzie had once blazed, and reports of cannibalism by some of the hired hands brought a good deal of notoriety to the expedition. On this journey, and another in the mid-1820s, Franklin and George Back mapped large portions of the continent's northern coast. Along Coronation Gulf, Melville Sound, the Beaufort Sea, and

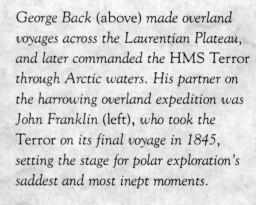

George Back (above) *made overland voyages across the Laurentian Plateau, and later commanded the HMS Terror through Arctic waters. His partner on the harrowing overland expedition was John Franklin* (left), *who took the* Terror *on its final voyage in 1845, setting the stage for polar exploration's saddest and most inept moments.*

James Clarke Ross (below) may have come by his early appointments through acts of nepotism, but his favorable place in history is based on his accomplishments. Ross added more to man's understanding of both poles than anyone of his era. Only Norwegian Roald Amundsen rivaled the Englishman's scope.

a number of nearby islands, Franklin compiled a great deal of geographic information. Natives had been familiar with these coasts for ages, and trappers had probably visited much of the region as well. But Franklin helped fill in the atlases, and for this he was knighted and eventually granted the governorship of Van Diemen's Land (Tasmania) on the other side of the globe.

Parry's return to the Arctic two years later concentrated on a more southerly approach, past Hudson Bay toward the Gulf of Boothia. He and his crew spent two winters in the region before being forced to return to England during the third summer as scurvy became increasingly prevalent. Parry didn't lose a man on either mission and established himself as the arctic explorer against which all who

followed would be judged. Even Parry's 1827 attempt on the North Pole itself was a respectable affair, ignorant of the southerly drift of the polar icecap that carried them continuously away from their goal. He and his crew returned safely, possessors of the farthest-north "prize" for nearly half a century.

John Ross also made a return visit to the Arctic, troubled with the same bad luck—or bad judgment—as his first. Ross went to retrace Parry's southern route and overshot the narrow straight between Somerset Island and the Boothia Peninsula that could have led him to complete the passage. He spent four winters in the Arctic, during which time his nephew, James Clark Ross, who had also accompanied his first expedition, became the first man to reach the magnetic North Pole in 1831. The younger Ross traveled throughout the region during those four years, across land and ice, learning a great deal from the Eskimo in the area. These accomplishments allowed Ross and his uncle to return to a more appreciative welcome than the one that had greeted their first expedition together and provided the training that prepared the younger Ross to lead his own expeditions.

While arctic explorers were moving closer to accomplishing their long-sought goals, another group was beginning to probe the mysteries of a relatively recent discovery. James Cook's travels along the Antarctic Circle and the increasing reports of seal hunters in the region, made it clear that the southern tip of the globe remained available for intrepid adventurers looking for new places to court fame. Cook had rightly assumed that if indeed there was land in the area, it would be difficult to reach and permanently covered with snow and ice. This, however, did not prevent a new generation from investigating the area.

The first two sightings of Antarctica are reported to have occurred within days of one another on oppo-

site sides of the continent. Investigating the recent discovery of the South Shetland Islands, Edward Bransfield explored that archipelago before proceeding farther south. On January 30, 1820, Bransfield's crew spotted something considerably more substantial than the small islands they had left behind. Out of the mists rose a chain of mountains stretching off to the south, what we now know to be the tip of the Antarctic Peninsula. Bransfield went ashore briefly before hurrying north to report his discovery. At the same time Bransfield made his discovery, a Russian captain named Thaddeus von Bellingshausen was piloting two ships through Antarctic seas in the name of Emperor Alexander I. He circumnavigated the continent, staying south of sixty degrees almost the entire way. Bellingshausen never actually touched down upon the Antarctic landmass, and probably didn't have a very clear picture of the continent he was circling. The region he christened Peter I Land was in fact a small frozen island located quite a distance away from the Antarctic mainland in the sea that now bears Bellingshausen's name.

Unfortunately, most of the successors to these two men were sealers who managed to decimate local wildlife populations in a few short decades. Men such as American Nathaniel Palmer and James Weddell, an Englishman, made Antarctic discoveries during the 1820s, juggling their roles as butchers and explorers. Weddell wandered into the sea since named for him during a period of unusually warm conditions. Those who followed his lead quickly learned that the Weddell Sea was a hazardous body to be avoided when possible, whose crushing pack ice figured prominently in one of the last great Antarctic explorations. The experiences of its discoverer would prove to be quite atypical.

In 1837, Jules Dumont d'Urville, a Frenchman, began the first of several visits to the Antarctic coast. Initially, d'Urville hoped to visit the great sea

Weddell had discovered. He was, however, thwarted by the region's normal expanse of ice and moved along to Graham Land on the Antarctic Peninsula, unaware that it had already been discovered. The Frenchman later christened a small portion of the opposite coast Adélie Land, though that discovery has since been "downgraded" to Adélie Coast. Americans were vying for similar recognition, and the period is marked by a number of coastal mappings and tenuous ventures along the periphery of the continent.

The first great name in Antarctic exploration, however, belongs to James Clark Ross, who had cut his polar teeth while serving on his uncle's arctic expeditions. In 1839, Ross set out in command of the *Erebus* and the *Terror*, stopping first at Tasmania and paying a visit to its governor, Sir John Franklin. While there, Ross heard that both the Americans and French had set out to locate the magnetic South Pole (Ross himself having discovered its northern equivalent), spurring his decision to explore elsewhere. If an Englishman could not be the first, he reasoned, it would be just as well to strike out in another direction altogether.

In January 1841, during the Antarctic summer, Ross' two ships broke through an outer layer of pack ice into the sea that has since been given

> "And now there came both mist and snow And it grew wondrous cold; And ice, most high, came floating by, As green as emerald."
> —Samuel Coleridge

171

his name. It was one of the first, and one of the finest, moments of pure Antarctic exploration; scientific, informative, and safe. Ross mapped 500 miles (800 kilometers) of coast, attained the most southerly point yet recorded, and encountered a pair of volcanic peaks that he named after his two ships. Eventually, the expedition came upon a great ice wall that stretched out along the horizon, a feature now known as the Ross Ice Shelf. Hundreds of feet high, offering no hope of a southern passage, the barrier was so imposing that Ross turned around and spent the next three navigable seasons exploring other Antarctic coasts. Despite, or perhaps on account of, Ross' safe, relatively uneventful journeys, northern interest in the southern polar regions remained mild. As events began to unfold in the Arctic, exploring the Antarctic lost its appeal, and it was nearly half a century before the nations of the world would redirect their attention south.

———————————

One of the most important incidents in arctic history, and certainly the prime motivation for an entire generation of polar exploration, was the return to the region by Sir John Franklin in the spring of 1845. A hero of the Napoleonic Wars and survivor of some miserable overland expeditions, Franklin was nearly sixty years old when he led 128 officers and crew members out on the two ships Ross had probed the Antarctic with, *Erebus* and *Terror*. Franklin was overweight, disdainful of indigenous adaptations to the environment, and, based on his previous expeditions, not likely to return with all of those with whom he had set out. There were many more qualified candidates for the position than Franklin, but politics, rather than practicality, played a greater role in the decision-making process, and the result was pathetically deadly.

Franklin's expedition spent its first winter frozen in off of Cornwallis Island, the second winter farther south

near King William Island. Side trips were undertaken early on, but the crew was ill-equipped for the harsh arctic conditions and often found themselves confined to the ships. Scurvy and other diseases began to crop up, and by June 1847, with no sign of the ice abating, Franklin and twenty-three others had already perished. Francis Crozier, captain of the *Terror*, took command of the expedition and led the men on a long, harrowing death march. Some died of starvation, others from exposure. Some awaited death alongside companions, while others wandered off to solitary ends. All were poisoned to some extent by the lead used in soldering cans of food shut, and this has been offered as an explanation for the fact that an incredible assortment of weighty, nonessential—often ridiculously frivilous—objects were being dragged along by men weak with scurvy plodding to their deaths.

All that we know of Franklin's expedition was pieced together long after the event. For years England awaited word from Franklin and his crew, and by 1847 the first search parties were dispatched. Two British expeditions traveled through the Bering Strait and overland across the Laurentian Plateau, while a third, marking Sir James Clark Ross' return to the Arctic, attempted to retrace Franklin's route. When it became clear that none of these had provided the answer to Franklin's fate, a spate of new expeditions were organized. Of these, Dr. John Rae's journey in the employ of the Hudson Bay Company was the first to uncover the grizzly facts. Rae, a veteran Arctic explorer, found numerous corpses and shocking evidence of cannibalism. He created a stir in the press, which engendered an outcry from Franklin's widow in defense of her husband.

While Rae was making his discoveries, another "rescue party" was connecting the final pieces of the Northwest Passage. Commander Robert McClure, a veteran of Ross' rescue mission, set out from the Bering Strait

" . . . we had discovered a new land, of so extensive a coastline and attaining such altitude, as to justify the appelation of a Great New Southern Continent"
—Dr. Robert McCormick

The Erebus *and* Terror *sit anchored off of the Canadian coast* (opposite page). *James Ross steered them safely through the icy waters of the Arctic, after which they were employed on a series of unsuccessful polar adventures.*

and headed east. He proceeded without his companion ship, either on account of his own ambitions or the tardiness of his partner, Captain Richard Collinson, in meeting up with him. McClure crisscrossed the southern reaches of the Beaufort Sea and headed north of Banks Island to the strait that now bears his name—and the realization of the Northwest Passage. Collinson managed to travel nearly fifteen degrees farther east than McClure along a southern route to the western entrance of Queen Maud Gulf, but graciously heralded his colleague's accomplishments. (Some have suggested that McClure was selfishly motivated in separating himself from Collinson and hindered the latter's efforts by leaving him without a translator. Collinson did not realize he was on the verge of discovering a more southerly, navigable passage—essentially the one Roald Amundsen would follow decades later in the opposite direction—since he misunderstood what the natives were telling him along the southern shores of Victoria Island. McClure's translator might have made the difference.)

McClure eventually had to be rescued by another Ross alumnus, Lieu-tenant Leopold McClintock, who would be responsible for negating the former's claims as discoverer of the long-sought passage. McClintock sailed from England in 1857 as a result of Lady Franklin's final effort to clear her husband's reputation in light of Rae's scandalous reports. On the western coast of King William Island, McClintock discovered a cairn erected by the crews of the *Erebus* and *Terror* before heading south in search of rescue. Captain Crozier's diary found at the site, reported the death of Sir John Franklin, his plans for an imposing march to the Great Fish River (since renamed for Franklin's early partner, George Back) 1,000 miles (1,609 kilometers) to the south and earlier observations that led Sir John Franklin's crew to the delineation of a Northwest Passage. Lady Franklin won her vindication, posthumous recognition for her husband, and an opportunity for the British Navy to put an honorable halt to its costly efforts.

The disappearance of the Franklin expedition led to the mapping of enormous portions of the western Arctic. The British do not seem to have learned from the mistakes of the Franklin expedition, but simply repeated them often enough to collect limited bits of information with which to construct a larger picture. Scurvy remained an ever-present threat, regulation navy gear was ludicrously unsuitable for polar conditions, and officers were still uninclined to adopt the practices of the natives. Toward the end of the Franklin era, rescue parties were being dispatched in search of rescue parties. Once the fate of the Franklin expedition was understood and the Northwest Passage charted, Britain could safely relax its arctic vigor. The Antarctic and other continents were gaining interest around this time, and the frozen north seems to have faded for a time from England's interest.

As a neighbor to the Franklin tragedy, the United States was eventually caught up in the search as well. Following the discoveries of Dr. John Rae, the extensive remains from Francis Crozier's last years were found by an American naval officer, E. J. De-Haven. He brought back hints of the madness that possessed the dying men and helped ignite an interest in the North Pole that set the stage for its conquest. DeHaven was accompanied by Elisha Kent Kane, whose subsequent arctic expeditions reached farther north than any of his predecessors, but not far enough to dispel his notions of an open polar sea. Kane's final expedition was a badly bungled, mismanaged affair that led to the defection of a large portion of his crew and a long, arduous journey down the coast of Greenland in search of help.

The most amateur and unprepared American explorer of this time must surely have been Charles Francis Hall of Cincinnati. Hall was a printer (and apparently an unsuccessful one at that) who bid farewell to his wife and children and caught a whaler out of New London, Connecticut, on the eve of America's Civil War. He disembarked at Baffin Island, where he was befriended by Eskimo and invited into their shelters. Though he sought relics of Sir John Franklin's expedition, Hall managed instead to uncover remnants of Martin Frobisher's sixteenth century visit to the region. Hall's second trip to the Arctic kept him there for five years, almost exclusively in the company of natives. He had heard of their encounters with Franklin many years earlier and was led to a great number of British remains. On his third visit, Hall attempted to reach the North Pole, besting Kane's farthest-north record by 200 miles (320 kilometers). Hall died on the way back, his ship was subsequently wrecked, and its surviving crew was rescued, near death, from a rapidly melting ice floe.

The British saw that the Americans were becoming a dominant force in the region and attempted to reclaim the territory following their post-Franklin lull. In the late 1870s they dispatched two expeditions to the Arctic, both attempting to travel farther north than ever before. They hauled their supplies across the polar cap and back, as opposed to relying on beasts of burden, but did little to generate much interest. In fact, their accomplishments were outshone at the time by one last invocation of the

Franklin legacy. American Frederick Schwatka set out in search of relics from the failed mission under the sponsorship of the same newspaperman who had dispatched Stanley to "rescue" Livingstone. Schwatka found a great number of artifacts, and laid to rest any questions regarding the specifics of Franklin's expedition.

Just after Schwatka set out, the same newspaper baron underwrote another arctic expedition under the care of George Washington De Long. A veteran of the north Greenland waters, De Long believed in an Arctic landmass, and passed through the Bering Strait in 1879 to search for it. De Long's ship soon became trapped in the ice north of the Chukchi Sea. After twenty months the ice broke up, leaving De Long's crew to make a perilous journey over unstable ice to the Laptev Sea. The drift of the polar ice cap had carried the ship and its crew away from the Bering and toward the pole. De Long's ship, the *Jeanette*, was crushed by ice, and his crews escaped in three small boats. The boats eventually set out upon the Laptev, and headed for the mouth of the Lana River, where they hoped to find relief. One boat was lost, and the entire crew of De Long's boat perished after touching down on an uninhabited region of the Siberian coast. Only one of the three boats was lucky enough to reach the sole inhabited village in the area and return alive.

While the survivors' tales and De Long's diary (found a year later) were of great interest to the public, polar explorers were more intrigued by the news that the wreckage of the *Jeanette* had washed up on the southwest tip of Greenland. This confirmation of polar drift was disavowed by those who still maintained the presence of land at the North Pole and scoffed at the possibility of a ship becoming frozen into the polar pack and actually drifting across the pole itself. Many Americans also failed to heed the requests of several European communities for limiting polar exploration to

"The poles of the earth had become an obsession of Western man. It could be argued against, but not argued away. Since the obsession was there, it had to be exorcised, and the sooner the better."
—Roland Huntford

Frederic Church's Icebergs *(opposite page) embodies the nineteenth century's romanticization of, fascination with, and fateful interaction with the Arctic. The wreckage in the foreground was added when inital reactions to the painting were less enthusiastic than the popular artist was accustomed to. Whaling ships followed (and occassionally preceeded) exploratory expeditions into the frozen north, and encountered most of the same difficulties. Currier and Ives, best known for their more idyllic compositions, attempted to capture the hazards of a whaling party (following pages) whose vessels have caught fire.*

scientific endeavors by continuing to seek an easy route to the pole and international acclaim. Mangled affairs such as A.W. Greely's pursuit of the pole continued, until a shift in the vanguard of polar exploration brought a number of Scandinavian adventurers to the forefront.

England's activities in the Arctic following the era of Sir John Franklin were tentative at best, while the Americans were represented by an assortment of thrill seekers and outcasts. The North American Arctic belonged to these adventurers, while more scientific endeavors were being undertaken on the opposite side of the polar icecap. Two Austrian soldiers, Lieutenants Karl Weyprecht and Julius Payer, made the first addition in a long while to arctic geography along the Barents Sea when they discovered Franz Josef Land. The expedition was admirably scientific in its approach, but sadly mistaken in its assumption that the islands represented an outer Arctic archipelago leading to a polar landmass similar to that of the Antarctic. It is fascinating to consider that barely more than a century ago there was still little agreement regarding the makeup of the earth's poles.

The scientific demeanor of the Austrians' expedition was adopted by the next important visitor to the region, a Finnish expatriate, Baron Nils Nordenskiöld. The first of the Baron's six Arctic enterprises was an attempt to reach the North Pole that relied on reindeer teams to haul provisions. Nordenskiöld eventually abandoned that attempt, but used the knowledge he gained from it to begin formulating a plan for undertaking a crossing of the Northeast Passage. The Baron made a preliminary voyage in 1875 and another the following summer. He plotted his route and finally set sail on August 10, 1878, with two ships and an international crew.

The voyage of Nordenskiöld's *Vega* stands in sharp contrast to those of most previous arctic expeditions. De-

the New Siberian Islands. On account of his sidetrack to this unfamiliar archipelago, Nordenskiöld just barely missed completing the first northeast passage in a single season. Had he done so, perhaps his speed would have compensated for the lack of peril and awarded the Baron a more lasting fame. Perhaps the passage itself would have been perceived more favorably. Instead, the *Vega* was held by a short expanse of ice just two days' sail from the warmer waters of the Chukchi Sea, leaving the crew sitting frozen in ice for ten months before completing their expedition. The frosty harbors Nordenskiöld visited are now stops along Siberian shipping lanes, the manifestations of a voyage that had greater effect on regional economy than world history.

One of Nordenskiöld's earlier arctic expeditions had involved a brief foray toward the center of Greenland's icecap. His account of this was read by a young Norwegian who subsequently attempted to cross the cap on skis from west to east despite recent disasters in the course of similar undertakings. Fridtjof Nansen set out in 1888 with Otto Sverdrup, who accompanied him on his next mission as well. The two became the first to cross the frozen wasteland, often employing sails to carry them quickly across the ice atop their rucksacks and skis. Nansen and Sverdrup just missed connecting with whalers for a ride back to southern latitudes and spent the winter with Eskimo as a result. The experience was useful in preparing him for his greatest voyage, four years later.

When the wreckage of George Washington De Long's ship washed up on the southern shores of Greenland a few years later, many were hard pressed to explain how such a thing might have happened. Proponents of a polar landmass were left grasping at lame theories, while Nansen's correct conclusion assumed the drift of arctic ice across the North Pole. To test this theory, and perhaps to attain the pole

spite its backing by a Russian merchant hoping to establish trade along the Siberian coast, the mission is a portent of the best to follow. Nordenskiöld was a cautious, learned individual, a scientist and philosopher who wrote about all that he encountered along his travels. Unlike many of his British and American predecessors (or contemporaries), the Baron never risked life nor limb unnecessarily. He was efficient and observant and ushered in an era of calm, "uneventful" polar advances that left several great Scandinavian explorers relegated to a secondary role behind more dramatic bunglers.

The *Vega* followed familiar waters into the Kara Sea before venturing off into unknown territory. Through foggy seas it made its way east toward

itself, Nansen commissioned the construction of a vessel that might withstand the crushing forces of the polar pack, allowing its crew to drift safely with the ice. Nansen named the product of his design the *Fram* (a Norwegian word meaning "forward"), which was by no means a great sailing ship, but would serve its crews well within the grip of frozen waves.

Nansen departed from Norway in June 1893, taking his ship along Nordenskiöld's northeast route into the Laptev Sea. Just west of the New Siberian Islands, Nansen pointed the *Fram* into the polar pack. The Arctic ice cooperated and surrounded the ship quickly. There was initial trepidation before the *Fram* could win the confidence of its crew, but during the course of the first arctic winter Nansen and his men settled into a comfortable routine. They took regular and in-depth readings in fields such as meteorology, hydrography, and cartography. In addition, Nansen himself introduced more information on the Arctic than any other single individual before or since. With a peace of mind regarding his immediate safety (unlike so many of his predecessors, contemporaries, and successors), Nansen's journals had the freedom to be appreciative of phenomena less secure observers viewed with dread.

The crew of the *Fram* went about their tasks for two winters before the vaguest signs of restlessness arose in any of the men. As it became clear that the ship's drift would not carry it over the pole, Nansen began to consider a dash north at an opportune time. Some suggest that Nansen was becoming stir-crazy or glory-hungry, and his diaries confirm a certain restlessness. Others accuse him of having abandoned his vessel. Assured of the *Fram*'s safety in the hands of his old companion Otto Sverdrup, Nansen set out with Frederic Johansen and a dog team for the elusive pole. The ship's uncertain movement within the pack would make it impossible to return to. Therefore, the pair would be forced to find their own way back.

Nansen and Johansen came within 224 miles (358 kilometers) of the North Pole, more than 150 miles (240 kilometers) closer than the previous record. They struggled back toward the edge of the pack ice, slaughtered their dogs for food, freed their kayaks from their runners, and set sail south. The two eventually reached the barren shores of Franz Josef Land, where they survived another arctic winter with considerably fewer provisions than those aboard the *Fram*. About the time Nansen and Johansen luckily boarded a passing whaler, Sverdrup

> *"Host after host marched on towards the north, only to suffer defeat. Fresh ranks stood ever ready to advance over the bodies of their predecessors."*
> —Fridtjof Nansen

Roald Amundsen (opposite page) *began his training and conditioning across the snow covered interior of Norway. Fritz Thaulow's 1886 painting of Norwegian skiers* (below) *reflects the ability of many northerners to travel the snow-covered, icy expanses of uninhabited terrain. Amundsen's early exposure to these hazards prepared him well for his later endeavors.*

was sailing the *Fram* out of the pack just above Spitzbergen.

The mission was deemed a great success by Norway, and Nansen received a hero's welcome upon his return. His rise to prominence introduced him to the world of international politics, where the honors bestowed upon him would rival those he received on account of his exploratory endeavors. For his humanitarian leadership in the aftermath of World War I, Nansen was awarded 1922's Nobel Peace Prize. He would remain the senior statesman of Norwegian exploration until his death in 1930, but Nansen's arctic expedition would be his last. From the shores of his homeland he watched the torch of active inquiry pass on to the next generation.

While Nansen was still frozen into the arctic night, his successor was lost in Norway's interior. Young Roald Amundsen was preparing himself for the rigors of arctic travel and hoped his country's snow-covered interior would serve as a training ground. Amundsen had been there to greet Nansen upon his return from the Greenland icecap, finding in him a more suitable role model than Sir John Franklin, whose exploits had inspired him as a youth.

Amundsen had decided early on that the life of exploration was for him and proceeded to train for it like a modern youth might train for the Olympics. He honed his physical and mental abilities with one single goal in mind—acquiring all of the skills he thought necessary for success in the Arctic. (Despite his early infatuation with Franklin's "martyrdom," Amundsen's practical side prevented him from ever making the mistakes that would have led to similar tragedies.) His earliest endeavors along these lines were ski trips into south-central Norway's frozen plateau. Amundsen repeatedly attempted a crossing of the Hardangervidda, Norway's version of the barren Arctic, and each time he was repelled.

After a handful of rather perfunctory arctic visits, Amundsen signed aboard a Belgian vessel headed for Antarctica. The crew of the *Belgica* also included its captain, Adrien de Gerlache, and the ship's doctor, Frederick Cook, who would soon become embroiled in a debate surrounding the conquest of the North Pole. All shared the distinction of spending the first Antarctic winter on ice, and only Amundsen seems to have actually enjoyed the experience. This was his preparation, his training, and the diary of the vaguely misanthropic Norwegian offers little of the despair that frequented his companions' thoughts. One Antarctic winter was nothing compared to the three polar nights Fridtjof Nansen and his crew had experienced, or John Ross' four. In fact, Amundsen was to have been one of four men aboard the *Belgica* to be stationed in Antarctica for the winter even if the ship had not become trapped, so his perception of the situation was sure to be different than most of the others.

Following Nansen's heroic dash for the North Pole, Amundsen came to see himself as the heir apparent to the polar crown. His season in Antarctica was perceived as an internship, while his attention remained focused on the opposite end of the globe. As a result, his next voyage, which was heralded internationally as a great accomplishment in its own right, was seen by Amundsen as still another stepping-stone toward his ultimate goal. The existence of several northwest passages had been confirmed, but no single ship had managed to make the entire journey. In 1903, with the flimsy rationale of seeking to determine the stability of the magnetic North Pole,

Amundsen sailed the *Gjøa* across the top of the Canadian Arctic out into the Beaufort Sea. Amundsen traveled light, accompanied by a crew of six, as compared to Sir John Franklin's three-digit complement. The Norwegian expedition was easy to maintain and well prepared for the conditions they were to face. They confirmed that the magnetic pole did move and spent a good deal of time learning from the Netsilik Eskimo they had befriended. In 1905, when the *Gjøa* slipped through the Bering Strait, the Northwest Passage had finally been sailed. Amundsen accomplished something that had escaped all of those who had preceeded him, many of whom had lost their lives in the process. The acclaim that greeted his return convinced him that the time had come to pursue his one great ambition: ninety degrees north.

As Amundsen was successfully petitioning Fritdtjof Nansen for the use of the *Fram* in an attempt to recreate his polar drift-and-dash approach, word reached Norway that two Americans had just returned from the Arctic claiming to have reached the pole. Initially, Frederick Cook, Amundsen's companion from the *Belgica*, was credited with the accomplishment. A flamboyant con man (eventually jailed for his role in an oil scam), Cook gave April 21, 1908, as the date for his arrival at the North Pole in the company of an Eskimo in his employ. A native of Brooklyn, New York, Cook returned to a hero's welcome in the United States, further accolades being bestowed upon the man already credited with having climbed the highest peak in North America (10,000 feet [3,000 meters]), Mount McKinley.

Robert E. Peary (opposite page) believed the North Pole to be some sort of birthright that belonged to him alone. His romanticization of that arbitrary geographic point was fueled by the general public, which had managed to glorify not only a long line of bunglers and failures, but those who waited patiently at home for their return. This painting by John Everett Millais (below), dated 1874, pays tribute to the exploration of the Northwest Passage and all of those who had a hand in it.

Peary and his companions are photographed (above) en route to the north and their final try at the pole. Peary, second from right, was accompanied, as usual, by Matthew Henson, the only African-American Arctic explorer of the era, and the man who was as responsible for Peary's survival and purported successes as was Peary himself. Although maps still show Peary's route leading to the pole (opposite page), and recent reports have reasserted his claims, it seems unlikely that he was even close to the pole itself. Had Peary echoed Nansen's sentiments that "to reach this point is intrinsically of small moment," he might have been forgiven his miscalculations. Instead, Peary's manipulation of the facts indicates that his priorities lay elsewhere.

To complicate the situation, three days after Cook's proclamations shattered Amundsen's dreams, Commander Robert E. Peary reported his own arrival at the top of the world a year after Cook claimed to have been there. (The two had been companions on an earlier, harrowing expedition atop Greenland, but their friendship gave way to Peary's burning ambition.) Peary considered his claim on the pole as "the thing which it was intended from the beginning that I should do," and he immediately questioned the veracity of Cook's reports. Peary had made many previous attempts at the pole, and this last one, a reprieve for a fifty-year-old explorer who had resigned himself to failure, seems to have convinced him that the recognition was destined to be his.

In time, Frederick Cook's claim on the pole loosened and slipped. A lack of substantiating evidence or wit-

nesses made his assorted indiscretions before and after the journey strong arguments against his credibility. In time, even Cook's claim of scaling Mount McKinley came into question. Robert Peary was eventually credited with the ultimate arctic achievement, the product of his life's ambition. Since 1898, Peary and his traveling companion, Matthew Henson, probably the only Afro-American Arctic explorer, had made several attempts on the North Pole, each of which met with unmitigated failure. Peary's second-to-last attempt had come in 1902 and fell pathetically short. He was greatly humbled and would not have returned were it not for the encouragement of President Theodore Roosevelt, who admired his courage and perseverance. Roosevelt needed no pretense of scientific usefulness to support a mission to the North Pole. The possibility of a determined American laying claim to it for all the world to see was sufficient incentive for this president.

Unlike the British polar explorers, who insisted on following "civilized" procedure regardless of the consequences, Peary and Cook were willing to employ any tactic that might speed them to the pole. Perhaps the one positive aspect of Peary's northern travels was his willingness to learn from the region's natives. He and Henson lived among them, learned their technology for igloo making, and adopted their methods of travel. Although it can be argued that Peary simply used the Eskimo to serve his blinding ambition, his appreciation of their adaptive abilities seems quite genuine. With them, Peary believed, he could reach the pole.

When the time came for Peary's final dash north, he proceeded exclusively in the company of Eskimo. Not even Henson, his most faithful traveling companion, was brought along for the mad scramble. The party had been advancing more slowly than Peary had anticipated, so he decided to make one last sprint, similar to a point in his previous expedition when a final solo run resulted in his claim of a new farthest north record. This time, Peary reports gaining ground at unimagined speeds, faster than any attained before or after, and arguably faster than anything credible at that point in time with the technology available to him. The culmination of Peary's "divine right" remained obscured by the notoriety that accompanied his ascension to the polar throne, and certain questions remained unanswered.

In 1988, the journal of the National Geographic Society introduced information that repudiated the findings of its predecessors nearly eighty years earlier. (The society had been instrumental in acknowledging Peary's claims and casting doubt over Cook's.) Even if Peary's estimations were to be believed, the society politely acquiesced, his failure to account for the drift of the polar icecap in his calculations would have placed him at least 30 to 60 miles (approximately 50 to 100 kilometers) from the top of the world. Other mysterious clues suggest Peary himself had doubts about his achievements. His attempts at covering them up were as incomplete as they were inefficient.

The fact that the North Pole is an imaginary point, floating atop the surface of drifting pack ice, renders much of this debate academic. Some argue that the accomplishment was essentially psychological, and that whether Peary stood at some specific spot in the vast arctic expanse is irrelevant. Perhaps Peary felt that to return empty-handed on either of his last two expeditions would have been a great embarrassment and disappointment. But for Peary to have questioned Cook's claims when his own assertions were so tenuous reflects the former's monomania. The North Pole was his goal from the start, and nothing must have seemed more unbearable to Robert Peary than to admit that it "belonged" to another.

If neither of these men was initially credited with having reached the North Pole, it is possible that the history of polar exploration would have unfolded much differently. If Roald Amundsen believed that no one had sat atop the globe, he would probably

"The poles of the earth had become an obsession of Western man. It could be argued against, but not argued away. Since the obsession was there, it had to be exorcised, and the sooner the better."
—Roland Huntford

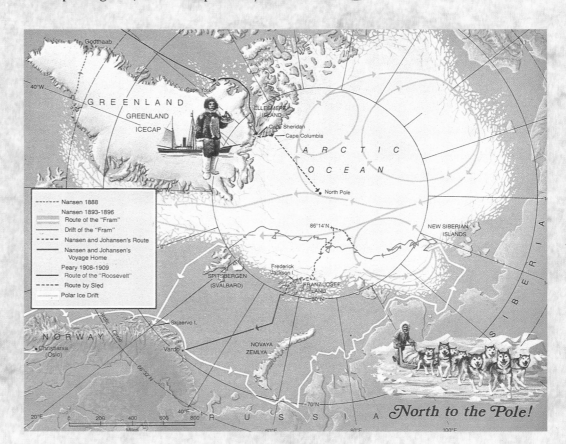

North to the Pole!

have sailed the *Fram* north out of Norway. Instead, he secretly decided that the remaining pole was his only alternative, and embarked upon a race of epic proportions. He dared to question England's claim to the remainder of the unexplored world and set his sights south. Following the great embarrassment of the Sir John Franklin era of arctic exploration, the British had begun to look to Antarctica for their final exploratory conquests. The continent remained essentially unknown at the turn of the twentieth century, and a new generation of adventurous and ambitious officers hoped to make names for themselves and to honor their king. The habitable world had been adequately probed, leaving the bitter polar wastelands as the last stage for the drama of terrestrial exploration.

Frederick Cook and Roald Amundsen's expedition to the Antarctic aboard the *Belgica* was one of several European exploratory forays around the turn of the century. They emphasized scientific inquiry, boasted prestigious international crews, and contributed many names to maps as blank as the continent itself. The outer limits of the last frontier were being determined, and it remained for an adventurous few to plunge south overland. Carsten Borchgrevink, another Norwegian, spent the first winter on the continent in 1899. During that time Borchgrevink established a farthest-south point, but this would change in a few short years. Germans, Swedes, Scotsmen, assorted Scandinavians, Americans, and Frenchmen all hovered about Antarctica, but the British led the pack until the very end. They thought of the continent as their own and developed an elite corps of polar explorers who spent the next decade wandering across it.

In 1902, Robert Falcon Scott commanded *Discovery* to the Ross Sea and then established a base camp on the mainland that he called home for the next three years. Parties were dispatched throughout the area, but

Ross' discovery of the twin volcanic peaks remained the most remarkable spotting in the course of the Antarctic's predominantly uneventful explorations. Without the accumulated histories that rivers and plains and mountain ranges acquire from their inhabitants in subpolar climes, the geographic features of Antarctica have little point of reference. That Scott's endeavors resulted in determining the limits of the Ross Barrier seems less tangible than the fact that his farthest trek south brought him within 500 miles (800 kilometers) of the pole and established a new farthest-south claim.

Ernest Shackleton accompanied Scott on this first mission and its

most important, most dangerous expeditions. In 1907, Shackleton returned to the southern continent with a command of his own. He undertook the charting and crossing of Antarctica, discovering that Ross' Mount Erebus was in fact active. Douglas Mawson led a number of parties for Shackleton and subsequently led two expeditions of his own. Mawson and a companion reached the magnetic South Pole in January 1909, while Shackleton and three others made an attempt at its geographic equivalent.

Shackleton's attempt to reach the pole was a valiant, exciting failure. After crossing the daunting Beardmore Glacier and discovering the Polar Plateau, the four-man expedition

managed to come within 97 miles (155 kilometers) of the South Pole. Shackleton had shattered Scott's farthest south point and returned to his base camp with no food remaining. The final days of the journey back operated under the conditions of a forced march, more harrowing than Shackleton had expected and perhaps only a day or so removed from dire consequences. Shackleton and a companion left two incapacitated colleagues at their final camp before embarking on the last leg of their journey, dispatching a rescue party immediately upon their return.

As he arrived back in England in 1909, Shackleton understood that now someone else was certain to have a crack at the pole before he could mount another expedition. The ambitious Captain Scott was likely to attempt it, and Shackleton would surely have preferred that to seeing another nation's flag fly over the pole. He had been close, closer than anyone on earth, and he had brought his entire crew home alive. But the opportunity

was lost, and Shackleton's hopes would soon be realized by others.

As Scott slowly prepared for an assault on the South Pole, Roald Amundsen was rapidly recalculating. The North Pole had been lost, but its antipode had yet to be claimed. Amundsen would alert Fridtjof Nansen, Scott, and the world of his altered intentions, but not until long after his departure from Norway. The consummate polar planner, Amundsen was never as comfortable with the politics and salesmanship that accompanied his line of work. His misanthropic inclinations allowed the public to create an image of Amundsen as a cold, indifferent man with few of the qualities they were prone to glorify. History has yet to formulate a consensus on this complex individual, and his actions on the eve of his greatest accomplishment would be used to discredit him in the aftermath of the events that followed.

In the waning months of 1911, with the first signs of what passes for summer in the Antarctic, Scott and

Today, dogs are still used to cover the terrain surrounding Scott Station (pictured, opposite page and above) *in Antarctica. Scott himself eschewed the canines, which was just one of many poorly advised decisions that led to the need for monuments* (above) *in memory of Scott and his fallen companions.*

Provisions for early Antarctic travel were a far cry from the nutritious rations that were developed later on. Robert Scott's supplies (some of which are pictured above) were comparatively primitive, but would have kept Scott and his men alive. Ernest Shackleton attempted to accomplish that which had proved too difficult for Scott, and to expand upon Amundsen's accomplishments by crossing the entire Antarctic continent. His plan, sketched roughly in 1914 (opposite page), was quickly interrupted by the unpredictable forces of nature.

Amundsen began the greatest race in the history of exploration. They were aware of one another, the magnitude of the task in front of them, and their opportunity to gain immortality. They were also complete opposites. Amundsen learned from the indigenous populations he lived among and then spent countless hours customizing their technologies to his peculiar needs. Scott, on the other hand, believed that his methods would work regardless of their practicality. The British way must be made to prevail over the conditions, whatever they might be, and for Scott there were much more important matters to concern himself with than the minutiae that surrounded such endeavors.

Amundsen led a streamlined expedition honed to maximum efficiency. He planned the slaughter of his dog teams, as they failed to serve a purpose, and reported his arrival at the pole with the same detached, laconic tone he employed when detailing weather conditions. Scott's undertaking was practically the realization of a satirist's imagination, fraught with inefficiency, petty politics, and short-sighted intransigence. Amundsen's efficiency would prove unexciting to the

masses, while Scott's grand gestures would cost him his life.

Roald Amundsen and four fellow Norwegians reached the South Pole on December 15, 1911. When forced to say something on the occasion, Amundsen reportedly expressed his disappointment at not standing on the opposite side of the globe. He then reminded his men of the return trip that lay before them and the importance of beating Scott back to civilization in light of the imbroglio that surrounded Cook's and Peary's contentions. Amundsen and his men departed the pole after a couple of days, leaving proof of their accomplishment and greetings to Scott, who arrived a month later. Unlike Amundsen, whose sleds were all pulled by dogs, Scott's party had been reduced to hauling its cargo themselves, something they perversely seemed to consider the most legitimate mode of polar travel.

Scott's arrival at the pole was a miserable moment in the course of an increasingly unpleasant expedition. The pathetic aftermath, in which all five of the final party perished on the journey back, lay the groundwork for Scott's canonization back home. He and his men had given it their very best. In fact, they had made the supreme sacrifice, and for this their country would honor them. Amundsen had his place in history, but it was Scott who came to occupy the hearts of millions. Nothing spoke louder than Scott's silence (and his heavily edited diary), while Amundsen's awkward attempts at suffering the inanities of the curious proved disastrous. Those who came to hear him speak of danger and adventure became exasperated with the Norwegian's perfunctory lectures and academic tone. Surely Scott would have proved more engaging.

The final pole had been conquered, and the great era of exploration was coming to a close. There were still numerous "firsts" left to accomplish, but the farthest corners of the globe had been broached and the maps of the

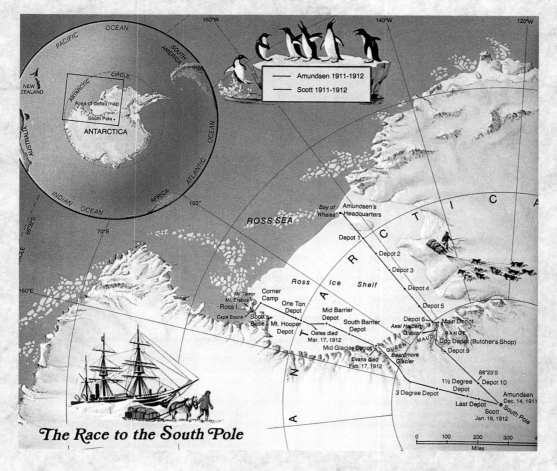

The Race to the South Pole

world were essentially complete. What lay between certain points may not have been totally understood, but the general public had all the information it needed. Any expedition that followed would have scientific study at its foundation, no matter how esoteric that research might be. Polar diaries were becoming hot literary properties, and soon various entertainment media would begin underwriting what passed for exploration. The handful of names that have emerged from the polar ice to claim a place in the history books begin to hint at the changes taking place in the face of exploration. Following one last, glorious tale of survival, expeditions to the Arctic and Antarctic began to reflect the changes in the civilizations that undertook them.

The last great tale of Antarctic adventure involves the return of Sir Ernest Shackleton to that continent. Following Scott's tragedy and Amundsen's triumph, the only thing left to be done was to cross Antarctica from one end to another. Shackleton made a series of arrangements in which his party would set out south from the Weddell Sea while another party left depots for it on the far side of the pole. Unfortunately, Shackleton was never able to attempt the crossing, since his ship, ironically named the *Endurance*, was quickly beset by ice and eventually engulfed.

Without a ship, Shackleton was forced to lead his men across the shifting pack ice that covered the Weddell Sea, dragging the *Endurance*'s three boats along until the coming summer would melt their tenuous perch. When that time came, Shackleton and his men abandoned the ice floes they had floated upon, boarded these small vessels, and sailed to Elephant Island, a cold, barren spot of land lying to the north of the Antarctic Peninsula. Before them lay the stormiest seas on the globe, which needed to be crossed if a rescue was to be effected before the onset of the next winter. Shackleton knew that all of his men would not survive another polar night with the limited supplies available to them, and he undertook one of the greatest boat journeys in recorded history to save them.

The story of Shackleton's epic journey is one of the most fascinating in the history of exploration. The fact that it added precious little to man's

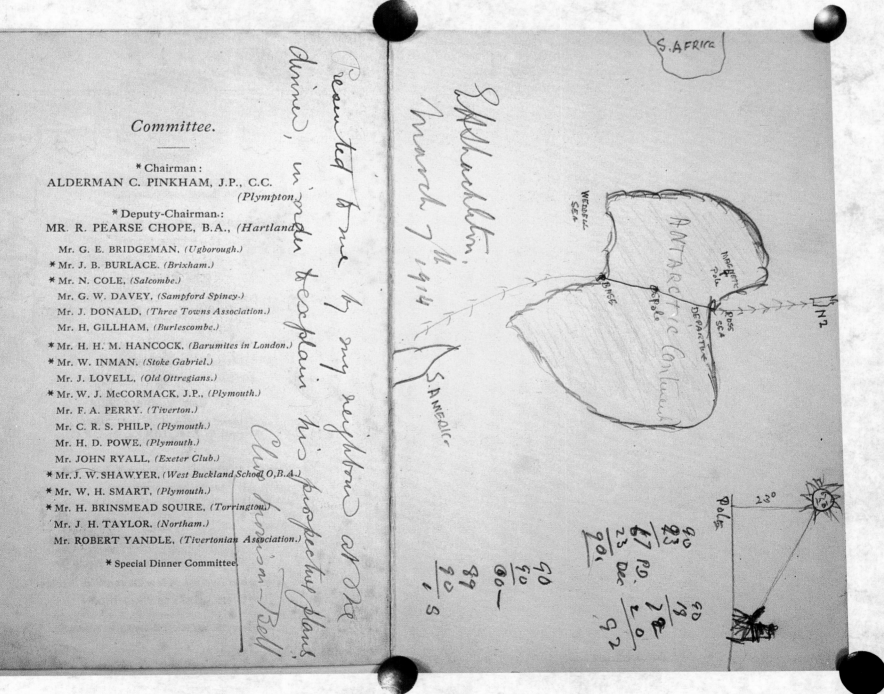

Commander Richard Byrd (above) heralded an age in which self-promotion was as important, if not more important, than the act of discovery. Byrd was never the first to arrive somewhere, but his method of accomplishing his goals, and the publicity that accompanied them, catapulted him into the public eye.

understanding of the region (the final leg's overland crossing of South Georgia Island was the greatest exploratory contribution made, and even that was negligible), has done nothing to diminish the feat's place in literature. Journals and reminiscences of those involved became immensely popular, as have the numerous volumes written about it since. Though Shackleton's own motives were sincere, the glorification of his failed expedition marks the beginning of an emphasis on life-threatening adventure for the sake of entertainment. Shackleton, the consummate leader of men, was lucky enough to bring all of his charges back alive. Yet not even this stirring tale of survival could match the power of Scott's ultimate failure.

Shackleton's undertaking also marks the end of an era during which polar expeditions relied on muscle and human ingenuity over machinery. The next accomplishments in polar exploration would come from the air, where newly improved flying ships were being put to the test. Roald Amundsen became involved in polar aviation and was preparing to attempt a flight over the top of the globe before he demurred to a wealthy American, Richard Byrd, who had entertained similar notions. In May 1926, Byrd flew the *Josephine Ford* across the polar icecap, confirming the absence of any great landmass and claiming to have circled the pole itself. While questions regarding Byrd's exact latitude are even more academic than those that surrounded Robert Peary's claim, some maintain that the former's calculations may have been as faulty as the latter's. If, in fact, this were the case, then Amundsen's subsequent flight shortly thereafter may actually have established that vessel, rather than Byrd's, as the first to hover above the pole. All of these claims are considered suspect by some, and, while it is unlikely that Amundsen and his companions were the very first to sit atop the North Pole, the concept of Amundsen laying claim to both poles and the North-

west Passage is a legitimate indication of his abilities and persistence in the field of polar exploration.

Richard Byrd would be branded the Last Explorer by his contemporaries, but his endeavors and results were often more self-serving than informative. His experiences during an Antarctic winter were chronicled in his book, *Alone*, and the well-connected Virginian was bestowed with a wide range of honors and accolades. Byrd made numerous visits to Antarctica before his death in 1957, by which time such expeditions were becoming increasingly commonplace. Englishman Vivian Fuchs eventually succeeded at Shackleton's ambition of crossing the Antarctic continent at this time, completing the task in 1958. Employing technologies unimagined in Shackleton's day, Fuchs' motorized crossing was supported by supplies laid on the far side of the pole by a New Zealand expedition led by Edmund Hillary, fresh from his conquest of Mt. Everest.

The same year that Fuchs completed his Antarctic crossing, the United States Naval submarine *Nautilus* traveled beneath the arctic icecap across the North Pole. It was the first sea-going vessel to surpass the *Fram*'s farthest-north point, established more than sixty years earlier. Ten years later, a surface crossing of the arctic icecap was attempted by yet another English explorer, Wally Herbert. In command of the British Trans-Arctic Expedition, Herbert (who later had a hand in debunking Peary's claims) led a group of scientists and sophisticated outdoorsmen across the expanse of arctic ice and completed human mastery over the poles. Events since that time have resulted in the increasing colonization and exploitation of the earth's poles, as well as environmental concerns about man's encroachment upon them. The twentieth century marked the end of our terrestrial discoveries, leaving only the heavens and the earth's crust to be explored. The poles were fittingly the final chapter in a story that has spanned the ages.

James B. Pond presents
Commander Richard E.
Floyd Bennett R E Byrd
BYRD
Telling His Own Story of
THE FIRST FLIGHT
TO THE NORTH POLE
WITH THRILLING MOTION PICTURES

10

THE END OF AN ERA

he face of exploration began to change drastically during the course of the twentieth century, as all that could be discovered upon the earth's surface had been, and the search for new areas to explore began to move away from the two-dimensional plane that had previously sufficed in plotting explorer's wanderings. The technology necessary for these new steps was far more complex than anything required of previous generations, and the result was a move away from individual efforts toward enormous undertakings that relied on massive support crews—technological advances on a scale that dwarfs anything that came before them—and astronomical bankrolls. The same kinds of political motivations, ethnocentricities, and scientific prejudices that fueled previous generations of explorers were at work here, but the effects of inflation—financial and factual—created a situation in which it became possible for only the largest, most powerful nations to enter the chase. Small, adventurous countries could no longer participate, making it impossible for the equivalent of ancient Grecian soldiers or fifteenth-century Portuguese sailors to emerge. Exploration was no longer a chance for smaller nations to rise up so much as it was becoming a way larger nations were able to widen the gap between themselves and their contemporaries. As the final pieces of the terrestrial puzzle were completed, it became apparent that the next steps would be taken by the geopolitical superpowers of the late twentieth century.

The exploration of our planet's polar regions was certainly the most conspicuous field of endeavor during the early decades of the twentieth century, but there were also scores of individuals who provided detailed information regarding more habitable climes. There are hundreds of travelogues and diaries available from this period of time, during which the wealthy and the curious, the intrepid and the inept, attempted to shed light upon

lands and peoples with which they were only vaguely familiar. The deserts of Arabia, the rivers of Africa and South America, and the wastelands of Australia continued to be mapped and charted until sophisticated satellites gave cartographers the ability to "see" places that had remained otherwise inaccessible and to precisely chart coastlines that hadn't yet been mapped with the greatest precision. As late as World War II, regions of Southeast Asia were being revisited for the first time since Marco Polo's tour of the region. Clearly, there was still a great deal to learn, but these concerns belonged to specialists and not the general population. There was no more *terra incognita*, just rugged terrain best avoided.

Twentieth-century exploration marks a period of transition during which the development of mass communication and intercontinental travel began to make familiar the distant corners of the globe that had always proved so alluring. Initially, it fell to eccentric adventurers to shed light on the remaining dark spots. Later it became necessary for enormous, heavily regulated, multimillion- (and eventually billion-) dollar undertakings to be conceived before anything new could be accomplished. The two-dimensional plane that had confined all exploration up until this time was giving way to probes above and below the planet's surface, and the results of these new endeavors have only recently begun to manifest themselves.

Despite the famous few who were chasing after historic firsts, much of arctic exploration became decidedly anthropological in nature, addressing the interests of botanists, meteorologists, zoologists, and psychologists. Some explorers, like Robert Peary, had adopted indigenous methods for personal gain, while others lived among Arctic natives to learn about their way of life. Vilhjalmur Stefansson spent nearly a decade in the Canadian Arctic, living with and like the Eskimo. In the process he undertook

the longest stretch of continuous polar exploration by a Westerner—nearly six years in length. In addition, Stefansson, born in Canada of Icelandic parents, charted a great deal of the Yukon Territory and its surrounding waterways. Long after the heroes of the halcyon days of polar exploration were gone, Vilhjalmur Stefansson remained a link to a forgotten time. He lived to the age of eighty-three, passing away in 1962.

During his lifetime, Stefansson watched others make their own contributions to civilization's global awareness, usually among more habitable climes. While his own expeditions contributed to the completion of North American maps, others were connecting the courses of the rivers running through its southern counterpart. Among those who braved these winding jungle waterways was a former president of the United States, Theodore Roosevelt. Teddy brought his son Kermit along in 1913 for an expedition with Candido Mariano da Silva Rondon, a native Brazilian who had already done a great deal of exploring throughout the Brazilian Highlands. Together they traveled to a spot where a river's source had been discovered and undertook a voyage to determine its course. It is a bit startling to consider a former president risking life and limb within the rain forests of South America during this century. He rode in dugout canoes, many of which were lost along the way and followed the river since named for him into the Amazon and subsequently the Atlantic.

Percy Fawcett was a less-fortunate Englishman who traveled about the region during this time as well. His surveillance of the Bolivian, Peruvian, and Brazilian boundaries provided the clearest such determination those fledgling nations had to rely on. Fawcett traveled along the Andes, back and forth across South America's continental watershed, and from ocean to ocean. Unfortunately, his great accomplishments in the region are belittled by his final search for a

Before, during, and after his presidency, Teddy Roosevelt traveled the globe. He was instrumental in the contruction of the Panama Canal (opposite page), built along the route first visited by Balboa, four hundred years earlier. Vilhjalmur Stefansson (below) was another adventurer who bridged the gap between historic and modern exploration. Stefansson lived into the 1960s, by which time he had been recognized for his contributions to our understanding of the inhabitants of the Arctic.

"Would it not be just as well to meet the gray old mower in full harness, struggleing for a grand object, as on a lingering bed of sickness?"
—Robert Peary

mythical lost city. In 1925, after two decades of surviving the perilous South American wilds, Fawcett and his son were lost in the same region Rondon had once explored. They had set out for the Xingu River in central Brazil, which empties into the same drainage basin as the Amazon, and were never heard from again.

The British maintained a presence around the globe during this time and could be found chronicling their travels across all of the continents. After Percy Sykes filled in the missing pieces for maps of Persia prior to the turn of the century, Aurel Stein spent three decades traveling throughout central Asia. During this time, Francis

Younghusband led a mission into Tibet in hope of swaying the Dalai Lama into an alliance with England. He is credited with a number of exploratory accomplishments, but was primarily working in the service of the crown and the British army. As is often the case, much of what would later be passed off as noble curiosity was in fact instigated by economic and/or military greed.

The northern deserts of Africa had always possessed some charm for the nations of western Europe, whose inhabitants took to roaming about the Sahara, Libyan, and Arabian deserts, as well as the Rub' al Khali. Despite the legends that surround all three, it

William Beebe and Otis Barton (below), ventured a half mile beneath the ocean in this primitive bathysphere. Their experiments paved the way for such advanced crafts as the Johnson-Sea-Link *(opposite page) to explore the majority of our planet's crust.*

This Vostok *spacecraft (above) is a replica of the one that carried Yuri Gagarin into space in 1961. Within a decade, Neil Armstrong (opposite page, top) set foot upon the moon, beginning a phase of human exploration whose repercussions have yet to be understood.*

is the "empty quarter" that has defied man's dominion. Bertram Thomas, in the employ of the Sultan of Muscat, made the first crossing of the Rub' al Khali in 1931, traveling north from the Indian Ocean coast of Oman to the country of Qatar, located on a peninsula. He was the first European to do so, but like all others of this generation, it was increasingly clear to Thomas that natives had long since wandered across most of these lands and had shared their experiences with others, who consequently knew enough to steer clear of the region. To this day, the boundaries of three nations lying within it are considered "undefined."

On account of the extreme conditions faced by polar explorers, their endeavors came to rely heavily upon the state of the art in certain areas of design and mechanized transport.

They developed clothing and shelters that protected them from the elements, leading to the development of synthetic creations that exceeded the abilities of the best natural materials. They came to rely on motorized sledges to carry their provisions and eventually turned to more rapid means of travel. Roald Amundsen, Richard Byrd, and Lincoln Ellsworth flew over great expanses of ice, and submarine technology eventually opened up a window on three-quarters of the planet's crust.

The diving-bell and deep-water suits gave way to bathyspheres and bathyscaphes. The former, which debuted in 1934, allowed its creators to be lowered to depths of several thousand feet or kilometers, but was unable to travel independently of the ship to which it was tethered. In 1953, Auguste Piccard introduced the latter, a navigable vessel that safely carried him 10,000 feet (nearly 3,500 meters) below the ocean's surface. Seven years later Piccard unveiled the *Trieste*, in which his son Jacques and Donald Walsh more than tripled the depth the elder Piccard had attained. (Jacques would later report on the effects of long-term confinement to representatives of America's National Aeronautics and Space Administration's program.) The *Trieste* was designed to dive down into the Marianas Trenches, a point southeast of Guam nearly 36,000 feet (approximately 12,000 meters) beneath the whitecaps of the Pacific. Its success was simply the most prominent of many contemporary attempts at sustaining human life beneath the crushing pressure of the oceans.

While the nations of the world have since assembled a fairly coherent picture of the bottoms of the oceans, the first visitors to the region were test pilots in much the same way as those men who preceded the astronauts. Their primary goal was to test the equipment they occupied. They were not explorers or discoverers, but their efforts were essential for those who followed to lay claim to such epithets. Despite the initial surge of enthusiasm for deep sea exploration, the pursuit seems to have entered a state of suspended animation. Whether it ever becomes desirable to encroach upon the oceans' floors for habitat or harvest remains to be seen. Those who have come before us made it possible for those who follow to use (or abuse) the earth's wet surfaces.

But the interest of the world, at a time when suboceanic exploration could have flourished, focused upward instead on man's first tentative steps into space. The Germans had advanced the art of rocketry, while much of Europe and America contributed to the science of aviation. The early steps were made by men of vision, wherever they might have been. As these advances created increasingly complex machinery, and computer technology burst upon the scene, only the most scientifically so-

phisticated and economically powerful nations were able to participate. Thus, the race to break free of the earth's atmosphere and enter upon a great new era of exploration became available to a select few.

Cosmonaut Yuri Gagarin was shot into space from the Soviet Union in 1961, and many fellow cosmonauts and American astronauts followed. Alexei Leonov left the safety of his capsule to float in space four years after Gagarin's mission, and both participants in the well-chronicled "space race" worked quickly to adapt their spacecraft to the demands placed upon them. While it took the Portuguese decades upon decades to edge along the African coast, the United States managed to reach its first target in less than ten years. Christened along the lines of all other famous ships of discovery, the *Eagle*'s landing on the surface of the moon certainly marks the first great step in a journey we can only imagine. It seems safe to say that Neil Armstrong's achievement will be recalled long after many of his peers are forgotten.

The long list of firsts we now compile when glorifying our ventures outside the protection of the earth's atmosphere are sure to be surpassed with time. If our present civilization gives itself the chance to act out the inexorable rhythms of history, expansion into the far reaches of our Solar System and beyond would appear practically inevitable. If such a scenario were to unfold, it is likely to be fueled by some of the same motives that have prompted previous voyages of discovery. Of course, to those concerned, the difference between those motivating factors would be great indeed. Whether the first interplanetary travelers undertake their journey on account of the kind of oppression that led to Iceland's discovery, the armies that carried generals across continents, or the curiosity of a prosperous people, will have an enormous effect on the nature of such an expedition.

It is, ironically, impossible to put humanity's most recent accomplish-

ments, arguably the greatest, in perspective. Only once we know in what direction they lead our heirs can we truly understand their importance. To imagine we have seen all there is to see would be small-minded and lead us into a period comparable to the Dark Ages. (The possibility should not be dismissed too casually.) Whether the human race manages to approach one of the futuristic utopias conjured up by fertile minds or plunges backward into fear and suspicion remains to be seen. Certainly, the potential for continued exploratory greatness exists. Perhaps, by examining those that came before us, we can better direct our own actions and those of subsequent generations. It is no exaggeration to suggest that the course of history, and the fate of life on this planet, hangs in the balance.

As man's ability to work in space becomes greater, so will his accomplishments. Extra-vehicular travel has progressed from the Apollo rocket (below) and Ed White's first tethered "space walk" (opposite page), but major technological steps still need to be taken before man can spread across the universe as he once did across the seas.

TIMELINE

c. 1500 B.C.	**c. 1400 B.C.**		**c. 1400 B.C.**
Queen Hatshepsut organizes a mission to Punt.	The *Argo* (Jason and the Argonauts) sets sail from Iolcus (Greece) for Colchis (Soviet Union).		Odysseus begins his return home to Ithaca from Troy.
c. 450 B.C.	**c. 400 B.C.**	**c. 336–323 B.C.**	
Herodotus writes *The Histories*.	Pytheas leads a mission that reached at least as far north as Norway, possibly even Iceland.	Alexander the Great amasses his empire.	
c. 500–600	**c. 870**	**c. 910**	**c. 960**
Irish monastics sail the north Atlantic, perhaps even reaching the New World.	The first permanent Norse resident settles Iceland.	Gunnbjorn Ulfsson, blown off course on his way to Iceland, finds an unknown coast far to the west.	Erik the Red leaves Norway for Iceland.
c. 990	**c. 1206–1224**	**c. 1230**	**c. 1273–1295**
Eriksson winters off a new landmass, christened Vinland, believed to be North America.	The empire of Genghis Khan extends from the Black Sea to the Yellow Sea, from the Danube River to the Yangtze River.	Guillaume de Rubrouck journeys into the heart of the Mongolian empire.	Marco Polo travels throughout the Mongolian empire with his father and uncle.

c. 1492		**c. 1497**	**c. 1497**
Christopher Columbus sets sail for a new route to the east, discovering a continent in the process. On this trip he discovered the Bahamas, Cuba, and Hispaniola (Haiti/Dominican Republic)—all the while believing he was in the East.		Vasco da Gama undertakes his first circumnavigation of Africa on his way to India.	John Cabot explores Newfoundland and possibly Nova Scotia.
c. 1513	**c. 1520**	**c. 1534–1542**	**c. 1540**
Vasco Nuñez de Balboa discovers a "Southern Sea," (the Pacific Ocean) off of Panama.	Ferdinand Magellan discovers a passage, now bearing his name, connecting the Atlantic Ocean with the Pacific Ocean.	Jacques Cartier explores the majority of southeast Canada, establishing the first European settlement at Quebec.	Francisco Basquez de Coronado discovers the American Southwest and the Great Plains.

c. 497–479 B.C.

Carthage defeats Persia in the Persian Wars.

c. 470 B.C.

Hanno leads an exploratory mission, possibly reaching as far south as the Cameroon region.

c. 470 B.C.

Himilco leads a voyage north, reaching the British Isles.

c. 300 B.C.

Egyptian King Necho orders a crew of Phoenicians to sail around the Strait of Gibraltar.

c. 200 B.C.

Sataspes, a Carthaginian, tries to circle the African continent, but fails.

0

c. 400

Chang Chíen travels from China south to Afghanistan, into northern Iran, and Europe.

c. 981–982

Erik finds Gunnbjorns land (see 910 A.D.), and establishes a settlement there.

c. 985–986

Erik leaves for Greenland (Gunnbjorn's land) with twenty-five ships, arriving with only fourteen.

c. 986

Bjarni Herjolfsson spots a new land, later thought to be somewhere near the Arctic Circle.

c. 990

Leif Eriksson sets out to find the land Herjolfsson had spotted.

c. 1324

Muhammad Ibn Batuta travels among the farthest outposts of Islamic expansion.

c. 1400

Prince Henry the Navigator establishes a School of Navigators.

c. 1481

Diogo Caõ travels a few degrees south of the Congo River, to what he believed to be the southern tip of the African continent.

c. 1487

Bartholomeu Dias reaches Port Elizabeth, in modern-day South Africa, realizing that he has rounded the southern tip of Africa.

c. 1498

John Cabot explores North America, possibly as far south as Long Island and the Chesapeake Bay.

c. 1500

Pedro Cabral inadvertently discovers Brazil, becoming only the second captain to encounter South America.

c. 1502

Columbus sets out on his fourth trip to the Caribbean, discovering Panama and Jamaica.

c. 1505

Amerigo Vespucci sails along the coasts of North and South America, discovering Florida, and parts of Brazil and Argentina.

c. 1541

Hernando de Soto travels into the lower reaches of the Blue Ridge mountains.

c. 1540s

Francisco de Orellana travels the breadth of the South American continent.

c. 1577

Francis Drake becomes the first Englishman to circumnavigate the globe.

c. 1580–1590

John Davis leads three expeditions to the Arctic region.

c. 1597

William Barents spends the winter farther north than any European before him.

c. 1605

Willem Jansz discovers and sails into the Gulf of Carpentaria along Australia's northern coast.

c. 1609

Henry Hudson becomes the first white man to ascend the river that now bears his name.

c. 1768

Captain James Cook begins his search for the legendary Terra Australius. He passes through the Society Islands, and drops down into unknown regions of the southwest Pacific.

c. 1769

Louis Antoine de Bougainville encounters the Great Barrier Reef on his way to divine the exact location of Australia. A crew member, Jean Bare, becomes the first woman to circumnavigate the globe.

c. 1773

Cook begins his second expedition, this time towards the Antarctic Circle in search of Terra Australius—he deduces that it is non existent.

c. 1796

Baron Alexander von Humboldt and Aime Bonpland begin their first mission in South America.

c. 1803

Meriwether Lewis and William Clark explore the Louisiana Purchase.

c. 1819

William Parry travels to the Arctic in search of the Northwest Passage.

c. 1820

Edward Bransfield sights Antarctica.

c. 1832–1835

The *Beagle* begins its circumnavigation. On board is the scientist, Charles Darwin.

c. 1837

Jules Dumont d'Urville begins the first of several visits to the Antarctic coast.

c. 1838

John Charles Fremont sets out to explore the Mississippi and Missouri Rivers.

c. 1845

Sir John Franklin leads an ill-fated journey to the Arctic, prompting two search parties, and leading to the mapping of enormous portions of the western Arctic.

c. 1870–1890

Heinrich Schliemann uncovers Troy, validating the existence of Ulysses.

c. 1873

David Livingstone and Henry Stanley meet and explore the region surrounding Lake Tanganyika.

c. 1899

Carsten Borchgrevink establishes a farthest-south point on the Antarctic continent.

c. 1905

Roald Amundsen becomes the first man to sail the Northwest Passage.

c. 1907

Ernest Shackleton crosses Antarctica.

c. 1909

Shackleton establishes a new farthest south point, coming to within 97 miles (155 km) of the South Pole.

c. 1642

Abel Tasman discovers the island that bears his name, the Fiji Islands, and New Zealand.

c. 1644

On his second voyage, Tasman manages to delineate the landmass of Australia.

c. 1767

Samuel Wallis encounters Tahiti.

c. 1789–1792

Alexander Mackenzie becomes the first man to cross the Americas north of Mexico.

c. 1790–1811

David Thompson travels from the Great Lakes to the Pacific Ocean, exploring the Northwest Territories, the upper region of the Mississippi and Missouri Rivers, and the Columbia River to the Hudson River.

c. 1795

Mungo Park sails for the Niger River by way of Gambia.

c. 1795–1799

George Bass explores the western and southern coasts of Australia.

c. 1820s–1831

Jedidiah Smith explores the western United States, becoming one of the first white men to see the Great Salt Lake.

c. 1828

Charles Sturt leads an expedition into the interior of New South Wales.

c. 1830

Richard and John Lander emerge out of the Nile Delta, completing the journey Park attempted in 1795.

c. 1831

James Clark Ross becomes the first man to reach the magnetic North Pole.

c. 1847

A party commanded by Robert McClure connects the final pieces of the Northwest Passage.

c. 1857

Richard Burton leads an expedition to find the source of the White Nile.

c. 1860

Charles Francis Hall establishes a new farthest-north record.

c. 1862

John Stuart successfully completes a south-to-north crossing of Australia.

c. 1878

Baron Nils Nordenskiold's expedition ventures off into unknown Arctic territory, just barely missing completing a Northwest Passage in a single season.

c. 1879–1884

Henry Stanley sets out on his third mission to central Africa, to rescue the Emin Pasha. The two discover the Semliki River and the Ruwenzori mountain range.

c. 1887

Samuel Teleki explores eastern equatorial Africa.

c. 1894

Fridtjof Nansen sets out with a dog team for the North Pole, coming 224 miles (358 km) closer than the previous record.

c. 1908

Frederick Cook claims to have reached the North Pole on April 21 of this year.

c. 1908

Commander Robert E. Peary claims to have reached the North Pole; instead, he fell at least 30 to 60 miles (50 to 100 km) short.

c. 1911

On December 15 of this year, Roald Amundsen reaches the South Pole.

The quotes that appear throughout this book have been chosen from a variety of sources. They are used, at times, to shed light on the subjects they were originally written about. In other instances, however, they have been removed from their historical context and applied to very different situations. The following biographies are meant to identify the sources of the quotes, shedding additional light upon them.

Brother Gaspar de Carvajal was a sixteenth-century Dominican friar who accompanied Francisco de Orellana on his journey along the length of the Amazon River, from the Andes Mountains to the Atlantic Ocean. His account of the journey was popular throughout Europe in its day.

Samuel Taylor Coleridge was an English romantic poet of great acclaim in the early nineteenth century. Among his writings is *The Rime of the Ancient Mariner*, from which this quote was taken.

Joseph Conrad was a nineteenth-century Polish sailor who adopted England as his home and English as his written language. Conrad wrote a number of famous novels, such as *Lord Jim* and *Heart of Darkness*, from which this quote was taken.

Roland Huntford is a contemporary British historian whose *Scott and Amundsen* was one of the inspirations for the undertaking of this book. He is also the author of a work of Sir Ernest Shackleton.

Harold Lamb was the author of literary histories, most of which focused on figures from the distant past. He describes his biography of Alexander of Macedon, from which he is quoted, as a "re-creation from imagination."

Dr. Robert McCormick served as ship's doctor on one of the earliest voyages to the Antarctic early in the nineteenth century.

Arthur Newton was a medieval scholar who edited *Travel and Travellers of the Middle Ages*, first published in 1926. The quote is taken from his introduction to that work.

Eileen Power was a medieval historian who is quoted from an essay that appeared in Newton's *Travel and Travellers of the Middle Ages*.

Seneca was a Roman philosopher, statesman, and dramatist who lived during the time of Jesus. In addition to *Medea*, from which he is quoted, he also wrote *Phaedra*, *Agamemnon*, and *Oedipus*.

Te Horete Te Taniwha was a young Tahitian native when James Cook first visited the island. His reminiscences were recorded during the early nineteenth century, in his old age, long after Cook had met his end in Hawaii.

Gerrit de Veer served as the ship's doctor on Willem Barent's sixteenth century foray into Arctic waters in search of the Northeast Passage. His log from that expedition is the most important source of information for that early visit into polar climes.

H.G. Wells was a successful twentieth-century author of both novels and histories. His *Outline of History* was immensely useful in helping us understand the state of the world at many different points in time.

BIBLIOGRAPHY

Allen, Oliver E. *The Pacific Navigators* (The Seafarers). Alexandria, Virginia: Time-Life Books, 1980.

Armstrong, Richard. *The Discoverers*. New York: Frederick A. Praeger. 1968.

Barnard, Marjorie. *A History of Australia*. New York: Frederick A. Praeger, 1963.

Beaglehole, J.C. *The Discovery of New Zealand*. London: Oxford University Press, 1961.

Becker, Peter. *The Pathfinders*. New York: Viking, 1985.

Berton, Pierre. *The Arctic Grail*. New York: Viking, 1988.

Boorstin, Daniel J. *The Discoverers*. New York: Vintage, 1983.

Bovill, E.W. *The Niger Explored*. London: Oxford University Press, 1968

Brendon, J.A. *Great Navigators & Discoverers*. Freeport, NY: Books for Libraries Press, 1967.

Bulfinch, Thomas. *The Age of Fable*. Boston: S.W. Tilton & Co., 1855.

Byrd, Richard E. *Alone*. Garden City, NY: International Collectors Library, 1938.

Cameron, Ian. *Magellan and the First Circumnavigation of the World*. New York: Saturday Review Press, 1973.

Cameron, Ian. *To the Farthest Ends of the Earth*. New York: E.P. Dutton, 1980.

Camóes, Luis Vaz de; translated by William C. Atkinson. *The Lusiads*. London: Penguin Books, 1985.

Casson, Lionel. *The Ancient Mariners*. New York: Macmillan, 1959.

Clark, Manning. *A Short History of Australia*. New York: Mentor, 1987.

Collis, John Stewart. *Christopher Columbus*. New York: Stein and Day, 1976.

Columbus, Christopher; translation by Fulson, Robert H. *The Log of Christopher Columbus*. Camden, Maine: International Marine Publishing, 1987.

Cook, Frederick A., M.D. *Through the First Antarctic Night*. Montreal: McGill-Queen's University Press, 1980.

Cumming, D. Duane and White, William Gee. *The American Frontier*. New York: Benzinger Brothers, 1968.

DeVoto, Bernard, edited by. *The Journal of Lewis and Clark*. Boston: Houghton Mifflin, 1953.

Downs, Robert B. *In Search of New Horizons*. American Library Association, 1978.

Edey, Maitland A. *The Sea Traders* (The Emergence of Man). New York: Time-Life, 1974.

Fagan, Brian M. *Quest for the Past*. Reading, Massachusetts: Addison-Wesley, 1978.

Fisher, Robin and Johnston, Hugh, edited by. *Captain James Cook and His Times*. Seattle: University of Washington Press, 1979.

Forrest, John. *Explorations in Australia*. New York: Greenwood Press, 1969.

Graves, Robert. *The Greek Myths: Volume Two*. Baltimore, Maryland: Penguin Books, 1955.

Hakluyt, Richard. *Hakluyt's Voyages*. New York: The Viking Press, 1965.

Hale, John R. *Age of Exploration* (Great Ages of Man). New York: Time Incorporated, 1966.

Hartwig, G M.D. *The Polar and Tropical Worlds*. Springfield, Massachusetts: Bill, Nichols & Co., 1871.

Helfrick, Gayle S., writer. "NOVA: Buried in Ice." Boston, Massachusetts: WGBH, February 2, 1988.

Henson, Matthew A. *A Black Explorer at the North Pole*. Lincoln: University of Nebraska Press, 1989.

Herbert, Wally. "Did He Reach the Pole?" Washington D.C.: *National Geographic*, September, 1988.

Herodotus; translation by Sélincourt, Aubrey de; introduction by Burn, A.R. *The Histories*. United Kingdom: Penguin Books, 1987.

Homer; introduction by Miller, Walter James. *The Odyssey*. New York: Washington Square Press, 1969.

Honnywill, Eleanor. *The Challenge of Antarctica*. England: Anthony Nelson, 1984.

Hoobler, Dorothy and Hoobler, Thomas. *The Voyages of Captain Cook*. New York: G. P. Putnam's Sons, 1983.

Hughes, Robert. *The Fatal Shore*. New York: Alfred A. Knopf, 1987.

Huntford, Roland. *The Amundsen Photographs*. New York: Atlantic Monthly Press, 1987.

Huntford, Roland. *Scott and Amundsen: The Race to the South Pole*. New York: Atheneum, 1984.

Innes, Hammond. *The Conquistadors*. New York: Alfred A. Knopf, 1969.

Jones, Gwyn. *The Norse Atlantic Saga*. London: Oxford University Press, 1964.

Kirwan, L.P. *A History of Polar Exploration*. New York: W.W. Norton, 1960.

Lamb, Harold. *Alexander of Macedon*. Garden City, NY: International Collectors Library, 1946.

Landström, Björn. *Bold Voyages and Great Explorers*. Garden City, NY: Windfall/Doubleday, 1964.

Langer, William L., compiled and edited by. *An Encyclopedia of World History*. Boston: Houghton-Mifflin, 1962.

Lansing, Alfred. *Endurance*. London: Granada, 1959.

Lee, The Rev. Samuel, B.D., translation by. *The Travels of Ibn Batuta*. New York: Burt Franklin, 1829.

Ley, Charles David, edited by; foreward by Prestage, Edgar. *Portuguese Voyages 1498–1663*. New York: Dutton, 1947.

Lomask, Milton. *Great Lives: Exploration*. New York: Charles Scribner's Sons, 1988.

Magnusson, Magnus and Pálsson, Hermann, translation & introduction by. *The Vinland Sagas*. Great Britain: Penguin Books, 1965.

McDonald, T.H., edited by. *Exploring the Northwest Territory: Sir Alexander Mackenzie's Journal*. Norman, Oklahoma: University of Oklahoma Press, 1966.

McEvedy, Colin. *The Penguin Atlas of Ancient History.* Hong Kong: Penguin Books, 1967.

Moorehead, Alan. *The Fatal Impact.* New York: Harper & Row, 1966.

Morison, Samuel Eliot. *The Great Explorers: The European Discovery of America.* New York: Oxford University Press, 1978.

Newton, Arthur Percival, edited by. *Travel and Travellers of the Middle Ages.* Freeport, NY: Books for Libraries Press, 1967.

Obregón, Mauricio. *Argonauts to Astronauts.* New York: Harper & Row, 1980.

Parry, J.H. *The Discovery of the Sea.* Berkeley, California: University of California Press, 1981.

Payne, Donald. *Lodestone and Evening Star.* New York: E.P. Dutton & Co., 1967.

Polo, Marco; translation & introduction by Latham, Ronald. *The Travels.* Great Britain: Penguin Books, 1958.

Power, Eileen. *Medieval People.* London: Methuen, 1924.

Prestage, Edgar. *The Portuguese Pioneers.* New York: Barnes & Noble, 1967.

Ralling, Christopher. *Shackleton.* London: Ariel Books/BBC, 1985.

Reid, Alan. *Discover and Exploration.* London: Gentry Books, 1980.

Rugoff, Milton, edited by. *The Great Travelers, Volume Two.* New York: Simon and Schuster, 1960.

Selsam, Millicent E., edited by. *Stars, Mosquitoes and Crocodiles: The American Travels of Alexander von Humboldt.* New York: Harper & Row, 1962.

Shackleton, Sir Ernest. *South.* London: Heinemann, 1970.

Sórensen, Jon, translated by J.B.C. Watkins. *The Saga of Fridtjof Nansen.* New York: W.W. Norton, 1932.

Stefansson, Vilhjalmer, edited by. *Great Adventurers and Explorations.* New York: Dial Press, 1947.

Wasserman, Jacob; translated by Paul, Eden and Cedar. *Bula Matari.* New York: Liveright, 1933.

Weems, John Edward. *Race for the Pole.* New York: Henry Holt, 1960.

Wells, H.G. *The Outline of History.* Garden City, NY: International Collectors Library, 1971.

Wilcox, Desmond. *Ten Who Dared.* Boston: Little, Brown and Company, 1977.

Wilson, Derek. *The World Encompassed.* New York: Harper & Row, 1977.

Worsley, F.A. *Shackleton's Boat Journey.* New York: W.W. Norton, 1977.

Wright, Helen and Rapport, Samuel. *The Great Explorers.* New York: Harper & Row, 1957.

Wright, Louis B. *Gold, Glory and the Gospel.* New York: Athaneum, 1970.

Zimmerman, J.E. *Diction of Classical Mythology.* New York: Bantam Books, 1964.

INDEX

Page numbers in italics refer to captions, illustrations, and quotations.

PHOTO CREDITS

Alinari/Art Resource, New York: 14, 20 (lower left)

Art Resource, New York: 18, 26–27, 36, 40, 47, 50, 80, 81, 115, 129, 138, 148, 157, 174

Tim Askew: 195

Courtesy of Australian Information Service: 141, 142–143

The Bettmann Archive: 189

Bridgeman/Art Resource, New York: 54, 55 (top), 70, 72 (upper right), 74–75, 77, 94, 100, 110, 117, 118 (lower left), 119 (bottom), 120–121, 122–123, 124–125, 130, 144–145, 148 (lower left), 149, 150, 151 (top), 152, 166, 167, 168, 169, 170, 171, 186, 187

George Buctel, reproduced from Great Adventures That Changed Our World, © 1978. The Reader's Digest Association, Inc. Used by permission: 37, 52, 79, 98 (top left, bottom left, bottom right), 1108 (bottom left), 109 (top left), 114, 119 (top left), 128, 151 (bottom), 162, 183, 186 (bottom)

Courtesy of the Cooper-Hewitt Museum, Smithsonian Institution/Art Resource, New York, photo © Scott Hyde. Frederic E. Church, U.S., 1826–1900, Icebergs at Midnight, Labrador, 1859, June–July, oil on paperboard, gift of Louis P. Church, 1917-4-711: 171

D.Y./Art Resource, New York: 55 (lower right)

Foto Marburg/Art Resource, New York: 21, 89 (upper right)

Giraudon/Art Resource, New York: 12 (lower left), 13, 16, 40 (upper left), 41 (upper right), 45, 58, 59, 60, 62–63, 66, 69, 76, 80 (lower right), 82, 88, 92, 93, 95, 102–103, 109, 110, 112, 113, 118 (upper left), 126, 127, 129 (lower right), 160, 179

Howard Jensen/Scala/Art Resource, New York: 161

Kavaler/Art Resource, New York: 47 (lower left)

Knudsens-Giraudon/Art Resource, New York: 56, 57

Lauros-Giraudon/Art Resource, New York: 38–39, 44, 111, 116, 131, 132, 133, 136–137, 158, 159

The Library of Congress: 180, 182

Joseph Martin/Scala/Art Resource, New York: 61, 104, 134–135, 146

David Mills/BMA-The Photo Source: 190

Albert Moldvay/Art Resource, New York: 184, 185

Courtesy of NASA: 197, 198, 199

The National Portrait Gallery: 163, 188, 193

New York Zoological Society: 194

North Wind Picture Archive: 9, 27 (top), 31, 33, 35, 154

Nicholas Sapieha/Art Resource, New York: 51

Scala/Art Resource, New York: 8, 10, 15, 17, 19, 22, 24, 25, 26 (top), 28, 41 (lower right), 42–43, 48, 53, 64, 67, 68, 72 (lower left), 73, 78, 84, 86–87, 89 (bottom), 90, 96, 97, 99, 107, 108, 176–177

SEF/Art Resource, New York: 164

Snark/Art Resource, New York: 155, 192

Tass/Sovfoto: 196

Tate Gallery, London/Art Resource, New York: 46, 124, 181

UPI/Bettmann Newsphotos: 178

Gian Berto Vanni/Art Resource, New York: 12 (upper left), 20 (top), 23, 30

Cordier Sculp.